Home Accountz® FOR DUMMIES®

by **Quentin Pain, David Bradforth, and John Taylor**

A John Wiley and Sons, Ltd, Publication

Home Accountz® For Dummies®

Published by
John Wiley & Sons, Ltd.
The Atrium
Southern Gate
Chichester
West Sussex
PO19 8SQ
England

Email (for orders and customer service enquires): cs-books@wiley.co.uk

Visit our home page on www.wiley.com

For general information on our other products and services, please contact our Customer Care Department within the U.S. at 877-762-2974, outside the U.S. at 317-572-3993, or fax 317-572-4002.

For technical support, please visit www.wiley.com/techsupport.

Wiley publishes in a variety of print and electronic formats and by print-on-demand. Some material included with standard print versions of this book may not be included in e-books or in print-on-demand. If this book refers to media such as a CD or DVD that is not included in the version you purchased, you may download this material at http://booksupport.wiley.com. For more information about Wiley products, visit www.wiley.com.

British Library Cataloguing in Publication Data: A catalogue record for this book is available from the British Library.

ISBN: 978-1-119-96892-4 (pbk); ISBN: 978-1-119-94055-5 (ebk); ISBN: 978-1-119-94057-9 (ebk); ISBN: 978-1-119-94056-2 (ebk)

Printed in Great Britain by TJ International Ltd, Padstow, Cornwall

WILEY

About the Authors

Quentin Pain is the founder of Accountz.com Limited, developers and publishers of Home Accountz and the Business Accountz range of software. He started his first company at the age of 23 when it dawned on him that he was practically unemployable after a series of failed jobs.

Having started his adult life determined to be a rock star, it quickly turned to stone as his interest in another kind of rock (the Jurassic type) took over. His interest in accounting was born out of a simple need to ease the burden of bookkeeping for his first business. How accounting, palaeontology, and music fit together is still a complete mystery to him.

David Bradforth has been a writer for longer than he can remember. He was first published at the age of 15 in a magazine called *Acorn Computing*. He describes that first experience of being published as exhilarating and as the main reason why he looked to get published further.

In his time, he's written for various magazines; has edited *eBay Advisor, Essential Website Creator, Essential OpenOffice.org,* and *Essential PC First Aid;* and has published a magazine that lost so much money he decided never to do it again.

John Taylor has assumed many roles in publishing over the years. With a background largely in computer magazines, he's been responsible for the launch of the award-winning Made Easy brand and has edited magazines such as *Windows Made Easy, PC Home, PC Basics,* and *Essential Website Creator.*

Dedication

I dedicate this book to all those who have ever struggled to make ends meet.
Quentin.

To Michelle — you've changed my world in a way I never before believed
possible. I love you. David.

Authors' Acknowledgments

We're deeply grateful to everyone at John Wiley & Sons, Ltd., without whom
this book would not have been published.

This began for David with a call from Accountz.com, asking if he'd be inter-
ested in writing a book about Home Accountz. He thought about it for a short
while, then said yes, as the experience would prove to be second to none.

We'd like to thank Laura Miller, our project editor. Her experience with the
For Dummies style has helped us to produce this end product.

Publisher's Acknowledgments

We're proud of this book; please send us your comments at `http://dummies.custhelp.com`. For other comments, please contact our Customer Care Department within the U.S. at 877-762-2974, outside the U.S. at 317-572-3993, or fax 317-572-4002.

Some of the people who helped bring this book to market include the following:

Acquisitions, Editorial

Project Editor: Laura K. Miller

Acquisitions Editor: Chris Webb

Assistant Editor: Ellie Scott

Copy Editor: Grace Fairley and Laura K. Miller

Editorial Manager: Jodi Jensen

Senior Project Editor: Sara Shlaer

Editorial Assistant: Leslie Saxman

Senior Editorial Assistant: Cherie Case

Cover Photo: © DNY59 / iStock

Cartoons: Rich Tennant
   (`www.the5thwave.com`)

Marketing

Associate Marketing Director: Louise Breinholt

Marketing Manager: Lorna Mein

Senior Marketing Executive: Kate Parrett

Composition Services

Senior Project Coordinator: Kristie Rees

Layout and Graphics: Carrie Cesavice

Proofreaders: Jessica Kramer, Linda Seifert

Indexer: Ty Koontz

UK Tech Publishing

   Michelle Leete, VP Consumer and Technology Publishing Director

   Martin Tribe, Associate Director–Book Content Management

   Chris Webb, Associate Publisher

Publishing and Editorial for Technology Dummies

   Richard Swadley, Vice President and Executive Group Publisher

   Andy Cummings, Vice President and Publisher

   Mary Bednarek, Executive Acquisitions Director

   Mary C. Corder, Editorial Director

Publishing for Consumer Dummies

   Kathleen Nebenhaus, Vice President and Executive Publisher

Composition Services

   Debbie Stailey, Director of Composition Services

Contents at a Glance

Table of Contents

Part II: Setting Up Your Accounts 91

Chapter 7: Coming to Grips with Home Accountz 93

Chapter 8: Changing Your Accounts Structure 103

Introduction

You can choose from many ways to manage your home finances. One way is to take a sheet of paper, write down all your income, take note of your expenditure, and then compare the difference between the two to see whether you're down or up at the end of the month. The other option is to buy a personal accounting package that's dedicated to the task.

Unlike Quicken or Microsoft Money, Home Accountz (published by Accountz.com Limited) is developed within the U.K. and is supported by PCs running Windows or Linux, or Mac OS X computers. If you have a technical query, the company has a lively forum available at www.accountz.com, where you'll quickly get assistance to resolve all major issues; and if you have a query about whether it will meet your needs, you can always telephone and ask. You'll get an honest answer, too.

About This Book

Home Accountz For Dummies addresses each of the different sections within Home Accountz and illustrates how you can use the program to meet your personal financial-management needs. The chapters have been logically divided up; you can dig into the book at any point if you want to better understand only certain parts of the package — there's no requirement to read from cover to cover.

The figures throughout this book contain fictional account and finance information. (We decided it wouldn't be wise to give out information about our personal finances in print.)

Although we essentially cover accounting as it relates to using Home Accountz in this book, we put the information together in a way that hopefully allows you to understand the subject matter easily, without using a lot of confusing terminology. If you need to know a particular term to understand a concept, we explain that term and how it relates to using Home Accountz, but we don't swamp you with jargon.

Conventions Used in This Book

Although we do talk about the foreign currency features of Home Accountz, this book focuses on U.K. currency (pounds sterling). Where we use British pounds, you can use other currency, such as U.S. dollars or Euros, in nearly the same way. If we address a feature of Home Accountz that differs in other countries, we highlight this difference.

The Home Accountz software is available for PC, Mac, and Linux computers, and the actual interface for the program is the same across all three platforms. Most of the figures in this book use Mac OS X, but the principals apply equally to each platform.

Home Accountz For Dummies offers many step-by-step guides, so if you don't already own Home Accountz, we recommend downloading the current trial from `www.accountz.com/dummies` so that you can follow along. This special 90-day trial allows you to make the most of the book, get a taste of the functionality available and (by inputting a code) turn your trial version into an unrestricted copy.

Foolish Assumptions

We assume that if you're reading this book, you're one of the following:

- ✔ A student preparing to go to university or college, with full control over your finances for the first time. You're looking to keep track of money coming in and payments going out for rent, bills, food, and so on.
- ✔ An individual who needs better control over your household finances. Perhaps you have to pay school fees in addition to rent or mortgage, car payments, food, and so on.
- ✔ A pensioner looking to better manage a limited income while still ensuring that you have enough money for essentials.
- ✔ Someone from any walk of life who is looking for control over your finances.

We don't assume that you have

- ✔ Any prior knowledge of accounting or accounts terminology
- ✔ An understanding of computer terminology

What You Need Not Read

There's no need to read this book from cover to cover. Each chapter is pretty self-contained, so if you want to dive straight into a particular chapter, you may do so. We include references to other chapters within the text to make navigation as easy as possible.

How This Book Is Organized

This book is divided into parts; and each part is further divided into chapters. The following sections describe what you can find in each part.

Part I: The Big Picture

This part introduces accounting and the Home Accountz software. We explain why you should account for your money and walk you through the first steps with Home Accountz. This part also covers some of the tools available within Home Accountz, as well as backing up and filing your data.

Part II: Setting Up Your Accounts

This part discusses setting up and altering the structure of your accounts, including importing data from Quicken, Microsoft Money, and bank and credit card online statements.

Part III: Exploring Transactions

In this part, we explore the various ways in which you can apply transactions, both template and automated, to your accounts, as well as how to deal with foreign currencies.

Part IV: Managing Your Money

In this part, we take a look at the different ways in which you can present and report your data from within Home Accountz. We discuss tables and views, how you can see your data with graphs and charts, and ways in which you can get the data out of Home Accountz itself. Also, you can find out how to customize the design of your reports by using the Documents Editor.

Part V: The Part of Tens

The Part of Tens appears in every *For Dummies* book. In this part, we take a look at ten of the most confusing accounting terms and explain them. This part also gives you amazing accounting and budgeting tips that Home Accountz can help you use, as well as advice for setting up accounts in Home Accountz.

Icons Used in This Book

We use these icons to highlight different essential subjects throughout the book:

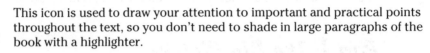

This icon is used to draw your attention to important and practical points throughout the text, so you don't need to shade in large paragraphs of the book with a highlighter.

This icon is a cautionary sign that warns about potential issues that could complicate your financial management through Home Accountz. Taking note of this material can ensure that you don't run into such issues on a regular basis — or at all. And we always try to offer ways to recover if you can't avoid these slippery situations.

This icon points out especially important ideas and concepts related to Home Accountz. Material marked by this icon covers the foundations of working with Home Accountz, so pay particular attention.

The Technical Stuff icon points out content that examines parts of accounting or the Home Accountz software that you don't need to know but might find interesting.

Where to Go From Here

You have two possible directions when leaving here. You can either download and install Home Accountz right away, making the most of the tutorials available within the program and using this book as a quick-guide reference if and when you get stuck or want more information. Alternatively, you can follow this book from the beginning, making your way through each component of Home Accountz.

Part I
The Big Picture

The 5th Wave   By Rich Tennant

"You know kids — you can't buy them just _any_ accounting software."

In this part . . .

In this first part, we give you a basic understanding of
the principles of accounting. We highlight a few
sources from which you can get help to manage your
money better, and then we go a little bit techie by showing you the procedure to follow to install Home Accountz
on your computer.

We also take a look at the Home Accountz Desk Diary and
Calculator, which you can use to help manage your money
with Home Accountz.

Finally, we explain how you can customize and configure
different aspects of the Home Accountz software to better
suit your needs.

Chapter 1

Accounting for Your Finances

*Y*ou've got hold of a book called *Home Accountz For Dummies* and, we assume, you've also bought or are looking to buy Home Accountz and have an interest in keeping track of your finances.

We don't make any assumptions about which computer you have because it doesn't really matter whether it's a PC or Mac. We've used an iMac to prepare the majority of this book, but if you're using a Windows computer, the interface and the screens for Home Accountz look very similar because it's written using a universal programming language called Java.

In this chapter, we guide you through some of very basic accounting techniques, look at why you should use Home Accountz to keep track of your finances, discuss some of the options for managing your money, and explore the principles of home accounting. We conclude with a look at some of the resources available on the Internet to help you with the Home Accountz software and to help you understand home accounting.

Why Account for Your Money?

There are more than a few reasons to account for your money:

> ✔ **Paying for expensive items:** Think back to when you first started working. It was probably tempting to go out and buy everything you'd ever wanted. However, it's more rewarding to save up your money for the

more expensive items you actually want, rather than spend it on two or three smaller items you *think* you want. If you want to buy an iPhone, for example, why not consider *budgeting* — splitting the cost of the phone over five months and putting aside that amount per month for five months? At the end of the five months, you have enough money to buy it without disrupting your cash flow.

✔ **Cars and consumables:** It's sensible to look around before buying a car. But cars are expensive: You not only have the financial commitment that comes with buying the car, you also need to pay any taxes due, insure it, and then buy fuel for it. You can't have a car without paying for all the other on-the-road expenses. To give yourself a chance to see the true cost of buying and running a car, you need to account for all this money somewhere.

✔ **House purchase or rental:** Whether you're looking to buy or rent, or indeed already own or rent a home, you must keep track of many upfront and ongoing bills, and make sure that you have the money in your account when it comes time to pay. If you're buying a house, you need a deposit, money for professional fees, and a sum of money upfront to help you get settled in your new home. Amassing a pot of money for the deposit on a house purchase is a serious commitment because it's probably a huge amount of money (not something you can pull from your monthly salary). You might also need a substantial percentage of your salary for a rental. You need to keep track of the payments to have a roof over your head, but how do you get this money together and keep an eye on it so that you don't spend it on something else?

✔ **Starting a family:** There comes a point in many of our lives when our thoughts turn to starting a family. This is a long-term commitment that must be sustained, regardless of your financial situation at the time you made the decision. For the first years of their lives, babies have needs that can't be ignored — food, drink, clothing, toys, a place to sleep, medicines — and these are in addition to any commitments that come with things such as renting a home. Tracking your finances means that you can allow for these costs and still ensure you have enough to live on.

✔ **Sending teenagers to college/university:** Higher education is expensive. You must pay yearly tuition fees, and earning a typical degree represents a substantial investment; then, on top of that, you have to consider costs for rent, food, drink, and the traditional entertainment side of university. If you're going to assist your child with his or her university costs, you need to ensure that you can do so without disrupting your cash flow. Many families plan ahead and start college funds when children are still babies, putting away a regular manageable amount that builds up over the years. Keeping track of this fund is vital.

✔ **Weddings:** If your son or daughter is getting married and you want to contribute to the costs, you may find you need many thousands of pounds. Can you allocate a certain amount each month towards this expense? The simplest way by far to make this decision is by viewing all your finances together and deciding how long before the wedding you need to commit to saving. That way, you easily can see how much you can afford and hence not over-commit yourself.

Life is a journey, and your financial circumstances change while you progress along that path, as the preceding list suggests; it just makes sense to keep track of your finances. You never know what's just around the corner.

Managing Your Accounts

You can bring together your personal finances in a number of ways. You can use manual systems — essentially accounting books in which you put your income in one column and your expenditure in the next, which might look something like this table.

Income	Amount	Expenditure	Amount
Salary	£350	Food shopping	£59
		DVD rental	£10
		Petrol	£40
		Gas	£40
		Electricity	£40
		TV, Broadband, Phone	£35
Total	£350	Total	£224

The amount carried over from the week's shopping in this table is £126 (£350 – £224), of which you could allow an amount for savings.

Obviously, this is only a simple example and assumes you're paid weekly, and nothing has been allowed for income from investments or other out-goings such as bank fees, car repairs, and so on.

There are significant flaws in this system of financial record-keeping. For example, you need to manually update the figures every day; although you have to do this with an electronic system, too, the benefit of the electronic system is that it makes these updates somewhat easier. Another flaw in a manual system is the difficulty of editing. After any edit, you then need to manually recalculate all totals.

Understanding the Principles of Home Accounting

The key principles of home accounting are very simple: You use it to ensure that you have

- ✔ Enough money to pay the household bills
- ✔ Enough money to eat
- ✔ Enough money to travel
- ✔ A little money for entertainment

Most of us don't live to work, we work to live — and as such, work and the money it brings are important for a healthy lifestyle. Whatever job you do, you need to balance work and play. Home Accountz uses a system of accounts to keep track of your money. These *accounts* are merely containers for money. In Home Accountz, everything has its own account — each of the people or companies to whom you pay money need an account, as well as people or companies from whom you receive money. For example, when you pay your mechanic for fixing your car, you might create an account called Car Maintenance and allocate the payment to that account. When you pay for your groceries, you can create an account called Food.

In fact, all transactions that involve money need to be allocated to or taken from the appropriate account.

Chapter 7 takes you through the process of creating and adding accounts and organizing those accounts into logical groups. You can use these accounts to manage your money and design reports whose views can help you compare your budgets with your actual balances and set a forecast for the future (which we talk about in Chapter 18). That way, you can ensure that you have enough for each upcoming bill.

Finding Accounting Help Online

Home Accountz has a built-in Help feature (which you can access by choosing Help⇨Help). This Help feature reflects the online Help available by choosing Help⇨Online Help. The online Help is constantly updated and may better reflect the current feature set of the application.

The built-in Help is useful, but online Help is both flexible and dynamic. The information contained online encompasses Frequently Asked Questions (FAQs), user forums, and video guides. This online Help tends to be more up to date and to address real issues that users have with the software.

Accountz.com Limited

At www.accountz.com, you can find the homepage for the developers and publishers of Home Accountz 2012. This site is worth a visit if you have an interest in any aspect of accounting. The company offers a number of solutions for businesses looking for accounting software, in addition to the Home Accountz product.

Also, look for user forums that contain the answers to the most common questions, an accounting glossary so that you can look up technical terms, and online technical guides for Accountz software.

Accounting for Everyone

Quentin Pain, the designer of Home Accountz and the chairman of Accountz. com Limited (and one of the authors of this book!), has produced a free 12-week course explaining accounting in depth. If you have an interest in understanding bookkeeping and generally want to make more of your home finances, you'll find much of interest here. You can sign up for this course at www.accountingforeveryone.com.

Home Accountz User Forums

In the Home Accountz User Forums, located at www.accountz.com/home/homeforum, you can immerse yourself in a community where other users can help you, and where the designers and programmers of the Home Accountz software don't just lurk — they get involved.

Unlike some products, Home Accountz has been developed entirely within the U.K. The support available for the product therefore has a certain bias towards the U.K. market, meaning that the people providing the support understand the types of situation you may find yourself in if you're based in the U.K. They also have an understanding of the way in which the U.K. economy works, particularly when it comes to managing money.

The user forums are truly global, and if you can't find the answers you need from the official support offerings, ask the global community — someone can probably help.

YouTube

Located at www.youtube.com/user/accountz99, this YouTube account features a number of training videos for the Accountz software packages. Although the information in the videos may relate to an earlier version of Home Accountz than the one you're using, because of the underlying structure of the software, it's easy to work your way through the videos and to gain a better understanding of the package.

Chapter 2

Getting Started with Home Accountz

*W*hether you download a trial version of Home Accountz or purchase a retail boxed copy, this chapter takes you through some of the primary considerations when purchasing Home Accountz. In this chapter, you can find a quick guide listing the system requirements for Home Accountz so that you can reassure yourself that the program will run smoothly on your computer. The chapter also helps you quickly get started. It has a simple installation guide, as well as instructions about how to use a license key to activate your copy of Home Accountz. And you can follow a short guide through the installation process.

Understanding the System Requirements for Home Accountz

Most computers purchased in the last few years have a system specification that can easily accommodate the needs of Home Accountz. The requirements of the package are so basic that, regardless of whether you're using a PC or Mac computer, the computer can most likely run it:

✔ **For PC users:** Windows XP, Vista, or 7 with 1GB of RAM installed and 350MB of space on the hard drive

✔ **For Mac users:** 1GB of installed RAM, an Intel processor, and 350MB of hard drive space

In each case, you need an Internet-connected computer because, to activate the program, you need Internet access. When first installed, Home Accountz runs in trial mode until you complete the activation procedure.

The following sections tell you how to identify the specifications of your computer.

Discovering your Mac's specifications

You can find your Mac's specifications by choosing ⌘⇨About This Mac. The About This Mac window that appears (shown in Figure 2-1) displays information about the Mac operating system, processor (you need Intel), and memory (anything over 1MB is fine). The computer in Figure 2-1 has a 2.4 GHz Intel Core 2 Duo processor and 2GB of SDRAM, which more than meets the specification required to use the software.

Figure 2-1:
The About
This Mac
window can
give you
details that
let you make
the most
of Home
Accountz.

About This Mac

Mac OS X
Version 10.6.6

(Software Update...)

Processor   2.4 GHz Intel Core 2 Duo

Memory   2 GB 800 MHz DDR2 SDRAM

(More Info...)

TM and © 1983–2011 Apple Inc.
All Rights Reserved.

Digging into your PC's specifications

Follow these steps to figure out your PC's specifications:

1. **Click the Windows Orb (or Start) icon on the taskbar at the bottom-left of the desktop.**

2. In the Start menu that appears, right-click Computer.

Computer appears in the right column of the menu.

A pop-up menu opens.

3. Click Properties.

The View Basic Information about Your Computer window opens, as shown in Figure 2-2, offering basic information about your computer. Within the System section of the window, you can see details of your system's specifications.

View basic information about your computer

Windows edition

Windows Vista™ Business

Copyright © 2007 Microsoft Corporation. All rights reserved.

Service Pack 1

Upgrade Windows Vista

System

Rating:	**3.0** Windows Experience Index
Processor:	Intel(R) Celeron(R) D CPU 3.33GHz 3.33 GHz
Memory (RAM):	1.50 GB
System type:	32-bit Operating System

Computer name, domain, and workgroup settings

Computer name:	DavidBradfor-PC
Full computer name:	DavidBradfor-PC
Computer description:	
Workgroup:	WORKGROUP

Change settings

Windows activation

Figure 2-2: This computer meets the specifications for Home Accountz.

The information in this window allows you to view a report of your computer's vital statistics. Listed in this report is the current hardware information, information about which Windows system is installed on your computer, and its current version (for example, Windows XP).

4. Locate the System section.

This section contains information about your computer's processor type and speed, as well as indicating how much random access memory (RAM) is installed.

5. **Look for Installed Memory (RAM) to find out the amount of memory installed in your computer.**

   For example, you might see Installed Memory (RAM) 4.00GB.

The computer in Figure 2-2 has an Intel Celeron processor clocked at 3.33 GHz and 1.50GB of RAM (meeting the minimum specification), and is running on a 32-bit operating system. In practice, the 32-bit/64-bit operating system variants have little bearing on Home Accountz because the application has been written in a programming language called Java, which works just as well on either platform.

Installing Home Accountz

You can get Home Accountz either as a download (if you order it via the Internet) or in a box that contains a Quick Start guide and a CD-ROM version of the software. In the following sections, we discuss the installation process for Home Accountz on a Mac or a Windows PC.

Whether you're downloading Home Accountz or installing the software from a CD-ROM, you need your computer to be connected to the Internet.

Installing on a Mac

To install Home Accountz on a Mac, follow these steps:

1. **Insert the Home Accountz installation CD-ROM into your computer.**

   If you're installing from a download, skip to Step 4.

2. **On your computer, open the Home Accountz CD-ROM folder.**

   The Home Accountz folder contains two folders named Pre OSX Lion 10.7 and OSX Lion 10.7+.

3. **Double-click the folder relevant to your operating system.**

   If you don't know the system you're running, see the section "Discovering your Mac's specifications," earlier in this chapter.

4. **Locate and double-click the file `install_home.dmg`.**

   The Installer file appears.

5. **Double-click the Home Accountz Installer file (see Figure 2-3).**

   A dialog box may appear, asking your permission to run the file.

6. **If the dialog box appears, click Open to continue.**

   The Installation Wizard opens. For details on the wizard, see the section "Using the Installation Wizard," later in this chapter.

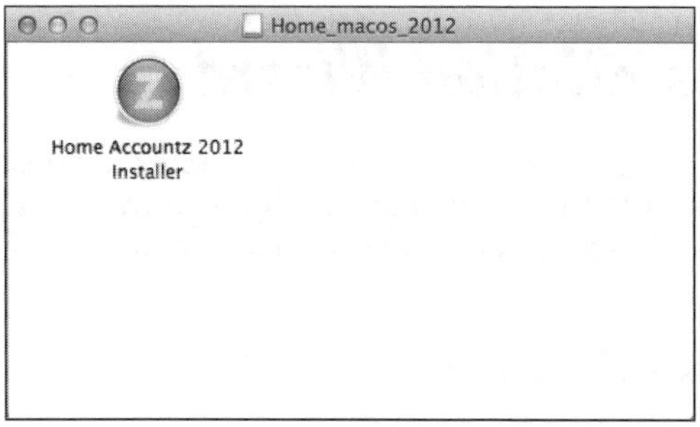

Figure 2-3:
Double-click
the Home
Accountz
Installer file
to install the
software.

Installing on a Windows PC

Follow these steps to install Home Accountz through Windows:

1. **Insert the Home Accountz installation CD-ROM in your computer.**

   If you're installing from a download, skip to Step 4.

   If the installer starts automatically, skip to Step 5.

2. **If the wizard doesn't automatically begin, choose Start⇨Computer.**

   The Computer window appears.

3. **Right-click the CD-ROM drive and select Open from the pop-up menu that appears.**

   The CD-ROM is represented by a red circle with a white Z.

4. **Locate and double-click the Home Accountz installer file (`install_home.exe`).**

   If User Account Control is activated on your PC, Windows prompts you for permission to install the application.

5. **If the dialog box appears, select Continue to proceed.**

   An Install dialog box appears, explaining that the Installation Wizard is being prepared and will guide you through the rest of the installation. A status bar keeps you informed of progress.

6. **Follow the Installation Wizard steps, as described in the following section.**

Using the Installation Wizard

After you start the installation process on your computer (as described in the preceding sections), the Home Accountz Setup window launches and displays the wizard's welcome screen. Follow these steps to complete the Installation Wizard:

1. **On the welcome screen, click Next.**

   The Select Destination Directory page appears.

2. **Select the folder on your hard drive in which you want to install the Home Accountz software (as shown in Figure 2-4).**

   If you have multiple hard drives, you can select an alternative drive that has enough free space available.

   You may want to use the default selection because it keeps your applications installed within the same location on your computer. Alternatively, you may want to change the location to allow portability — for example, you can install Home Accountz on a memory stick.

   The program verifies that your hard drive has enough available space for the application.

3. **Click the Next button.**

   Mac users, skip to Step 6.

   The Select Start Menu Folder window appears, from which you can choose whether to have the wizard create shortcuts and where to place them.

4. **To create shortcuts and have them available to all users of the computer, select the Create Shortcuts for All Users check box.**

   To create shortcuts just for yourself, ensure the Create Shortcuts for All Users check box is deselected. For example, you might want to make the shortcuts available to only yourself if you don't want your children to have access to the application, and along with it, all your financial data.

Figure 2-4:
Select
where to
install the
software
and verify
you have
the space
available on
your hard
drive.

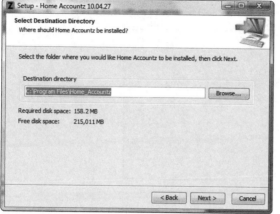

5. **From the list of folders, select where you want the program's shortcuts to appear.**

   If you want to locate the shortcut in the default folder (Home Accountz), skip this step.

6. **Click Next.**

   The screen that appears displays the status while the program downloads the latest files it needs to your hard drive and then extracts those files (see Figure 2-5). This may take a few minutes.

   You can cancel the download process by clicking the Cancel button, if you want.

   When the files are copied and extracted, the Completing the Home Accountz Setup Wizard window opens, telling you that Home Accountz has been successfully installed on your computer.

7. **Click the Finish button.**

   The Installation Wizard closes. Your browser opens to the Home Accountz Help page.

   You can use Home Accountz for 30 days before you need to license your software. To license your copy of Home Accountz, choose Help⇨Set License Wizard, and then follow the instructions.

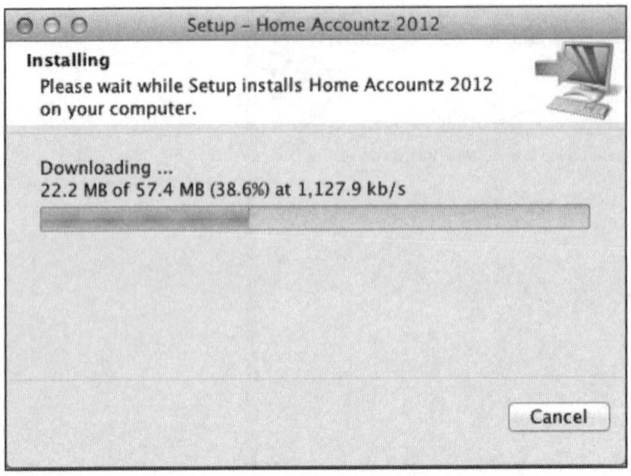

Figure 2-5:
The status
screen
displays
how the
installation is
progressing.

Running Home Accountz for the First Time

After you install the program, you're almost ready to launch Home Accountz for the first time. However, before you use Home Accountz, you need to verify that you have the most up-to-date version of the program. Just follow these steps:

1. **Double-click the Home Accountz shortcut.**

   The Installation Wizard created this shortcut and placed it on your desktop. (See the preceding section for more about this wizard.) The shortcut is a red circle with a white letter Z inside it.

   The eaZy Button screen appears.

2. **To connect to the online system at Accountz.com, choose Help⇨Check for Update.**

   If an update is available, the Download Progress dialog box appears, and a bar keeps you informed of the download progress.

   Note: You can cancel this process at any time by clicking the Cancel button.

   After the download is completed, a dialog box opens, which presents you with two choices: Carry on with the installation or cancel the installation.

3. **Click the Install button.**

The update is now installed, and a bar is displayed keeping you informed of the upgrade progress.

After the upgrade finishes, a message appears, informing you that the application will close and the upgraded version will be started next time you launch the application.

4. **To exit Home Accountz, click the OK button.**

Home Accountz closes.

Home Accountz is now the latest version, so you benefit from any upgrades that have been made to the software in the time since the disc or download file was created.

Using the Home Accountz Setup Wizard

The Home Accountz File Setup Wizard, which appears when you first open Home Accountz, guides you through the initial configuration of your copy of Home Accountz.

Home Accountz allows you to import data from third-party sources (such as online banks or legacy bookkeeping apps) in the following formats:

✔ CSV (Comma Separated Values)

✔ QIF (Quicken Interchange Format)

✔ OFX (Open Financial Exchange)

Follow these steps to use the setup wizard:

1. **Double-click the Home Accountz shortcut.**

Home Accountz launches, and the Home Accountz Setup Wizard opens.

The first page presented by the wizard contains three options:

• Set up Home Accountz from scratch.

• Import data from the earlier application Personal Accountz.

• Import data from Intuit's Quicken or Microsoft's Money.

2. **Click the appropriate radio button, based on whether you want to work with existing data or start from scratch.**

    In our example, we chose to create a new file from scratch, so we selected Use This Option if You Want to Set Up Home Accountz without Importing Any Previous Data.

3. **Click Next.**

    The New File Name and Location page appears.

4. **Click the Browse button.**

    The Set Filename dialog box appears. The text box at the top of this dialog box displays the current name for the file.

5. **(Optional) Click in the text box and enter a different filename.**

6. **Navigate to the location where you want to save the file.**

    For example, you might want to save it in your Documents folder.

7. **In the File Format field, select HAZ Files.**

8. **Click the Set Filename button at the bottom of the dialog box.**

    The location of the file and its name appear in the Enter Your Filename field.

9. **Click the Next button.**

    The Setup Bank Accounts page appears (see Figure 2-6). You're prompted to enter the names for your bank, deposit, and savings accounts. By default, a Current account has already been added. You're also prompted to enter the names for any credit card accounts. By default, one Credit Card account has already been added.

10. **(Optional) To add more accounts, fill in the Account Name and Current Balance text boxes, and then click the green plus sign (+) button to the right of these text boxes.**

    You can add or remove accounts at a later date by using tools in Home Accountz, as we discuss in Chapter 3.

11. **(Optional) To remove one (or both) of the example accounts, click the account to highlight it, and then click the Delete button.**

    The Delete button displays a red circle with a white X.

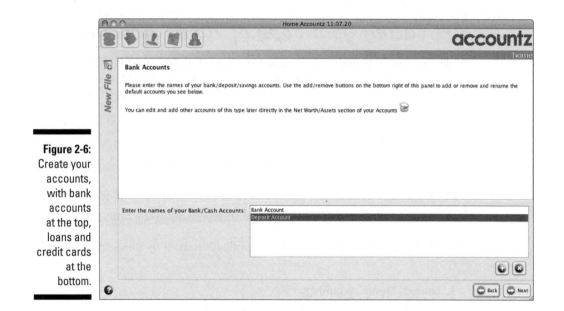

Figure 2-6:
Create your
accounts,
with bank
accounts
at the top,
loans and
credit cards
at the
bottom.

12. **Rename the default Credit Card account by clicking in the named field and entering the new name.**

    For example, you could name it Visa.

13. **(Optional) To add multiple cards, simply fill in the Card/Loan Name text box and the Amount Owed text box, and then click the green plus sign (+) button to the right of these boxes.**

14. **Click the Next button.**

    The Action page appears. This page informs you that when you click the Finish button, your new file will be created. It also tells you where your new file can be found.

15. **Click the Finish button.**

    After the file is created, the eaZy Button window appears. (See Chapter 3 for details about the eaZy button.)

Activating your copy of Home Accountz

When you install Home Accountz and run it for the first time, it runs in Evaluation mode, which means you have full usage of the program, but only for a limited time. You can run the program in this mode for a period of 30 days. Each time you start the program, a reminder appears, telling you how many days are left in the evaluation period and offering you a chance to activate your product.

You can activate your copy of Home Accountz in two ways:

✔ Accepting one of the offers on the opening screen of the application

✔ Requesting to activate Home Accountz from within the application

Activate Home Accountz through the application itself by following these steps:

1. **Launch Home Accountz.**

2. **Click Help in the menu bar at the top of the screen.**

   A drop-down list appears.

3. **Select Set License Wizard.**

   The Set License Wizard page appears. On this page, you can enter your serial number and register your software so that a license can be generated.

4. **Click in the Type Your License Key Here text box and enter your license key.**

   Your license key appears either on a sticker stuck on the Home Accountz CD case or in the confirmation e-mail you received after purchasing the download version.

5. **Click the Next button.**

   The page that appears prompts you to enter your name.

6. **Click in the Please Enter or Edit Your Name text box and type in your name; then click Next.**

   Subsequent screens request your address, contact number, and e-mail address.

7. **Fill in the text boxes as appropriate and click the Next button to move on.**

   Note: The data collected is for use by Accountz.com only.

   The Accountz Opt-In Monthly Newsletter page appears.

8. **Click the appropriate radio button to select whether you want to receive a newsletter, and then click the Next button.**

   The Action page appears. This page explains that when you click the Finish button, the Accountz License server will be contacted.

9. **Click the Finish button.**

   Your Home Accountz software is activated. When the activation concludes, an information window opens, informing you that the software has been successfully licensed.

   If you have trouble licensing, send an e-mail to `support@accountz.com`.

Home Accountz is now fully registered, and the next time you launch the program, the Evaluation reminders don't appear.

Chapter 3

Simplifying Your Accounts with the eaZy Button

In This Chapter

▶ Accessing transactions with the eaZy button

▶ Specifying bank and credit card information

▶ Using the eaZy button to set up your accounts

*N*ew to Home Accountz 2012 is the eaZy button. This button provides quick and easy access to, and use of, various features within Home Accountz. The eaZy button window is divided into three panels — Transactions, Bank/Credit Card, and Set Up/Reports. Each panel has a number of options, which we call eaZy processes. In this chapter, we take a look at the processes within the Transactions, Bank/Credit Card, and Set Up panels. (The Reports processes are covered in Chapter 16.)

Looking into the Transactions Panel

The Transactions panel of The eaZy button window handles transactions — income and expenditure. In this section, you have six options (as shown in Figure 3-1):

✔ Pay a Bill

✔ Buy Something

✔ Record Income

✔ Add Recurring Income

✔ Add Recurring Transfer

✔ Add Recurring Payment

Figure 3-1:
The
Transac-
tions panel,
showing
the six eaZy
processes.

Entering single transactions

The Transactions section allows you to enter one-off transactions. You can pay a bill, buy something, or record your income.

Pay a Bill

By using the Pay a Bill option, you can record when you pay a bill, such as a mobile phone bill. Follow these steps:

1. **Click the Pay a Bill button in the Transactions panel, and then select the payee from the Select the Payee of This Bill list.**

   The *payee* is the person whom you're paying. If you're paying a mobile phone bill, for example, the payee could be Orange.

   Alternatively, to add a new payee, click Add New Payee, enter the name of the new payee in the Name field, and then click Done.

2. **Click Next, which appears at the bottom-right of the eaZy Process panels.**

   The Select the Date the Bill Was Paid window opens, displaying a calendar.

3. **Click in the calendar to select the date the bill was paid.**

   Alternatively, click Select Today at the bottom of the calendar to select today's date (as shown in Figure 3-2).

4. **Click Next.**

5. **In the Enter Total Amount of the Bill That Was Paid field that appears, enter a value, and then click Next.**

6. **In the From Account window that appears, select the account you used to pay the bill, and then click Next.**

   In the case of a phone bill, you probably make a regular payment from your current account.

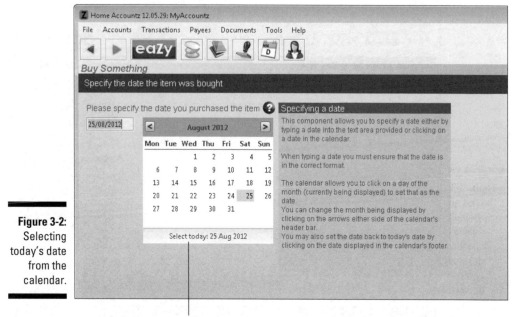

Figure 3-2:
Selecting
today's date
from the
calendar.

Select Today

7. **Click Next.**

8. **Select the Expense account to which you want to transfer the money; then click Next.**

   In the case of Orange, you probably want to choose an account such as Telephone.

   The Assign Default Values window opens.

9. **(Optional) Enter information in any of the fields you want (as shown in Figure 3-3).**

   This window contains three fields:

   - *Description:* Record a meaningful description for the transaction, such as **paying mobile phone bill**.

   - *Reference:* Record identifying information about the payment — perhaps a check number or payment reference.

   - *Notes:* Record some additional information about the transaction. For example, you can use the Notes field to identify different accounts.

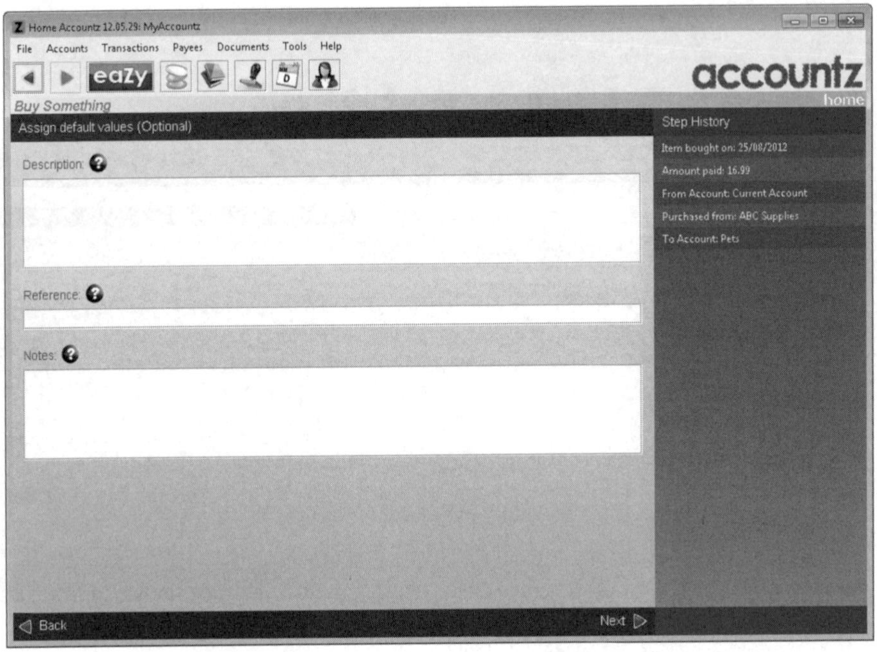

Figure 3-3:
The Assign
Default
Values
window
includes
three
optional
fields.

10. **Click Next.**

    The Action panel opens, displaying a summary of this transaction.

11. **Click Finish.**

    The Finish button appears on the bottom-right of the panel and is always the last step for every eaZy process.

Buy Something

You can record a payment for something you buy by using the Buy Something option. Just follow these steps:

1. **Click the Buy Something button in the Transactions panel.**

   The Specify the Date the Item Was Bought window opens.

2. **Select the date you bought the item from the calendar window.**

   If you bought the item today, click Select Today at the bottom of the calendar.

3. **Click Next.**

4. **Type a value in the Enter the Total Amount You Paid for the Item field, in pounds and pence.**

5. **Click Next.**

   The From Account window opens.

6. **Select the account you used to purchase the item from the list of accounts, and then click Next.**

   If you paid in cash, you choose your Cash account.

7. **In the Purchased from Payee list that appears, select the business from which you purchased the item.**

   If the business doesn't appear in the list, click Add New Payee, and then enter the name of the business.

8. **Click Next.**

   The To Account list appears.

9. **In the To Account list, select the Expense account for the transaction, and then click Next.**

   The Assign Default Values window opens.

10. **(Optional) Enter values in any of the fields you want.**

    You can enter information in the Description, Reference, and Notes fields.

11. **Click Next.**

    The Action panel opens.

12. **Click Finish.**

Record Income

You use the Record Income option to record money you receive. You can make the most of it by following these steps:

1. **Click the Record Income button in the Transactions panel.**

   The Specify the Date the Income Was Received window opens.

2. **Select the date you received the income from the calendar.**

   If you were paid today, click Select Today at the bottom of the calendar.

3. **Click Next.**

4. **Enter the total amount received, and then click Next.**

5. **In the From Account window that appears, select the account that's the source of the income.**

   For instance, you might select Interest Received or Salary.

6. **Click Next to open the To Account window.**

7. **Select the account into which the income was paid, such as Current Account, from the To Account list; click Next.**

   The Assign Default Values window opens.

8. **(Optional) Fill in the Description, Reference, and Notes fields if you want to document this transaction in more detail.**

9. **Click Next to open the Action panel.**

10. **Click Finish to complete the transaction.**

Recurring transactions

For any of the three recurring transaction eaZy processes (Add Recurring Income, Add Recurring Transfer, and Add Recurring Payment), you need to select how often the transaction occurs in the Select the Frequency of the Payments panel, as shown in Figure 3-4. (We explain how for each process in the following sections.) You can choose from these options:

✔ Never

✔ Daily

✔ Every 30 Days

✔ Every 1 Week (Weekly)

✔ Every 2 Weeks

✔ Every 3 Weeks

✔ Every 4 Weeks

✔ Every 5 Weeks

✔ Every 12 Weeks

✔ Every Month (Monthly)

✔ Every 2 Months

✔ Every 3 Months (Quarterly)

✔ Every 4 Months

✔ Every 6 Months (Half-Yearly)

✔ Every Year (Annually)

✔ Every 2 Years

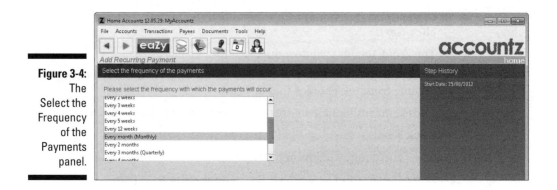

Figure 3-4:
The
Select the
Frequency
of the
Payments
panel.

Add Recurring Income

The Add Recurring Income option deals with money you receive on a regular basis. Follow these steps to use this option:

1. **Click the Add Recurring Income button in the Transactions panel.**

   The Enter the Start Date of the Recurring Income window opens.

2. **Select the date from the calendar window for the date you want to begin the recurring income.**

   If you want to start the income today, click Select Today at the bottom of the calendar.

3. **Click Next.**

   The Select the Income's Frequency window opens.

4. **From the list, select the frequency with which you'll receive the income.**

   The list includes options covering everything from daily to every two years (see the preceding section).

5. **Click Next.**

6. **In the Please Enter the Total Number of Income Payments You Will Receive window, enter a value.**

   If you're not sure how many payments you'll receive, enter a large number (such as **9999**) to ensure the recurring transactions continue until you decide to stop them.

7. **Click Next.**

   The Amount to Be Received window opens.

8. **In the Enter the Amount Received Each Cycle field, enter a value; then click Next.**

   The From Account window opens.

9. **Select the account that you want to be the source of the recurring income from the choices that appear.**

   These choices include Interest Received, Other Income, and Salary.

10. **Click Next.**

    The To Account window appears.

11. **Enter the account into which the income should be paid.**

    The Assign Default Values window opens.

12. **(Optional) Enter values in the fields that appear in this window.**

    The three fields are

    - *Description:* Record a meaningful description for the transaction.
    - *Reference:* Record information to identify the payment, such as a check number.
    - *Notes:* Record information about the transaction for personal reference.

13. **Click Next.**

    The Action panel appears.

14. **Click Finish.**

Add Recurring Transfer

With the Add Recurring Transfer option, you can record recurring transfers from your account. Follow these steps:

1. **Click the Add Recurring Transfer option in the Transactions panel.**

   The Enter the Start Date of the Recurring Transfer window opens.

2. **Select the date from the calendar window for the date the recurring transfer should begin.**

   If you want it to start today, click Select Today at the bottom of the calendar.

3. **Click Next.**

   The Select the Frequency of the Transfer window opens.

4. **From the list, select the frequency with which the transfer will occur.**

   Your options range from daily to every two years (as described in the section "Recurring transactions," earlier in this chapter).

5. **Click Next.**

6. **In the Please Enter the Total Number of Transfers That Will Take Place field, enter a value.**

   If you're setting up a payment for a 12-month period, enter **12**.

7. **Click Next.**

8. **Enter a value in the Enter the Amount to Transfer Each Time field that appears, and then click Next.**

9. **In the From Account list that appears, select the account from which the money should be taken; click Next.**

   The To Account window appears.

10. **Enter the account to which the money is to be transferred, and then click Next.**

    The Assign Default Values window opens.

11. **(Optional) Enter information in any of the three fields — Description, Reference and Notes.**

12. **Click Next to open the Action panel.**

13. **Click Finish.**

Add Recurring Payment

By using the Add Recurring Payment option, you can record a payment made on a recurring basis — such as a council tax bill. To set up a recurring payment, follow these steps:

1. **Click the Add Recurring Payment option in the Transactions window.**

   The Enter the Start Date of the Recurring Payment window opens.

2. **Select the date of the recurring payment from the calendar window.**

   If you want to start the payment today, click Select Today at the bottom of the calendar.

3. **Click Next.**

   The Select the Frequency of the Payments window opens.

4. **From the Frequency list, select how often you'll make the payment.**

   The options available go from daily to every two years, as we outline in the section "Recurring transactions," earlier in this chapter.

5. **Click Next.**

6. **Enter the total number of payments to be made, and then click Next.**

   The Amount to be Paid window opens.

7. **Enter the amount to be paid each time; click Next.**

   The From Account window opens.

8. **From the list that appears, select the account from which the money should be taken, and then click Next.**

9. **Select the payee from the list that opens.**

   Alternatively, you can add a new payee by clicking the Add New Payee button, entering the name of the payee, and then clicking Done.

10. **Click Next.**

    The To Account window opens.

11. **Select the account to which the payment is to be made from the list.**

    Or you can add a new account by clicking the Add New Account button, entering the name of the account, and clicking Done.

12. **Click Next.**

    The Assign Default Values window opens.

13. **(Optional) Enter information in the Description, Reference, and Notes fields.**

14. **Click Next.**

    The Action panel opens.

15. **Click Finish.**

Dealing with the Bank/Credit Card Panel

The Bank/Credit Card panel of The eaZy button handles bank and credit card transactions — payments, charges, and so on. This section includes 14 options (as shown in Figure 3-5):

- ✔ Pay Off a Credit Card
- ✔ Transfer to Another Bank
- ✔ Add a Direct Debit

- ✔ Add a Standing Order

- ✔ Add a Direct Credit

- ✔ Record Bank/Finance Charges

- ✔ Create a Loan

- ✔ Pay Off a Loan

- ✔ Add a Bank Account

- ✔ Add a Credit Card

- ✔ Close an Account

- ✔ Re-Open a Closed Account

- ✔ Delete an Account

- ✔ Undelete an Account

In the following sections, we explain a little more about each in turn and explore how to use each section.

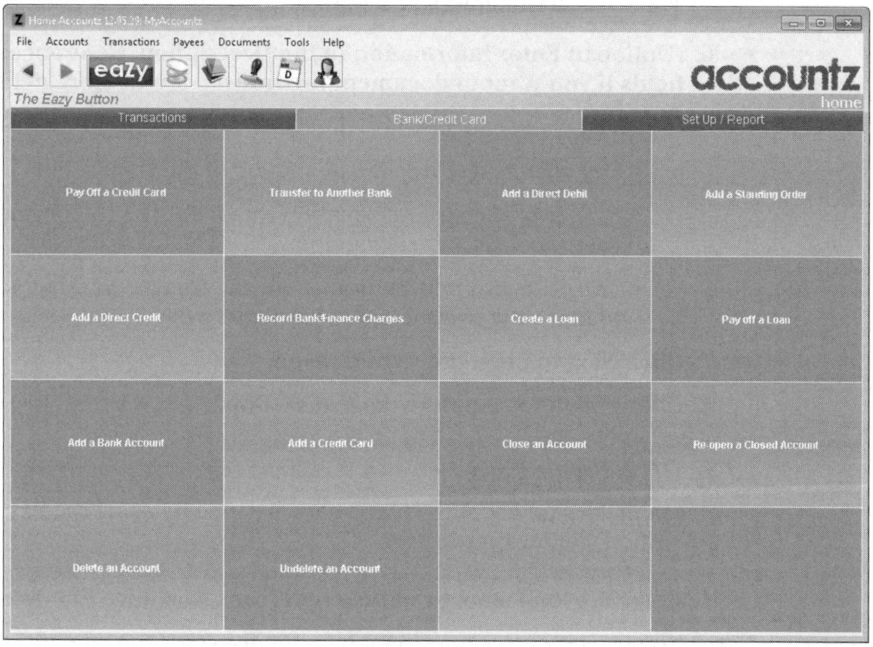

Figure 3-5:
The Bank/
Credit Card
panel's
options.

Entering transactions

Each eaZy process has very similar steps, so this section gives you an overview of the general steps — we detail the differences in the following sections. Follow these steps to enter a single transaction:

1. **Click the appropriate eaZy process button in the Bank/Credit Card panel.**

   A calendar appears, prompting you to specify the date of the transaction.

2. **Select the date from the calendar.**

   If the transaction occurred on the day you're entering the transaction, the default date is correct, so you don't have to change anything.

3. **Click Next.**

4. **Follow the steps for the particular option you selected in Step 1.**

   The following sections offer this information for each option.

5. **Click Next.**

   The Assign Default Values window opens.

6. **(Optional) Enter information in the Description, Reference, and Notes fields if you want to document the transaction in more detail.**

   Here's how you can use these fields:

   - *Description:* Record an explanation of the transaction.
   - *Reference:* Record information that identifies the payment specifically, such as a check number.
   - *Notes:* Record information about the transaction that you can use to place the transaction in context.

7. **Click Next to open the Action panel.**

8. **Click Finish to complete the transaction.**

Pay Off a Credit Card

You can make a payment to clear a card balance by using the Pay Off a Credit Card option. Follow these steps:

1. **Enter the total amount of the credit card's balance that was paid.**

   You can enter this information in detail — so if the amount paid was £209.21, enter **209.21**.

2. **Click the Next button.**

   The From Account window appears, asking you to select the account you've taken the money from to make the payment. In most cases, you probably select either Current Account or Savings Account.

3. **Select the appropriate account from those listed, and then click Next to open the To Account window.**

   You need to select the credit card account that you're paying off. If you have more than one credit card, they appear in the list.

Transfer to Another Bank

To transfer funds to another bank account, follow these steps:

1. **Enter the total amount of the transfer in the field provided, and then click Next.**

   In the window that appears, you're asked to select the account from which you want to transfer money.

2. **Click the most appropriate account in the To list; click Next.**

3. **Select the account to which you want to transfer money from the list that appears.**

Record Bank/Finance Charges

To record any bank charges, or finance costs, follow these steps:

1. **In the Amount Charged window, enter the total amount you were charged in the field provided, and then click Next.**

   If this amount includes pounds and pence, such as £20.99, enter the figure in the form **20.99**.

2. **Select the account on which you incurred the charge from the list that appears.**

   For your credit card, you might be paying the interest charges; whereas for your bank account, it may be simply normal bank charges (for example, bank fees, overdraft fees, and so on).

   If the account doesn't already appear in the list, click Add New Account and enter the name of the new account in the Add New Account window that appears (as shown in Figure 3-6).

3. **Click Next.**

   The Select the Payee Who Charged You screen appears.

4. **(Optional) Select the payee from the drop-down list.**

5. **Click Next.**

6. **Select the account to which the charge was paid from the list of options.**

Add New Account

Name:

Account Type: Bank Account ▼

✓ Done   ✗ Close

Create a Loan

Create a loan account by following these steps:

1. **In the Loan Account screen, enter the total amount you borrowed, and then click Next.**

   The From Account window appears.

2. **Select an account from the Select the Account That Is the Source of the Loan list.**

   Default options include Mortgage and Other Loans.

   Alternatively, you can add a new account that has the name of the new loan. Click the Add New Account button, enter the name of the new account, and then click Done.

3. **Click Next.**

4. **In the Loan Supplier list that appears, select the payee who supplied you the loan, and then click Next.**

   If this person or business doesn't already appear in the list, click Add New Payee, enter the name of the payee, and then click Done.

5. **From the list of available accounts, select the account into which you want to pay the loan charge, and then click Next.**

Pay Off a Loan

To pay a loan debt in full, follow these steps:

1. **In the Repayment Amount screen, enter the total amount you repaid; click Next.**

2. **In the From Account screen that appears, select the account that you're using to repay the loan from the list provided.**

   Default options include Cash, Credit Card, and Current Account.

3. **Click Next to open the Loan Supplier window.**

4. **Select the payee from the Please Select the Payee Who Supplied You the Loan list, and then click Next.**

   If you've already entered the detail by using the Create a Loan button (which we describe in the preceding section), this payee appears in the list.

5. **In the To Account window that appears, select the loan account to which the repayment was made.**

Adding recurring transactions

The Bank/Credit Card section provides you with a common way to handle recurring transactions, including the Add a Direct Debit, Add a Standing Order, and Add a Direct Credit eaZy processes. Follow these steps to add a recurring transaction:

1. **In the Bank/Credit Card panel, click the button for the recurring transaction you want to enter.**

   A calendar appears, prompting you to specify the date of the transaction.

2. **Select the transaction date from the calendar.**

   If you're entering the transaction on the day the transaction occurred, the default date is correct.

3. **Click the Next button.**

   The Frequency window opens, asking you to select the billing cycle.

4. **Select an option from the Select a Billing Cycle panel.**

   You can choose from the options outlined in the section "Recurring transactions," earlier in this chapter.

5. **Click Next.**

   The Total Number of Payments panel appears, prompting you to enter the total number of transactions.

6. **Enter the number of transactions, and then click Next.**

   The Installment Amount panel appears.

7. **Enter the amount, and then click Next.**

8. **In the From Account panel that appears, enter the account the money will be coming from.**

9. **Click Next.**

   The Select Associated Payee panel appears.

10. **(Optional) Select a payee, if relevant.**

11. **Click Next.**

    The To Account panel appears.

12. **Enter the account the money will be going to, and then click Next.**

    The Assign Default Values panel appears.

13. **(Optional) In the appropriate fields, enter a description, a reference, or notes to be assigned to each future transaction of this type.**

    For example, you could enter DD in the Reference field to identify the transaction as a direct debit. If you're entering a mortgage payment, you could reference your mortgage account number. Or you could enter your employee ID number if you're creating a transaction for your salary.

14. **Click Next.**

    The Action panel opens.

15. **Click Finish to complete the recurring transaction.**

Adding accounts

To add a bank or credit card account, follow these steps:

1. **Click the appropriate option in the Bank/Credit Card panel.**

   Click either Add a Bank Account or Add a Credit Card Account.

   The Bank Account Name or Credit Card Name panel appears.

2. **Enter the name for this new account in the Bank Account Name or Credit Card Name text box, and then click Next.**

3. In the Set the Opening Balance panel that appears, enter a value in the Enter the Current Account Balance text box.

How you enter this information depends on the details of the account:

- *New bank account that contains money:* Enter a positive amount. For example, if you have £1,000 in your bank account, then enter **1000**.

- *New bank account that's overdrawn:* If you owe your bank money, then enter a negative amount. For example, if you're overdrawn by £300, then enter **-300**.

- *New credit card account for which you owe money:* Enter a positive amount. For example, if you owe £500 on your credit card, enter **500**.

- *New credit card account for which your credit card company owes you money:* In this very rare case, enter a negative amount. For example, if your credit card owes you £25, enter **-25**.

4. Click Next.

The Action panel opens

5. Click Finish to create the new account.

Your new account appears in the Chart of Accounts tree (as shown in Figure 3-7 and which we talk about in Chapter 6).

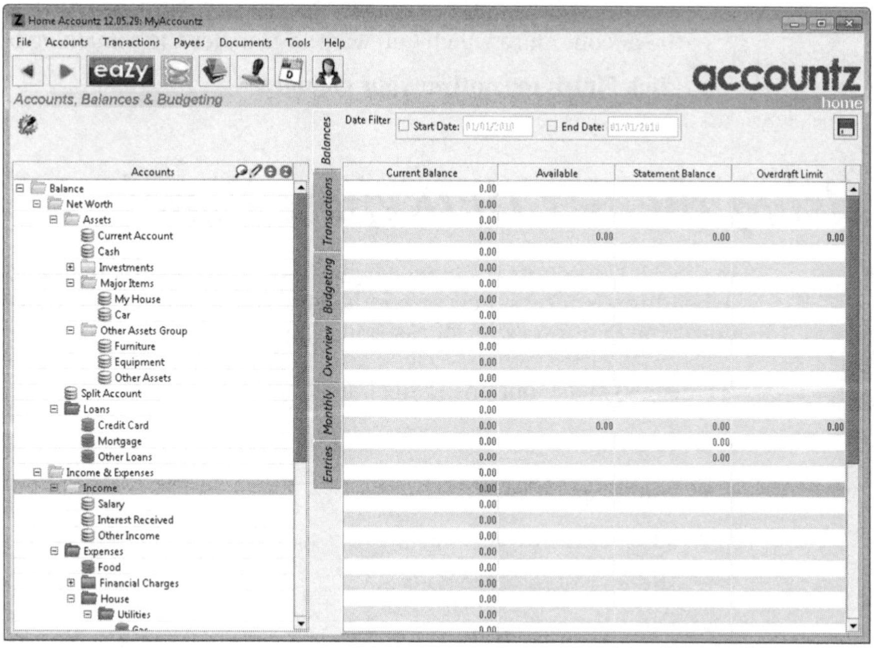

Figure 3-7:
The Chart of Accounts tree shows all the accounts in the system.

Working with accounts

Four eaZy processes can help you manage your accounts:

- ✔ Close an Account
- ✔ Re-Open a Closed Account
- ✔ Delete an Account
- ✔ Undelete an Account

Follow these steps to use one of these processes:

1. **Click the appropriate button in the Bank/Credit Card panel.**

   A list of accounts appears.

2. **From the list of accounts, select the one that you want to change.**

   Depending on which option you selected in Step 1, specify the account you want to close, reopen, delete, or undelete.

3. **Click Next.**

   A summary of the account details appears.

   If you're deleting an account, the Transfer Balance to Account panel appears if a balance remains in the account you want to delete. Select the account into which you want to transfer the remaining balance.

4. **Click Finish to confirm your changes.**

Using the Set Up/Report Panel

In the Set Up/Report panel (see Figure 3-8), you can create new income and expenditure sources, new or continuation files, payees, and reports. (We cover the Report eaZy processes in Chapter 16.)

We discuss these options in the following sections:

- ✔ New File
- ✔ Continuation File
- ✔ Add an Income Source
- ✔ Add an Expenditure Source
- ✔ Add a Payee
- ✔ Delete a Payee

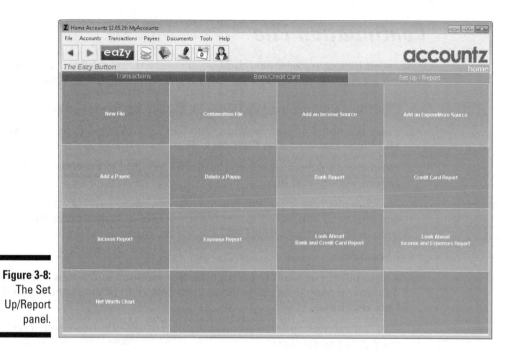

New File

To create a new set of accounts for your home or personal finances, follow these steps:

1. **In the Set Up/Report panel, click the New File button.**

2. **Select the first option in the New File panel that appears, and then click Next.**

3. **Type a filename in the Enter Your Filename text box.**

   You can also save the default path to your file by clicking the Browse button to the right of the text box.

4. **Click Next.**

5. **Add any new bank, credit card, or loan accounts by entering their names in the Account Name text box.**

6. **Add any opening balances to these accounts in the Current Balance text box.**

7. **Click Next.**

   The Action panel appears.

8. **Click Finish to create your new file.**

Continuation File

If you want to create a new file based on the current file — for example, to create a file that includes only this year's transactions — follow these steps:

1. **Click the Continuation File button in the Set Up/Report panel.**

2. **Enter the name of your continuation file in the Please Type Your New File Name text box, and then click Next.**

3. **Enter the date from which you want the new file to continue in the Enter the Date text box.**

   For example, if your current file consists of the transactions from 2011 and 2012, and you want the new file to contain only the transactions from 2012, then enter **01/01/2012** in the Enter the Date text box.

4. **Click Next.**

5. **(Optional) If you want to restrict the transactions in the new file to a date in the past, then enter the appropriate date in the Enter the End Date text box.**

   You can use this option if you want to create a file that consists of only your 2011 transactions.

6. **Click Next.**

7. **Select the account you want to use from the Opening Balance list.**

   Home Accountz automatically creates new opening balances if the date set in Step 3 is later than the transactions that already exist in your current file.

8. **Click Next to open the Action panel.**

9. **Click Finish to create your continuation file.**

Add an Income Source

If you want to add a new account to track a new income source, follow these steps:

1. **Click the Add an Income Source button in the Set Up/Report panel.**

   The Income Source Name panel appears.

2. **Enter a name for the income source in the Give the Income Source a Name text box, and then click Next.**

   The Action panel appears.

3. **Click Finish to create the new income source.**

Add an Expenditure Source

To create a new expenditure source to track a new category of expense, follow these steps:

1. **In the Set Up/Report panel, click the Add an Expenditure Source option.**

2. **Enter a name in the Give the Expenditure Source a Name text box, and then click Next.**

3. **In the Action panel that appears, click Finish to add the new expenditure source.**

Add a Payee

Add a payee to Home Accountz that you can attach to your payments by following these steps:

1. **In the Set Up/Report panel, click the Add a Payee button.**

   The New Payee's Name panel appears.

2. **Enter a name in the Please Enter the New Payee's Name text box, and then click Next.**

3. **(Optional) Enter information for the payee in the Address, Post Code, and Country text boxes.**

4. **Click Next.**

   The Action panel opens.

5. **Click Finish to add the new payee.**

Delete a Payee

To remove a payee from Home Accountz, follow these steps:

1. **Click the Delete a Payee button in the Set Up/Report panel.**

2. **Select the payee that you want to remove from the Please Select the Payee You Purchased From list.**

3. **Click Next.**

   The Action panel appears.

4. **Click Finish to delete the payee.**

Chapter 4

Backing Up and Filing

*B*acking up your data is the single most important action you can take to protect your accounts files. Computers are pretty reliable, but data loss can happen at any time. In order to make sure you have your data protected, you need to create a backup copy of the data on a separate hard drive. You can even make several copies on removable devices, such as DVD disc or USB stick.

Home Accountz does its best to protect your data by automatically saving on a regular basis. In addition to this, Home Accountz gives you the ability to swap data files. In this chapter, we highlight the different ways in which you can manage (and retain) your data and show you the best procedures to adopt when doing so.

Storing Your Data in Home Accountz

Home Accountz stores its data in HAZ format files. These are proprietary format files, much the same as you get from Quicken or Microsoft Money. By using a proprietary format such as this, the team developing the application can ensure that the format extends to meet the needs of the application.

You can apply a number of properties to Home Accountz files to help protect those files. These properties help you keep track of your files by providing you with more information so that you can track down the file you're looking for.

You can use the Home Accountz file properties to change your file's name and add a description, if necessary. You can also set a transaction lock date to prevent you from accidentally editing entries that you've cleared or finished with. Just follow these steps:

1. **Choose File⇨Properties.**

   The Properties window opens (shown in Figure 4-1). This window presents a series of fields that represent the properties associated with a Home Accountz HAZ file.

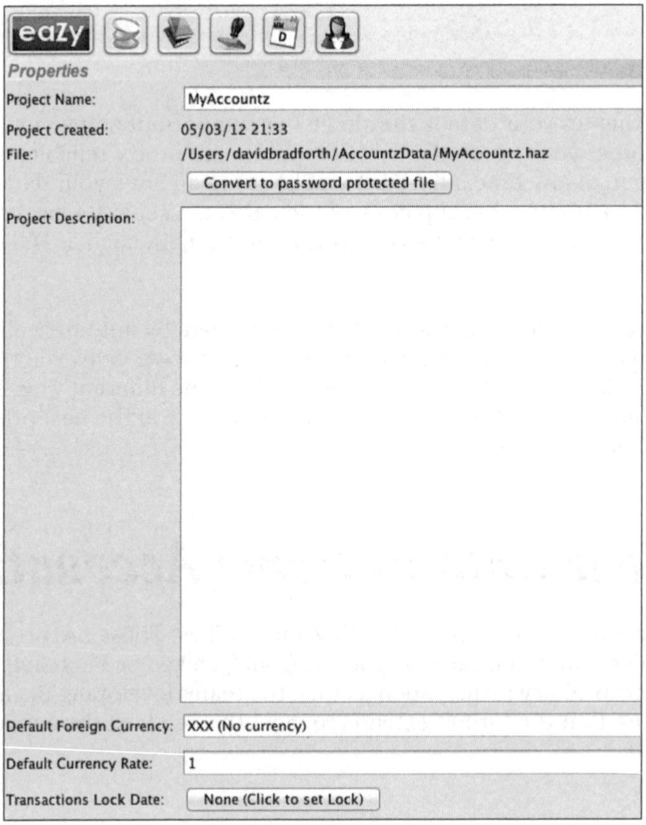

Figure 4-1:
The Properties window contains settings specific to your file, and can also contain a description of that file.

2. **(Optional) To change the project name to something other than the filename (which appears by default), click in the Project Name text box and enter a new name.**

   The project name applies to this set of accounts, and it appears in the title bar for Home Accountz. *Note:* The name in the title bar doesn't change until you exit and then restart the application.

   The Project Created field is read-only, displaying the date and time that the file was created. You can customize how this information appears within the Configuration section of Home Accountz (which we talk about in Chapter 6).

   The read-only File field indicates the location of the file on your computer.

3. **If you want to add password protection to your Accounts file, click the Convert to Password Protected File button.**

   It's the large gray button that appears above the Project Description text box.

   A message appears, telling you that your data is being prepared for data conversion.

   After the conversion finishes, the Home Accountz: Password Protected File Loading dialog box appears (see Figure 4-2).

4. **Enter the password you want in the Please Enter Your Password For text box, and then enter it again in the Please Repeat Password text box.**

   Keep this password simple, but not obvious: Use a mixture of numbers and letters. The password is case sensitive, adding an extra level of security — make sure Caps Lock is off before you set your password.

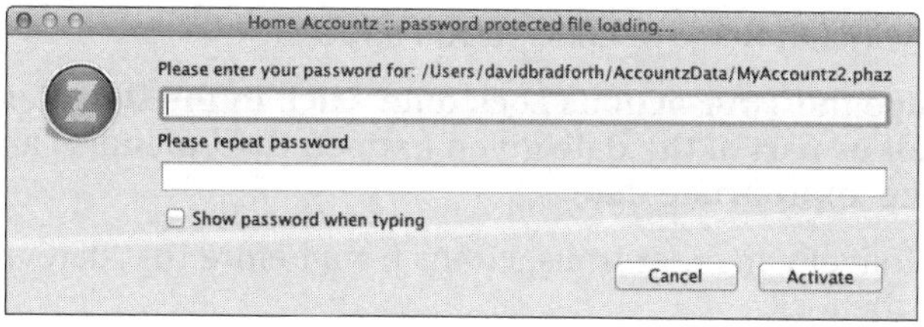

Figure 4-2:
Enter a
password to
secure your
file — just
don't
forget it!

Home Accountz :: password protected file loading...

Please enter your password for: /Users/davidbradforth/AccountzData/MyAccountz2.phaz

Please repeat password

☐ Show password when typing

Cancel   Activate

5. **Click Activate to confirm your password.**

   Make sure you make a note of your password. If you lose it, your file will be permanently locked.

   The password window closes, and you return to the Properties window.

   The next time you open your accounts, you're prompted to enter this password.

6. **To add a description, click in the Product Description text box and enter your description.**

   The information contained in this box is effectively a large note. You can use this section to leave reminders for yourself or others who use this file in the future.

7. **If you're working in multiple currencies, click the Default Foreign Currency button and select an option from the drop-down list that appears.**

   The Default Foreign Currency field appears below the Project Description form. By default, the field is set to be XXX (No Currency).

   You can type the three letter descriptor (for example, EUR for Euro, USD for American dollar, AUD for Australian dollar) directly into the Foreign Currency field.

8. **To change the currency conversion rate, click in the Default Currency Rate text box and type in the rate.**

   For example, if the current U.S. dollar rate against the pound is 1.49, you can enter **1.49**.

9. **If you want to prevent yourself from accidentally editing entries you've cleared or finished with, click the None button next to Transactions Lock Date.**

   Any cleared or finished transactions are locked.

   A Date field and Remove Lock button appear.

10. **To change the Transactions Lock date, click in the Date field and delete all or part of the date given to open the Calendar, and then select the appropriate date.**

    You no longer can enter transactions from before that date unless you remove the lock.

11. **After you finish customizing the properties attached to your accounts file, close the Properties window by clicking any of the options in the toolbar.**

    When the Properties window closes, the changes you made are applied.

Creating Backups

Home Accountz is set to automatically create a backup of your data every 30 minutes. However, you can take control of how, when, and where your backups occur.

When you change any of these settings, the new settings don't take effect until you restart the Home Accountz application. These changes don't affect manual backups: If you choose File⇨Backup, you immediately create a backup of your file.

Setting up the automatic backup

To create and customize the automatic backup function in Home Accountz, follow these steps:

1. **Choose File⇨Backup.**

   The Backup window appears, as shown in Figure 4-3.

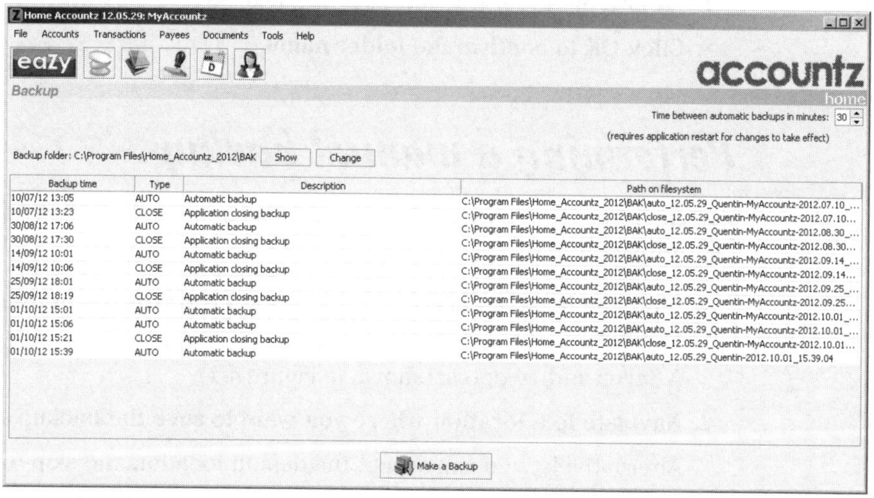

Figure 4-3:
The Backup window.

The time between automatic backups is set to 30 minutes by default.

2. **To change the amount of time between backups, click in the Time between Automatic Backups in Minutes text box and type in the number of minutes.**

   Alternatively, you can click the up and down arrows to the right of the text box to alter the time within that field.

You may want to reduce the time period between backups if you're entering a large number of transactions so that you can prevent losing a lot of data. You can increase the backup time period beyond 30 minutes, but you probably don't want to because you run a higher risk of losing your data in the event of a computer crash, power failure, and so on.

3. **Click the Show button on the left side of the screen.**

   The File window for the current backup folder and all current backup files appears.

4. **To change the location of the backup folder and where the backup files are stored, click the Change button.**

   The Open dialog box appears.

5. **Navigate to the location where you want to create a new backup folder.**

   Choose a location other than your current hard drive (for example, a removable USB drive) to prevent a hard drive failure from taking out both your data files and your backups.

6. **Click the Create New Folder button on the top-right of the dialog box.**

   The New Folder dialog box appears.

7. **Enter a name for this folder in the text box.**

8. **Click OK to confirm the folder name.**

Performing a manual backup

You can force Home Accountz to create a manual backup at any time. Just follow these steps:

1. **Click the Make a Backup button located towards the bottom of the window.**

   A Save window opens (shown in Figure 4-4).

2. **Navigate to a location where you want to save the backup.**

   Alternatively, you can accept the default location and skip to Step 4.

3. **(Optional) If you want to create a new folder, click the New Folder button at the bottom of the window, enter a filename for the folder, and then click OK.**

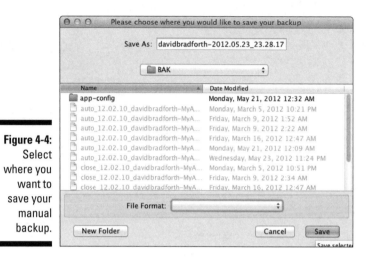

Figure 4-4:
Select
where you
want to
save your
manual
backup.

4. **Click in the File Name text box and enter a new name for your backup file.**

   Alternatively, you can leave the name automatically generated by the program.

   The automatically generated backup filename has the format of the username, followed by the account file creation date, the backup file creation date and the time the backup was created — for example, `user_12.04.13_Sony-2012.04.17_14.59.00`. This file naming convention allows you to easily track down the backup file if something happens to your original file.

5. **Click the Save button at the bottom of the dialog box.**

   A line is added to the bottom of the Backup report (shown in Figure 4-5), which appears when you choose File➪Backup.

   The report is divided into four columns:

   • *Backup Time:* When the backup was created

   • *Type:* Whether this was an automatic backup or a user backup

   • *Description:* A brief explanation of this backup

   • *Path on File System:* The save location of the backup file

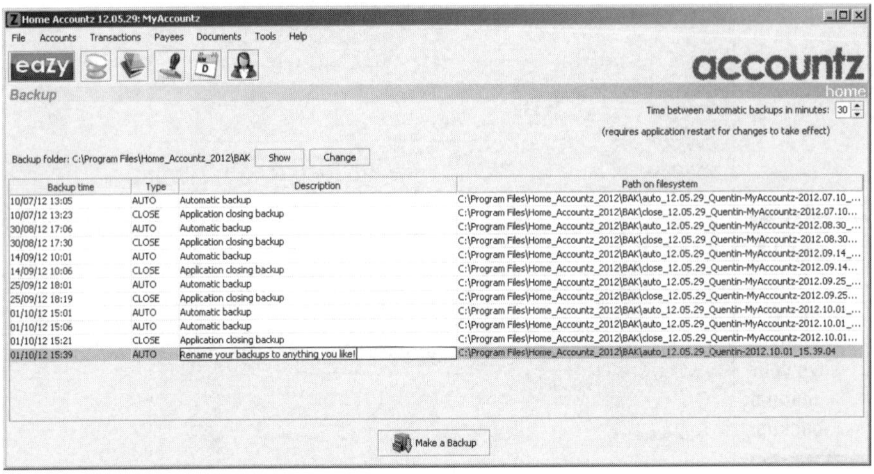

Figure 4-5:
With each
type of
backup,
a line is
added to
the backup
report.

6. **Double-click in the Description field, and then type in a description.**

   This description can reflect any major activity in your accounts files, and it can provide a useful pointer to how you've developed your personal accounting file.

7. **Press the Return (or Enter) key to confirm your description.**

8. **To leave the Backup report, click any of the icons located at the top of the screen.**

Working with Multiple Accounts

Home Accountz allows you to create as many accounts as you need — you're not limited to producing one set of accounts. You can save each set of accounts with its own unique filename, allowing you to use Home Accountz to manage several different sets of accounts. For example, you could make two sets of accounts, one of which is your personal home accounts and the other being accounts for a local club.

Creating multiple Home Accountz files

You can create as many files as you have sets of accounts. Each accounts file has the extension HAZ; for example, myhomeaccounts.haz or myclub.haz.

To create a new accounts file, follow these steps:

1. **Choose File⇨New File.**

   The New File Welcome page appears.

2. **Select the appropriate radio button for how you want to set up Home Accountz.**

   This page has three options:

   - Set up Home Accountz without importing any previous data.
   - Upgrade from Personal Accountz, importing your Personal Accountz data.
   - Move to Home Accountz from Intuit Quicken or Microsoft Money.

3. **Click the Next button.**

   The New File Name and Location page opens (shown in Figure 4-6).

4. **Enter the filename for your new set of accounts in the File Name text box, and then press the Return (or Enter) key.**

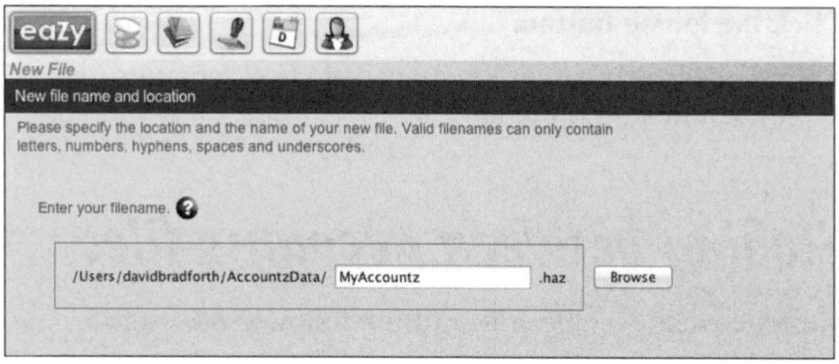

Figure 4-6: Enter the filename for the new set of accounts in the File Name text box.

New File

New file name and location

Please specify the location and the name of your new file. Valid filenames can only contain letters, numbers, hyphens, spaces and underscores.

Enter your filename.

/Users/davidbradforth/AccountzData/ | MyAccountz | .haz | Browse

5. **Click Next.**

   The Setup Bank Accounts page appears.

   A Current account appears by default.

6. **To add another account, enter the account name in the blank Account Name text box.**

7. **Click the green plus sign (+) button to the right of Current Balance.**

8. **Enter the opening balance for the account in the Current Balance text box to the right of the new account name you've entered.**

9. **(Optional) Rename the default Credit Card account by clicking in the Card Name field, entering your own text, and then pressing Return (or Enter) to confirm the entry.**

   If you don't have any credit cards or loans to enter, you can ignore the Credit Card section.

10. **To add another card, enter the appropriate information in the Credit Card section.**

    Follow these steps:

    a. Fill in the blank Card/Loan Name text box.

    b. Click the green plus sign (+) button to the right of the Amount Owed text box.

    c. Enter a name for the card in Account Name and the current balance of that card in Amount Owed.

11. **When you finish adding accounts and balances, click the Next button.**

    The Action page appears. This page informs you that when you click the Finish button, your new file will be created. It also tells you where you can find your new file.

12. **Click the Finish button.**

    Your new file is created. You now have two accounts files, which are separate and self contained.

Switching between accounts files

To switch between one file and another, follow these steps:

1. **Choose File⇨Open.**

   The Open Existing File dialog box appears.

2. **Click a file from the list of available files.**

   The file is highlighted and copied into the File Name text box.

You can also navigate to a folder in which you save accounts and type the filename directly into the File Name text box. For absolute beginners, you can always more easily locate a file by clicking its name. More proficient users may have multiple files that contain multiple sets of data, so you can more easily navigate to a file by simply entering its name.

3. Click the Open Existing File button.

A dialog box opens, informing you that your selected file is being opened.

After the file is opened, the Accounts, Balances & Budgeting page appears.

Restoring Files

If something happens to your accounts file but you have automatic backups set up, you normally lose only anything you added to the accounts file in the last 30 minutes (or however long you've set Home Accountz to perform an automatic backup, as described in the section "Setting up the automatic backup," earlier in this chapter).

You can use the automatic backup files or files that you manually created to restore your accounts file to any past backup point. Just follow the steps in the preceding section to open a backup file.

You can keep track of recently opened files by using the History list (shown in Figure 4-7), which you can access by choosing File⇨History. This list provides one-click access to each of the previous working files in the order they were last opened in Home Accountz.

Figure 4-7:
The File History details all recent files opened within Home Accountz.

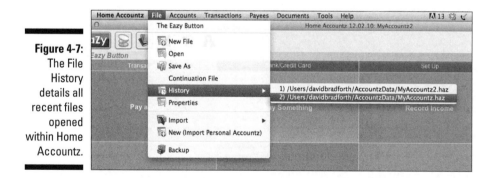

If you attempt to open the file you're already working with, the application prompts as to whether you want to do that. Reopening your current data file removes any changes you made to that file and restores it to the point at which the backup file was created.

The History option is useful if you're managing two different sets of accounts — for instance, yours and your partner's. It provides one-click access to the most frequently used files. Follow these steps to use the History option:

1. **Choose File⇨History.**

   A pop-up menu of recently opened files appears.

2. **Select the file that you want to open.**

   The file opens in Home Accountz, and the Accounts, Balances & Budgeting page appears.

Chapter 5

Using Tools to Keep Track of Your Finances

In This Chapter

▶ Working with the Desk Diary

▶ Calculating directly in Home Accountz

*H*ome Accountz features a Desk Diary and Calculator, both of which can help you manage your budget.

The Desk Diary is a virtual diary and scheduling tool; it includes features that can help you keep track of appointments, milestones, and deadlines. It also allows you to build to-do lists. These lists can help you prioritize any tasks that you need to carry out.

The built-in Calculator tool allows you to perform simple calculations. You can add as many rows of calculations as you want, and they're all saved with your file. The most common use of the Calculator is to add up checks that you're about to deposit in the bank or to add up petty cash receipts.

Writing in the Desk Diary

The Desk Diary component consists of two panels (as shown in Figure 5-1):

✔ **Calendar:** The left panel contains the calendar itself. Today's date is highlighted in blue by default, and dates that include events or appointments are highlighted in red.

You can select a date by clicking it. When you do, the selected date is highlighted in blue.

✔ **Entries:** In the right panel, you can create, edit, copy, and delete entries. You can view all future diary entries and create a prioritized to-do list. There are four tabs across the top of this table:

- Diary Entries
- Update Diary
- Future Entries
- ToDo List

The following sections guide you through how the Desk Diary works, highlighting some important features.

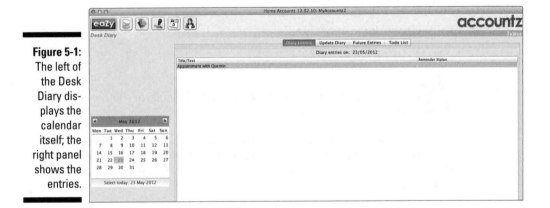

Figure 5-1:
The left of the Desk Diary displays the calendar itself; the right panel shows the entries.

The Diary Entries tab

The Diary Entries tab shows all your diary entries in the right panel. This panel is divided into two columns:

✔ **Title/Text:** Stores the title of each Diary entry

✔ **Reminder Status:** Stores the fields that show whether you have any reminders set for these entries.

If this is the first time you use the Diary, both these columns are blank.

The Update Diary tab

The Update Diary tab allows you to create, edit, and delete calendar entries and set reminders for those entries.

The Desk Diary toolbar on the right of the screen contains three buttons:

- ✔ **Add Entry:** This button contains a green circle with a white plus sign (+) in the middle. Click this button when you want to add a new diary entry for the selected date. (Adding a diary entry is explained in the following section.)

- ✔ **Repeat Entry:** Use this button to create recurring diary entries based on existing entries. For example, you might create a repeat entry for a regular monthly budgeting meeting that's scheduled to occur on the first Thursday of every month. You can instruct the Desk Diary to set all future meeting dates automatically, as we explain in the section "Adding a repeating meeting," later in this chapter.

- ✔ **Remove Entry:** You can use the Remove Entry button to delete the current entry, as well as any recurring entries derived from the current entry. We describe using this button in the section "Deleting a diary entry," later in this chapter.

The following sections cover the likely scenarios with Diary entries: adding Diary entries reflecting repeating or one-time activities, as well as removing entries if they're no longer required.

Adding a diary entry

The top half of the Update Diary table (shown in Figure 5-2), which appears when you select the Update Diary tab, has two fields:

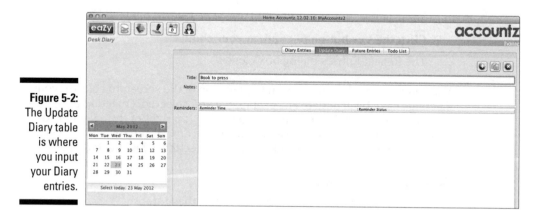

Figure 5-2:
The Update Diary table is where you input your Diary entries.

- ✔ **Title:** Enter the title of your new entry by clicking in the Title text box and typing a descriptive name.

- ✔ **Notes:** Enter a more in-depth description of this entry by clicking in the Notes text box and typing your notes.

Data entered into these fields is automatically saved when you add another entry or switch to another tab.

Adding a repeating meeting

You can set how often and how many times you want an entry to appear in your Desk Diary by following these steps:

1. **Click the Diary Entries tab.**

2. **In the list of diary entries, select the entry that you want to repeat.**

   The Update Diary tab opens, displaying your selected meeting.

3. **Click the Repeat Entry button.**

   The button has an image of two pieces of paper.

   The Repeat Entries dialog box appears.

4. **Select how often you want the meeting to occur from the Days drop-down list.**

   The default is Days, but if you want to schedule a meeting once a month, select Months from the drop-down list.

5. **Click in the Do It Once Every text box and type in a number.**

   For example, if your meeting occurs once a month, type **1**.

6. **Click in the Until text box and enter the number of times you want your meeting to repeat.**

   For example, if you want to add one year's worth of meetings, type in **12**.

7. **Click the Yes button to confirm your changes.**

   The Repeat Entries dialog box closes.

You can now use the calendar on the left side of the screen to confirm your meetings have been added. For example, if you selected a meeting to recur once a month, click the Forward button at the top-right of the calendar to move through the months or select the Future Entries tab to view the list. The day of the month you selected for your meeting is highlighted in red.

Deleting a Diary entry

To delete an entry that you're viewing, follow these steps:

1. **Click the Remove Entry button.**

   The button features a red circle with a white X inside.

   The Remove Repeated Entries dialog box appears.

2. Select the appropriate option.

You can choose to remove

- *All Repeated:* All repeated meetings that follow the selected meeting

- *This:* Just this meeting

- *Both:* This meeting and all the following repeated meetings

Or you can select Cancel to not remove any meetings.

After you make a selection, the Remove Repeated Entries dialog box closes.

Adding reminders

In the lower half of the Update Diary table, you can set reminders for a calendar entry. The Reminder section of the page is divided into two columns:

- ✔ **Reminder Time:** Fields in this column contain the date and time of your scheduled reminder. After you set a reminder, a dialog box appears on your screen at the specified time.

- ✔ **Reminder Status:** A check in this field shows that a reminder has been set for this entry.

To create a reminder, follow these steps:

1. Click the Add Reminder icon.

This green button features a white plus sign (+).

The Add Reminder Alarm dialog box appears (as shown in Figure 5-3).

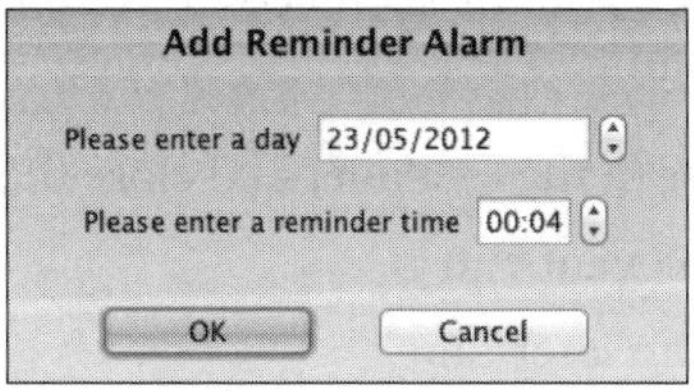

Figure 5-3:
The Add Reminder Alarm dialog box allows you to set up a reminder.

Add Reminder Alarm

Please enter a day 23/05/2012

Please enter a reminder time 00:04

OK   Cancel

2. **(Optional) In the Please Enter a Day text box, change the date the reminder will be displayed by clicking in the box and entering the date.**

   Alternatively, you can click the up and down buttons to the right of the text box.

   The date of the meeting appears by default.

3. **Click in the Please Enter a Reminder Time text box and enter a time for the reminder to appear.**

   Alternatively, you can click the up and down buttons to the right of the text box to set the time.

   You can also use the up or down buttons to the right of the text box.

4. **Click OK to confirm the reminder.**

The reminder appears when your chosen date and time is reached, reminding you about the selected event (shown in Figure 5-4).

If Home Accountz isn't running at the scheduled time, the reminder doesn't appear.

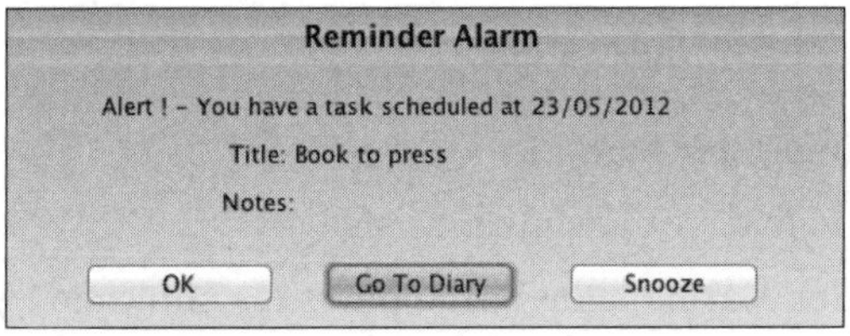

Figure 5-4:
A reminder alarm alerts you about a scheduled task.

Reminder Alarm

Alert ! – You have a task scheduled at 23/05/2012

Title: Book to press

Notes:

| OK | Go To Diary | Snooze |

The Reminder Alarm dialog box gives you three choices. Click one of these buttons, depending on what you want to do:

- ✔ **OK:** Acknowledge that you've seen the reminder and close the dialog box.
- ✔ **Go to Diary Entry:** View the relevant entry.
- ✔ **Snooze:** Reset the reminder for a later time.

If you need to remove a reminder, click the reminder to select it, and then click the Remove Reminder button, which appears on the bottom-right of the screen.

The Future Entries tab

The Future Entries tab (shown in Figure 5-5) displays all your future Diary entries in one place. The page is divided into three columns:

- ✔ **Text/Title:** The event or meeting name
- ✔ **Reminder Status:** Whether you have any reminders set for an event, represented by a white check in a green circle
- ✔ **Date:** When the event is scheduled to occur

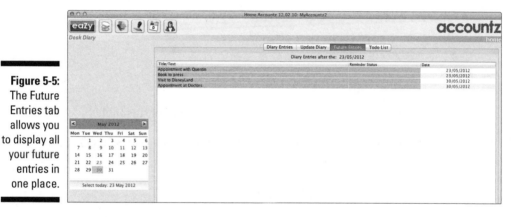

Figure 5-5:
The Future Entries tab allows you to display all your future entries in one place.

Double-clicking on any entry takes you to the Update Diary tab, described in the section "The Update Diary tab," earlier in this chapter.

The ToDo List tab

The ToDo List tab (shown in Figure 5-6) allows you to create a list of pressing tasks and give them a priority value (on a scale of 1 to 10, 1 being most urgent).

The table is divided into two columns:

- ✔ **ToDo:** Details a description of any task you've added to this list
- ✔ **Priority:** Relates the task's level of urgency

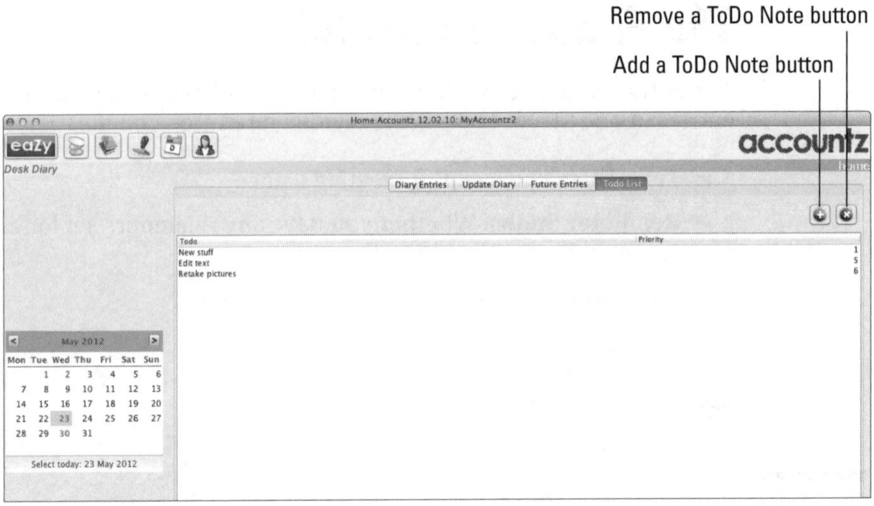

Remove a ToDo Note button

Add a ToDo Note button

Figure 5-6:
The ToDo
list allows
you to
prioritize
pressing
tasks.

You can find two buttons above and to the right of this table:

✔ **Add a ToDo Note:** A green circle with a white plus sign (+)

✔ **Remove a ToDo Note:** A red circle with a white X inside

Add a ToDo note by following these steps:

1. **Click the Add a ToDo Note button.**

   A new, blank line appears in the ToDo list.

2. **(Optional) Double-click in the ToDo field.**

   The ToDo Editor dialog box appears.

3. **Click in the Note text box and enter text that accurately describes the task you need to be reminded of.**

4. **Click the number in the Priority field and select the item's priority, from 1 to 10.**

5. **Click the OK button to close the dialog box.**

   Your task description and priority are added to the appropriate fields.

The ToDo list automatically sorts itself in order of priority. To edit an item, simply click in the field you want to change.

You may need to remove a reminder that no longer applies. For example, a set task that you normally do may be given to someone else to do in the future. To delete a ToDo note, click the item you want to delete, and then click the Remove a ToDo Note button.

Your selected task is removed as soon as you click Remove a ToDo Note. You don't get a warning, and Home Accountz doesn't double-check that you really want to remove the task. So make sure that you really do want to remove it.

Using Home Accountz's Calculator

A Calculator tool is built in to Home Accountz. With this tool, you can cut and paste the answers to your calculations directly into Home Accountz transactions.

Adding, editing, and deleting calculations

To use the Calculator tool, follow these steps:

1. **Choose Tools⇨Calculator.**

2. **To start a new calculation, click the Add a New Calculation Line to the Table button.**

   This button displays a green circle with a white plus sign (+) in the center.

   A new calculation line is added to the table.

3. **Click in the Calculation field and type in your calculation (as shown in Figure 5-7).**

   For example, you might enter **1+2+3+100+123+6789**.

Figure 5-7:
A calculation's result appears in the Result column.

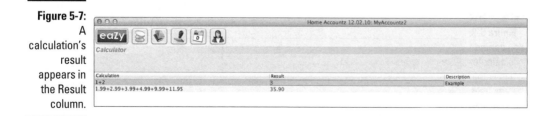

The calculation field allows you to enter figures just like you can in a spreadsheet, but they must be numerical constants. You can also carry out larger calculations by including calculations within calculations — using parentheses to build a larger calculation (see Figure 5-8).

When you enter your figures into the calculation field, the result is computed and displayed in the adjacent Result field.

Figure 5-8:
You can
include part
of a cal-
culation in
parentheses.

Calculation
1+2
1.99+2.99+3.99+4.99+9.99+11.95
2.99+9.99+(21.99-599)

4. **(Optional) Add a description of the calculation in the Description field so that, in the future, you can easily determine what data the calculation uses.**

   For example, you could enter **Total Gas Receipts for October 2012**.

5. **Repeat Steps 2 through 4 for all the calculations you want to create.**

   You can add as many rows of calculations as you want, and they're all saved with your file.

6. **After you finish adding calculations to the table, leave the Calculator tool by clicking another section of the Home Accountz program.**

   All the calculations you've entered in the Calculation table are automatically saved and available the next time you use the Calculator tool.

You can change a calculation after you enter it by clicking in the calculation's field and making your changes (see Figure 5-9). The Results field for that line changes when you confirm the entry by pressing Return or Enter.

Figure 5-9:
You can edit
a calcula-
tion within
its field.

Calculation
1+2
1.99+2.99+4.99+4.99+9.99+11.95
2.99+9.99+(21.99-599)

Deleting a calculation is as easy as removing the row that contains the calculation: Select that row in the Calculator table, and then click the Delete the Current Calculation Line from the Table button. After you click the button, the row that contains the calculation is removed from the table.

Calculating directly in tables

You have the option of using the basic Calculator features directly in the Home Accountz tables (see Figure 5-10).The preceding section explains how to add single transactions to the Transaction table. You may need to add a transaction that's made up of several elements — for example, daily lunches for the month would include Sandwich and Drink. You can use the built-in calculation capabilities of Home Accountz to enter these transactions.

Figure 5-10:
You can enter multiple values in the Total Amounts column.

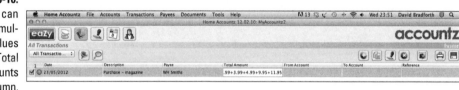

To use calculations in the Transaction table, follow these steps:

1. **Click the All Transactions button on the toolbar.**

   The All Transactions window opens.

2. **Click the Add a New Transaction button.**

   This button displays a green circle with a white plus sign (+) and appears at the top-right of the screen.

3. **Click in the Total Amount field and type in a calculation.**

   For example, you could enter **=1.99+2.99+5.99+10.99**.

   Note: The calculation must be preceded by an equal sign (=).

   Home Accountz calculates the total and places it in the Total Amount field.

Chapter 6

Configuring Home Accountz

. . . .

In This Chapter

▶ Exploring the Home Accountz Configuration panel

▶ Specifying how elements appear in Home Accountz

▶ Dealing with validation and statuses

▶ Displaying dates, times, and numbers the way you want

▶ Choosing which application elements appear

. . . .

In common with other computer software packages, there are a number of areas within Home Accountz that you can customize. For example, you can change the date format, location of documents, presentation of tables, and other settings that are specific to individual components of the application.

This chapter can help you work through the configuration section of Home Accountz. You can make all kinds of changes to the Home Accountz configuration. For example, you may want to change the number and order of the buttons in the main toolbar so that the tools you use most often are closer to hand. If you're an expert, you may want to turn off some of the warning messages. Maybe you prefer working more with the keyboard rather than the mouse, in which case, you can add and change your keyboard shortcuts.

Navigating the Home Accountz Configuration Panel

To open the Configuration panel (shown in Figure 6-1), choose Tools⇨ Configuration. The Configuration page of Home Accountz appears. On the left side of the page, a number of folders are listed. Each folder contains further folders or tabs that you may configure.

The Configuration panel contains the folders discussed in the following sections. To open any of these folders, either double-click the folder name in the Configuration panel list or click the plus sign (+) immediately to the left of the folder icon.

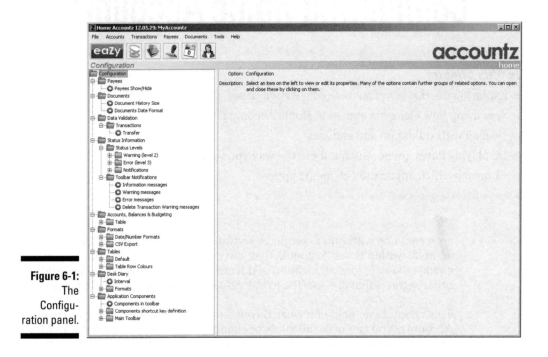

Figure 6-1:
The
Configuration panel.

Payees

This folder allows you to configure the database and default settings to show or hide payees from any menus. The folder contains an option setting called Payees Show/Hide, which you can set to specify whether hidden payees appear in any drop-down list or database.

Documents

The Documents folder allows you to specify how different elements of the document component appear, including how dates are displayed on documents. This folder contains two configuration option settings:

✔ **Document History Size:** Enter the maximum number of documents that you want to save in the Documents History menu, which you can access by choosing Documents➪Documents.

✔ **Documents Date Format:** Control how a date is presented.

Data Validation

You can use the Data Validation folder to set the level of interaction between data entry and data checking. For maximum security, you can turn on all the validators. For example, you can specify whether you want Home Accountz to warn you if you enter a transaction that has a zero amount. The Data Validation folder contains another folder called Transactions, which allows you to alter the transaction data validation configuration.

The Transactions folder contains a setting called Transfer, which you can use to apply to or remove from your transaction any of a number of validation rules. The data-type columns that remain in the Show list are used to validate your data while you work with it: The data-type columns that remain in the Hide list aren't applied at all.

Status Information

The Status Information folder contains the configuration of how status information appears onscreen. In this folder, you can specify the background color for transactions that contain mistakes. Also, you can turn on and off toolbox notifications. For example, display (or hide) information messages and tips that relate to changes you've recently made.

The Status Information folder contains a folder called Status Level, which contains settings that control both information and warning-level values for how status information appears. There are two warning-level values:

- **Level 2:** The application can resolve the issue for itself.
- **Level 3:** The application can't resolve the issue and needs your help.

Accounts, Balances & Budgeting

This folder, which allows you to control various aspects of the Accounts, Balances & Budgeting page, contains the Table folder. In this folder, you can select the Show Account Code setting if you want the account codes to appear in the Chart of Accounts and when you look at your accounts.

The Account Manager dialog box is split into three vertical portions:

- **Chart of Accounts tree:** In the far-left of the window
- **Button panel:** In the middle of the window
- **Properties panel:** On the far-right of the window

Accounts are stored in the Accounts, Balances & Budgeting table in the Accounting pane. To display this table, when you have the Accounts, Balances & Budgeting window open, follow these steps:

1. **Click the Accounts, Balances & Budgeting button in the toolbar.**

   The Accounts, Balances & Budgeting page opens, displaying the Accounts pane and the Accounts, Balances & Budgeting table.

2. **Click the Create/Edit Your Accounts button in the Accounts pane.**

   The Account Manager dialog box appears.

Formats

The Formats folder contains settings that control the default general application configuration options. It contains a folder called Date/Number Formats, which contains settings that you can use to change the display format for dates, time, and numbers. It also contains the CSV Export folder, where you can change the comma separated value to another separator.

Tables

The Tables folder allows you to change the table display properties. For example, you can change features such as background colors and add alternate row coloring (which some people prefer so that they can more easily follow data in rows). The Tables folder contains two folders:

- **Default:** Contains default options that other tables can link to.
- **Table Row Colors:** Lets you change the default row colors in all tables, including the selected row color and error transaction colors. You can also alternate row coloring to make tables easier to read (make the Background color the same as the Alternate Row Colour if you want all rows to be the same color).

Desk Diary

The Desk Diary folder is used to configure the Desk Diary, allowing you to set date and time formats. It contains a setting called Interval, which lets you specify how often the Desk Diary checks whether alarms are due. The Desk

Diary folder also contains a folder called Format, which contains settings that allow you to configure the Desk Diary time and date formats.

Application Components

Change what items appear in the main toolbar and the order in which they appear in the Application Components folder. Also, you can edit, add, and delete keyboard shortcuts. You can show or hide any the components in the main toolbar by selecting them from the Show or Hide lists and moving them to the opposite side. You can also choose the order in which to display them by selecting a component in the Show list and moving the component up or down within the list. (The new toolbar isn't configured until you move to another view.)

Adjusting Document Display Settings

The Documents folder offers two different tabs that allow you to alter settings: Document History Size and Document Date Format.

Document History Size

This tab allows you to enter the maximum number of documents that appear in the History submenu. (Choose File ⇨History to access this submenu.) To change the number of documents that appear in the History submenu, follow these steps:

1. **Click the plus sign (+) to the left of the Documents folder, and then select Document History Size from the drop-down list that appears.**

   A window opens in the working pane to the right of the configuration list.

2. **Click in the Value text box and type the number of documents that you want to display.**

3. **Click another folder or setting to save the changes.**

   Alternatively, you can click the button that displays a pile of coins to leave the configuration screen.

   Your change is saved automatically.

Document Date Format

In this section, you can configure the format in which dates appear in your documents. Click the Document Date Format setting in the Documents folder. This setting follows the Simple Date format specified by Java (the language in which Home Accountz is written).

Click in the Text text box at the bottom of the Document Date Format screen, and then type in a format string (for example **d MMMMMMM yyyy**).

You specify the year with the letter **y**; the month with the letter **M**, and the day of the month with the letter **d**. Be sure to use the correct uppercase and lowercase letters because the case of the letters is important (for example, you use capital **M** for months, lower case **d** for days).

So, if you wanted to display the date 23 October 2011 as 23/10/2011, you enter **dd/MM/yyyy**. On the other hand, if you wanted to display the date as 12 March 2012, you enter **dd MMMM yyyy**.

The number of letters you place within the month section affects how the month is displayed; for instance, MM means the display will show 01, MMM will result in Jan, and MMMM will result in January.

Specifying How to Validate Your Data

The Data Validation folder in the Configuration panel handles the aspects of Home Accountz that check whether the data you enter into the application is valid. This setting allows you to specify the level of interaction between data entry and data checking. (For maximum security, turn on all the validators.)

This folder contains a folder called Transactions, which offers a configuration setting called Transfer (see Figure 6-2). This setting allows you to transfer a rule from the Show column to the Hide column, and vice versa. The items in the Show list are checked when you enter transactions; those in the Hide list are ignored.

These rules are particular practices that should be applied to your data — they include Account Missing, From and To Account Same, Date Missing, Amount Is Zero, Quantity Is Zero, and No Negative Amounts.

A warning appears if any part of a transaction breaks a validation rule. For the best level of data integrity, include all the validators in the Show list.

Here's a list of validators:

✔ **Empty Transaction:** A Transaction must have values in the Date, From Account, To Account, Amount, and VAT Code fields.

✔ **Account Missing:** One of the accounts hasn't been set. If you haven't created either the From or To account within Home Accountz (which we describe in Chapter 3), an error message appears because Home Accountz doesn't have an account to receive the money or to which it can send the money.

✔ **From and To Account Same:** The same account is used in both the From Account and To Account columns.

✔ **Amount Is Zero:** The Amount value shouldn't be zero.

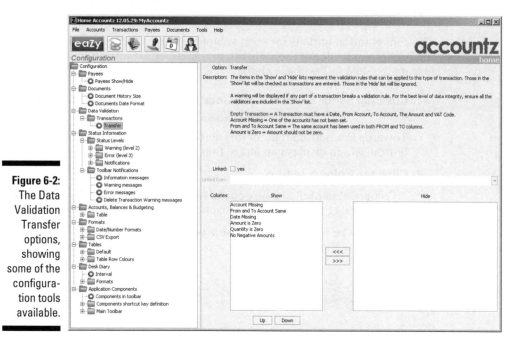

Figure 6-2: The Data Validation Transfer options, showing some of the configuration tools available.

A warning appears if any part of a transaction breaks a validation rule. To ensure data integrity, make sure all the validators are in the Show list (and none are in the Hide list).

To move an option out of the Show list and into the Hide list, click that option, and then click the right-arrow button. Alternatively, to move something from the Hide list to the Show list, select the option, and then click the left-arrow button.

Personalizing Your Status Information

The Status Information folder of the Configuration panel is focused around information that appears within the Home Accountz windows.

Status Levels

The Status Levels folder contains three subfolders:

- Warning (Level 2)
- Error (Level 3)
- Notifications

The configuration options for each subfolder are the same — you can alter the background color of the status to one that better suits your personal preference. Just follow these steps:

1. **Click the Status Background Colour setting in the folder you want to alter.**

   Towards the bottom-right of this setting, you can find the Colours button, which displays an image that looks like 16 square colors.

2. **Click the Colours button.**

   A Colour Selector dialog box opens (as shown in Figure 6-3), from which you can select the color for the background of these status reports.

3. **When you're happy with the color you've chosen, click the OK button to close the dialog box.**

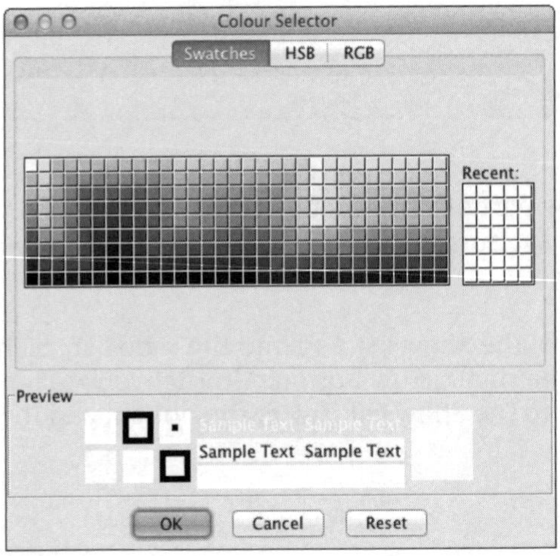

Figure 6-3: The Status Background Colour setting's Colour Selector dialog box.

Toolbar Notifications

The Toolbar Notifications folder includes the following settings:

- ✔ Information Messages
- ✔ Warning Messages
- ✔ Error Messages
- ✔ Delete Transaction Warning Messages

In these settings, you can enable or disable the appearance of information, warning, and error messages within the application. To specify whether these messages appear for each setting, select or deselect the check box at the bottom of the window. If it's selected, you get that type of notification; if it's deselected, you don't.

Formatting Dates and Numbers

The Formats folder contains a number of settings related primarily to how numbers are displayed within the system. They're all located in the Date/Number Formats folder.

You can link the format for any of the following options from another area of the Home Accountz system. Just select the Link check box, and then select the format that you want to link from the list that appears below the check box.

Formatting dates and times

You can represent dates in many different ways, and Home Accountz gives you the choice of how you want your dates to appear.

ISO 8601 Date

The International Standard for the representation of dates and times is called ISO 8601. Here are some typical ways to enter date formats into Home Accountz:

- ✔ **Year:** YYYY (2012)
- ✔ **Year and month:** YYYY-MM (2012-09)
- ✔ **Complete date:** YYYY-MM-DD (2012-03-17)

Date (Tax Date Etc)

The Date (Tax Date Etc) setting allows you to control the display format for dates within the Home Accountz system. To specify this setting, use the letters discussed in the section "Document Date Format," earlier in this chapter, to represent the date format of your choice.

Date/Time

The Date/Time configuration options control the date and time format. Check out the section "Document Date Format," earlier in this chapter, for how to format dates and the section "Configuring the Desk Diary," later in this chapter, for information on formatting time of day.

Date Consolidated By

Some reports within Home Accountz allow you to consolidate transactions by week, month, quarter, and half-year. In the Date Consolidated By setting, you can specify how you want the date to be represented.

To consolidate transactions, follow these steps:

1. **Click the All Transactions button at the top of the screen.**

   This button displays an image of a green book.

   The All Transactions window opens.

2. **Click the Open/Close View Editor Panel button, which looks like a blue funnel.**

   The View Editor panel appears.

3. **Click the Filter tab, located to the top-left of the All Transactions window.**

4. **To group transactions by a particular column, select a column from the Group on Column drop-down list.**

   If you pick a column that stores dates as the one by which you want to group your transactions, an additional drop-down list appears next to each ID below the Group on Column drop-down list.

5. **If the By Each drop-down list appears, select an option from it.**

   This option allows you to specify how you want the transactions to be grouped together. You can choose

   • Day

   • Week

   • Month

   • Quarter

- Half Year

- Year

The selections you make in Steps 4 and 5 are confirmed the moment you select them.

Time

This setting lets you set the time format for use within Home Accountz. Use the letters (and any separators) that we outline in Chapter 5.

Specifying how numbers appear

Different countries treat numbers — particularly finances — in different ways. In this section, we look at how you can specify the number format.

To open the Date/Number Format options, follow these steps:

1. **Choose Tools⇨Configuration.**

   The Configuration page appears.

2. **Click the plus sign (+) to the left of the Formats folder to open it.**

   The Formats folder contains the Date/Number and Formats folder.

3. **Click the plus sign (+) to the left of this folder.**

   A list of settings appears.

4. **Click the Number setting.**

5. **Specify number formatting in Home Accountz by entering a string of characters (and separators) in the Text text box at the bottom-right of the screen.**

   Here are the formatting codes used to specify the number format in Home Accountz:

   - *0 (zero):* Digit. If no digits are entered in the Text text box, then a 0 appears in place of the missing digits. For example, if the format is set to 0.00 and the actual amount entered is 1.2, then it's reformatted as 1.20. You use this format to force amounts to two decimal places; for example, when you're displaying currency.

   - *# (hash):* Digit. If no digits are entered, then no zeros are displayed. For example, if the format is #.#### and the number entered is 1.2, then it appears as exactly 1.2.

   - *. (period):* Decimal separator or monetary decimal separator.

   - *, (comma):* To separate different groups of numbers.

- *; (semicolon):* To separate, and treat as unique formulae, positive and negative sub-patterns.

- *- (dash):* Minus sign.

- *% (percentage sign):* Multiply by 100 and show as percentage.

- *Currency sign:* Add any currency symbol. If you want the currency to appear at the start of each number and for both positive and negative numbers, add the currency sign at the beginning of the string you enter in the Text text box and again after the semicolon.

    For example, to display a number as £123,456.78 for both positive and negative numbers, enter this format in the Text text box: **£###,###,##0.00;£– ###,###,##0.00**.

The Number tab also allows you to define the number format used throughout Home Accountz, including integers, decimals, currency, prices, and more:

- ✔ **Integer:** The Integer setting allows you to define the integer format used throughout Home Accountz. By default, the Integer setting uses the format ###,###,##0;–###,###,##0, which presents currency as whole numbers (no decimal place).

- ✔ **Decimal, Money, Currency, Price, and Price Currency:** These settings allow you to define the format used throughout Home Accountz to display these types of figures (whether standard decimal places or some form of currency). You use the same characters that you do for the Integer tab.

    The default format for these number displays — ###,###,##0.00;–###,###,##0.00 — looks like 12.99.

For any of the Number tabs, you can link to the format that you want to use from another part of the application (such as the Documents folder). Select the Linked check box, and then select the format that you want to use from the list that appears.

In most cases, CSV (Comma Separated Value) files use a comma (,) to separate data on a single row. However, with some language or country settings, Microsoft Office may expect a CSV file to use a semicolon (;). Other systems may expect a different separator. These options let you change to the relevant separator.

Setting Your Tables

The Tables folder contains two folders:

- ✔ **Default:** Sets default keyboard shortcuts that allow quick access to many parts of the application

- ✔ **Table Colours:** Sets the default table colors within various components of Home Accountz

Working with table keyboard shortcuts

The Default folder contains default keyboard shortcut settings for various areas of Home Accountz. Here's a list of the default shortcuts:

- ✔ **Add Transaction:** Ctrl+N
- ✔ **Copy Transaction:** Ctrl+C
- ✔ **Reload Transaction:** Ctrl+R
- ✔ **Print Transaction:** Ctrl+P
- ✔ **Export as CSV File:** Ctrl+E

To remove a keyboard shortcut for a particular control in Home Accountz, follow these steps:

1. **Click the setting that you want to change.**

   For example, click Copy Transaction Key Shortcut.

   The default keyboard shortcut for that control appears in the Key Shortcuts text box in the bottom-right pane.

2. **Click the shortcut that appears, and then click the Remove Key button.**

   This button looks like a red circle with a white X inside and appears at the bottom-right of the screen.

   That shortcut is removed.

Customizing table colors

The Table Row Colours settings let you change the default row colors in all tables in Home Accountz.

The Tables Row Colours folder deals with the display properties for tables in Home Accountz. To specify a setting, follow these steps:

1. **Click the small plus sign (+) to the left of the folder.**

2. **From the list that appears, select the color element that you want to manipulate.**

   For example, click Default Background to change the background color of table rows.

The available settings are

- *Default Background/Text Colour:* The default background or text color that appears on all transactions.

- *Alternate Row Background/Text Colour:* The default color for the background or text of every other row in a table. Change this setting from the default if you want to alternate row colors.

- *Transaction Selection/Text Colour:* The background or text color used for selected transactions in a table.

- *Focus Background/Text Colour:* The background or text color used for the field in a table that has the cursor or focus.

- *Warning Background/Text Colour:* The background or text color displayed when something may be wrong within a transaction (for example, if an amount has no From or To account, or the two sides of the account don't add up).

- *Error Background/Text Colour:* The background or text color used to display transactions that contain an error (for example, if a VAT Code isn't set or an account is missing).

- *Non-Editable Background/Text Colour:* The background or text color that appears on all fields that you can't edit.

- *Highlight Colour:* The color used to highlight search results.

- *Other Search Result Colour:* The color used to highlight search results that don't fit in your main search.

3. **Click the Colour Selector button towards the bottom-right of the screen.**

   This button looks like a small box with tiny colored squares inside.

   The Colour Selector dialog box opens.

4. **Click the tab for the color model that you want to use.**

   You can choose to select a color from one of three available color models:

   - Swatches

     We use the word *swatch* to mean the range of colors available in Home Accountz — in this case, the colors available via the Configuration table.

   - HSB

   - RGB

   We talk about the HSB and RGB color options in the following sections.

   A color pallet containing a selection of colors appears.

5. **To select a color, click the box that contains your chosen color.**

6. **Click the OK button at the bottom of the dialog box.**

   The color is set, and the dialog box closes.

Setting colors with HSB or RGB

A color model defines the range and depth of colors available. For example, the RGB color model defines color by using Red (R), Green (G), and Blue (B) light. Each color has a value ranging from 0 to 255, where 0 is no light and 255 is maximum intensity. The combination and amounts of red, green, and blue light defines the resulting RGB color that appears on your monitor.

The HSB color model use three properties to define color:

✔ **Hue:** This model works on the theory that every color originates from a single pure color (called the *hue*). Other colors are made by mixing this original color with defined amounts of white and/or black, or another color, creating shades of the original color.

Hue is measured in degrees from 0 to 360.

✔ **Saturation:** A measurement of the purity of the original color — the amount of pure color mixed with white. Saturation can range from white to pure color. Saturation is measured in percent, ranging from 0 to 100 (the closer to 100, the greater the purity of the color).

✔ **Brightness:** Controls the intensity of the color. The intensity of a color is changed by mixing the pure color with black. Brightness can range from black to pure color, measured in a percentage.

The Colour text box in the right-hand pane at the bottom of the screen has the color code for your chosen color already filled in.

Coloring with HSB

HSB lets you control the hue, saturation, and brightness of colors (hence the abbreviation). Each of the options is represented by three numbers.

The range of each setting is from 0 to 360, and you can change the value of a setting in any of the following ways:

✔ In the Colour Selector dialog box, click the HSB tab. You can now type a new number directly into the Colour text box, and then press the Enter or Return key.

✔ Select a color by clicking the up- or down-arrow button to the right of the text box.

✔ Drag the slider up or down to change the color in the Colour Selector box.

✔ To select a hue, in the Colour Selector box, click the color that you want to use, and then click OK.

You can see the effect of each option in the main color box on the left side of the Colour Selector dialog box.

Using RGB colors

To access the RGB option, which stands for Red, Green, and Blue, click the RGB tab in the Colour Selector dialog box. This tab includes three sliders, one for each color. The range for each is from 0 to 255. A value of 0 represents no color at all (or white). A value of 255 represents the maximum for that color.

So, if you want pure red, then drag the slider for Red to 255 and leave the other two sliders at 0. *Note:* If you want the color black, drag all three sliders to 255.

Configuring the Desk Diary

The Desk Diary configuration options allow you to customize the Desk Diary in Home Accountz. (We talk about the Desk Diary in detail in Chapter 5.) The Desk Diary folder contains the Interval tab and Formats folder.

The Interval tab allows you to set how often Home Accountz checks for Desk Diary alarms. This setting, which you specify in seconds, ensures that the application doesn't miss any of your alarms.

Tabs within the Formats folder configure the time and date formats for the Desk Diary:

- **Date:** These configuration options format the date as it appears in the Desk Diary. This formatting follows the same rules as the settings in the Documents folder (see the section "Adjusting Document Display Settings," earlier in this chapter).

- **Date/Time:** These options control the date and time format in the Desk Diary. You use the same formatting that you do in the Documents folder (which we describe in the section "Adjusting Document Display Settings," earlier in this chapter). In addition to the date letters, you use the following letters to format the time of day:

  - *H:* Hour, using the 24-hour clock (from 0 to 23)

  - *h:* Hour, using a.m. and p.m.

  - *m:* Minute

  - *s:* Second

  - *a:* Include an a.m. marker (if it's p.m., you don't include anything)

  For example, to format information as 23/01/06 14:08, you'd input **dd/ MM/yy HH:mm**.

> ✔ **Time:** Using the same sequence of letters as for the Date/Time tab, you can set the time format of your choice. (See the section "Formatting dates and times," earlier in this chapter, for the details.)

Changing Application Components

The Application Components folder of the Configuration panel is focused on configuration of the toolbar and other components within Home Accountz. You can choose which buttons appear in the main toolbar, and also the order of those buttons.

Components in Toolbar

The Components in Toolbar tab allows you to configure which components appear within the main toolbar of Home Accountz.

You can move any of the components in the main toolbar from the Show list to the Hide list (or vice versa). Select the option that you want to move into, or out of, the toolbar, and then click the appropriate button. (Click the right-arrow button to hide something or the left-arrow button to show something.)

You can change the order in which components appear by selecting a component within the Show list and then moving it either up or down by clicking the Up or Down button.

The new toolbar isn't configured until you move to a different window within Home Accountz.

Components Key Shortcuts Definitions

In the Components Key Shortcut Definitions tab, you can change the keyboard shortcuts used to open different components of the program. If a keyboard shortcut exists, you can change it. Definitions you can change in this tab include the keyboard shortcuts that launch

> ✔ Backup (no default)
>
> ✔ Documents (no default)
>
> ✔ Payee (Ctrl+Alt+U)

✔ Transfer Transactions (Ctrl+Alt+T)

✔ Properties (Ctrl+Alt+Shift+U)

✔ Calculator (no default)

✔ Error Report (no default)

✔ Desk Diary (no default)

Follow these steps to change a keyboard shortcut:

1. **Click the item relating to the keyboard shortcut you want to alter.**

   The Key Shortcuts dialog box that opens contains any existing defined shortcut for that option.

2. **Click the green plus sign (+) icon, and then press the keys you want to use for that shortcut.**

   Ctrl, Shift, ⌘ (on the Mac), and Alt can be used, in addition to any letter or number.

3. **To confirm the shortcut, click OK.**

To remove a shortcut, click the shortcut in the Key Shortcuts box and then click the Remove button, which looks like a red circle containing a white X.

Main Toolbar

The Main Toolbar tab is used to change configuration settings that are applied to the main Home Accountz toolbar. You can adjust these options as follows:

✔ **Toolbar Text:** If you select this check box, this option displays all the main toolbar buttons with their text descriptions below them. If you change your mind and decide you don't want the text to appear below the icons, deselect the check box.

✔ **Scroll Offset:** If your toolbar is longer than the space available within the window, you can scroll across the toolbar by a given number of pixels. For example, if you enter a value of **5**, you get very fine scrolling, whereas a value of **40** scrolls approximately on an icon-by-icon basis.

   To change the Scroll Offset setting, enter a value in the Value text box, which appears towards the bottom of the page, and then click outside that window.

Part II
Setting Up Your Accounts

Account Manager

Balance
▼ 📁 Net Worth
  ▶ 📁 **Assets**
    💲 Split Account
  ▶ 📁 Loans
▶ 📁 Income & Expenses
  💲 Opening Balance

[Add Account]

[Add Group]

[Edit Selected]

[Delete Selected]

☐ Show Deleted

Move Accounts

You can move any Account to a different Group by dragging and dropping it from one Group to another

Re-order Accounts

⬆ ⬇

Account Properties

Name: Assets

Ref Code:

Reconcilable: ☐ (if set entries will not auto clear)

Type: Assets Group

Can Contain: Asset Account
Bank Account
Cash Account
Deposit Account
Assets Group

Notes:

[Done]

In this part . . .

This part takes a look at how you start setting up the account structure within your Home Accountz software. We start by exploring the structure of your accounts, and then move on to ways in which you can edit the accounts and the account structure. This part concludes with an exploration of how you can import data to Home Accountz from other programs and documents, such as Quicken or online bank statements.

Chapter 7

Coming to Grips with Home Accountz

- -

In This Chapter

▶ Working with transactions

▶ Getting the balances of your accounts

▶ Recording money you make and money you spend

▶ Seeing if things balance in the balance sheet

- -

*I*t sounds simple enough: managing your money. It's frequently not as simple as it should be, however — using Home Accountz can help you simplify the process. Before you start using Home Accountz, you do need a basic understanding of accounting and the way Home Accountz uses accounts.

This chapter uses a few transactions and some simple guidelines to reveal the logic behind bookkeeping and explain the jargon. If you read through this chapter, you'll be able to talk, and understand, the language that your bank manager, accountant, and tax inspector use.

At the heart of Home Accountz is a powerful bookkeeping system known as double-entry bookkeeping. This method of keeping accounts has stood the test of time (over 600 years) and is the standard used worldwide. The purpose of this system — and the purpose of Home Accountz — is to record every financial transaction that takes place. So, double-entry bookkeeping is at the heart of the Home Accountz program.

This chapter gives you a very simplified view of accounting, from an initial transaction through to its effect on your account balances. It shows just how simple accounting really is. Before computers came along, the whole process was carried out manually by using books of entry known as journals and ledgers.

Understanding Transactions

A *transaction* is the term used to describe the recording of the flow of money from one place to another. In double-entry accounting, these cash-flow places are called *accounts*. For example, recording your salary and paying it into your bank requires two accounts — Salary and Bank. In order to start any transaction, you need the following information:

- **Where the money came from:** The source of the money. It could be your bank or credit card account if you buy something, or your salary or some other income account if you receive money.

- **Where the money went:** What you did with the money. Maybe you purchase food or fuel, or you could send money to your bank or credit card.

In a single-entry accounting system, entries are recorded one after another in a book that typically has a column for the account used and a column to describe the goods or service. However, single-entry systems have no simple way to verify that your accounts are correct, which is why double-entry has become the global standard. If you care about your money, double-entry is the system to use.

Although you probably have no problem viewing money stored in the bank as an account, what's more difficult to understand is the concept of goods, services, and income as accounts in their own right. For example, filling up your car is a transaction that involves you receiving goods (fuel) and paying for these goods with cash or credit card. A double-entry bookkeeping system requires two entries; in this example, you use two accounts:

- **Cash:** Where the money came from
- **Fuel:** Where the money went

This from-and-to aspect of each transaction is known as *crediting and debiting,* which is what the term *double-entry* means. Home Accountz achieves the whole transaction in a single entry in the Transactions table.

In Home Accountz, everything is an account, whether it's a bank or credit card, fuel, food, or cash. You have a Bank account, a Food account, an Electricity account, a Telephone account, and so on. And Home Accountz places these accounts in groups. For example, you can use an Expenses group to hold your Food and Clothing accounts.

Recording Your Transactions

The double-entry system uses books — often known as day books, cash books, or journals — to record entries. Home Accountz, on the other hand, uses a panel called All Transactions to do the same thing. The panel contains a spreadsheet-like table that records transactions. Each transaction is displayed on a single row in the table (see Figure 7-1). The minimum number of columns required to fully record a transaction is five:

- ✔ **Date:** When the transaction took place
- ✔ **Reference:** Used to associate a transaction with a relevant document, such as a payslip or receipt
- ✔ **Account From:** The source of the money; for example, Salary or Bank
- ✔ **Account To:** Where the money went; what you spent it on or where you paid it
- ✔ **Total Amount:** How much was spent or received

You can enter transactions one after another in any date order you want. You can sort all your transactions by date order, if you want, by clicking the Date column heading.

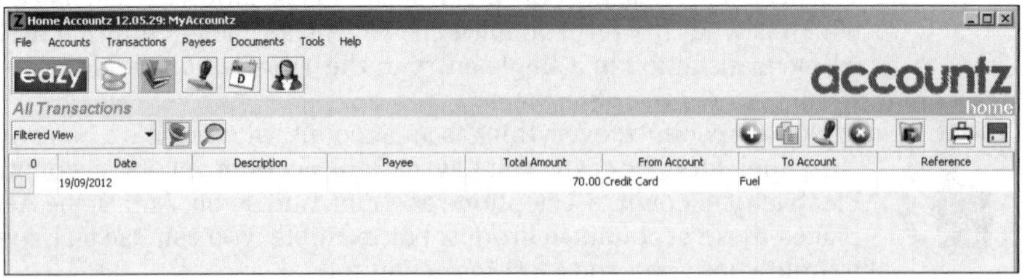

Figure 7-1:
The All
Transactions
table, show-
ing a single
complete
transaction.

Figure 7-1: The All Transactions table, showing a single complete transaction.

Keeping track of purchases

When you pay cash for fuel, for example, two accounts are involved (Cash and Fuel). Every time you make a purchase, add a new transaction to the All Transactions table and specify the date, account from, account to, and total amount (you also have the option to add a reference).

By recording every purchase in this way, you can keep track of everything you buy. To see the balance of those transactions, choose Accounts⇨Accounts, Balances & Budgeting to open the Accounts, Balances & Budgeting panel.

Keeping track of income

Whenever you receive any income, you can record it in the All Transactions table in exactly the same way as anything you buy. For example, receiving money from your salary and depositing it in your bank account involves two accounts: Salary and Bank.

By recording every form of income you receive, you can track your income over time and compare that income with your expenses to ensure that you stay within budget.

Within Home Accountz, the Accounts, Balances & Budgeting panel lists all your accounts, the balances, and the totals (see Figure 7-2).

Posting from the journal to the ledger

In a traditional double-entry accounting system, your transactions are manually copied from the day books or journals into another book known as a ledger. (You can see just how tedious that must have been for people before computers came along.)

Posting into the ledger reordered the entries by account from the long chronological list of entries in the journals. The ledger shows all your transactions grouped together by account. The ledgers were also split into different books to show the different aspects of a business: sales, purchase, and nominal.

Home Accountz does a similar job automatically, so you don't have to worry about copying everything yourself. Whenever you

add a transaction, the relevant balances of the accounts that the transaction affects are balanced immediately. So, if you transfer £100 from your bank to your credit card, your bank account balance decreases by 100 and your credit card balance increases by 100.

Because your accounts can be grouped together into categories and subcategories, those groups balances are also affected. For example, a Revenue group contains an Income group and Expenses group. If you add a transaction that increases your income by 1,000 and another that adds 400 to your expenses, your Revenue group total shows 600 (1,000 income less 400 expenses). So, you can instantly see that you're not spending more than you're earning.

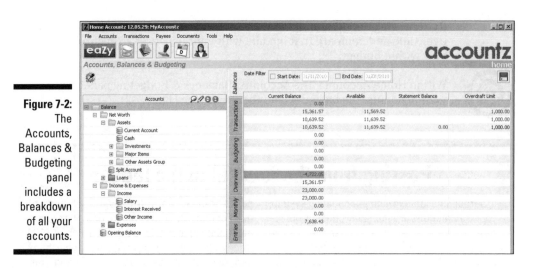

Figure 7-2:
The
Accounts,
Balances &
Budgeting
panel
includes a
breakdown
of all your
accounts.

Tallying Up Account Balances

A traditional double-entry system uses something called a trial balance in order to verify that a set of accounts balances. A *trial balance* is a complete list of account balances from the ledgers (see the sidebar "Posting from the journal to the ledger," in this chapter, for more on ledgers). A trial balance involves bringing together in the Debit and Credit columns all the balances of all accounts in all the ledgers. You prepare a trial balance at the end of every reporting period to help you ensure the transactions entered so far are correct. The layout is similar to the ledger, except that only three columns are required: Account Name, Debit, and Credit.

You copy only the final balance line of each account into the trial balance; use the Debit column if the account has a debit balance or the Credit column if the account has a credit balance.

The Debit and Credit columns are then totalled and checked; the columns must match each other to satisfy the first rule of accounting (all the debits must equal all the credits).

If the total debits and total credits are not equal to each other, you have proof that a mistake has been made. You then have to carry out an audit to find the error. An *audit* involves going through each entry in the journal to check whether it matches the original paperwork. In accounting, an *audit trail* is the sequence of paperwork that validates or invalidates accounting entries. Each entry in the journal needs to be matched up with the paperwork associated with the transaction. If you don't find an error in the journal, then it must be due to a mistake made when you posted the entries to the ledger. The audit then continues by checking each journal entry against the ledger entries until you find the error.

You can see just how difficult accounting was using a manual system. Home Accountz removes all the complexity. Every transaction you ever make in Home Accountz is automatically posted to the correct accounts, and all the accounts' and groups' balances are automatically adjusted. Provided you complete each transaction, your books will always balance. You don't need to use any of the traditional books, processes, and tools associated with the double-entry system.

Dealing with Income and Expenses

In a business, the difference between your sales and the money spent on expenses is recorded in the Profit and Loss (or P&L) account. As its name implies, it tells you whether you're making a profit or suffering a loss. Are you earning more money than you're spending (a profit) or vice versa (a loss)?

When you look at your home accounts, you do something very similar — but you don't refer to it as profit or loss. Instead, you're looking at the difference between your income (for example, from a salary, gifts received, dividends from shares, or interest from a savings account) and your expenses (money spent on food, rent, mortgage interest, and so on).

Your income and expenses fall into the Revenue group. The difference between your income and expenses is the money you have available (or how much you owe), as shown in Figure 7-3.

Traditionally, you'd do this sort of analysis once a year, but because of the automatic nature of Home Accountz, the information is available at any time. Whenever you add a new transaction (or edit an existing one if you find a mistake), all the balances are automatically updated for you.

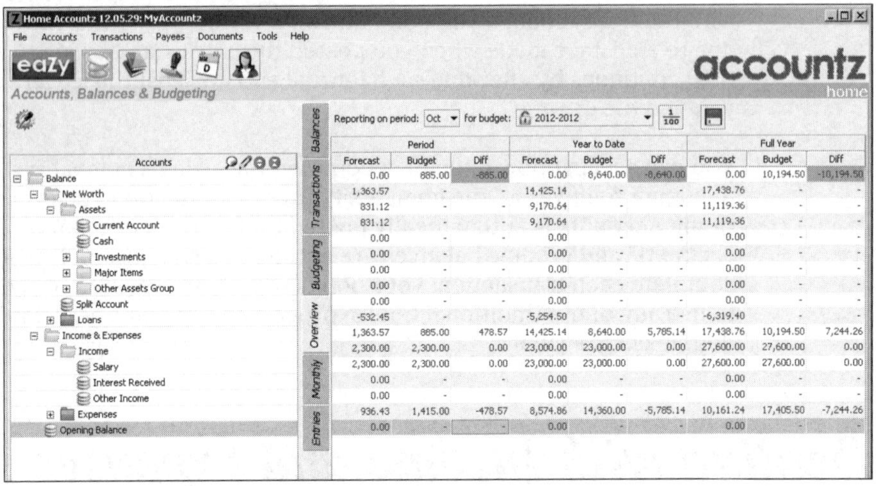

Figure 7-3: Use the Budgeting panel's Overview tab to compare your budget with your actual spending.

Keeping Your Eye on the Balance Sheet

The double-entry accounting system is based on the following equation: Equity = Assets – Liabilities. This equation outlines the first rule of accounting (the debits must equal the credits), and this rule is applied at every stage in the accounting process, from a single transaction to a journal right through to the ledger.

The P&L account (discussed in the preceding section) reflects the balance of a specific area of your finances over a particular period of time. The *balance sheet* is a financial statement that summarizes assets and liabilities.

This is much simplified in Home Accountz because you don't have to deal with the complexities of a business and accounting rules and regulations. You can simply have Home Accountz show you only the parts that matter to you.

The balance sheet in Home Accountz is represented in the Accounts, Balances & Budgeting panel (shown in Figure 7-2). You can open this panel at any time to see all your account balances in an instant.

There are two main groups:

✔ **Net Worth:** Your assets and cash

✔ **Income and Expenses:** All the accounts you need in order to analyze your income and expenses

The Accounts, Balances & Budgeting panel consists of two main sections — the accounts appear on the left, and the right displays different aspects of each account. We describe this panel in detail in Chapter 8.

Chapter 8

Changing Your Accounts Structure

. . . .

In This Chapter

▶ Regrouping your Home Accountz accounts

▶ Hiding accounts you don't need anymore

▶ Recovering accounts

▶ Closing unused accounts

. . . .

As we explain in Chapter 7, accounts are set up in a tree structure. If you click the plus sign (+) beside an account group, the group expands to reveal further accounts and groups contained within that group.

Your set of accounts isn't static, however. You may need to shuffle them around because of a change in circumstances or to try a different structure to make your accounts easier to use. In this chapter, we explore the ways to move, hide, or delete your accounts and to ensure these changes don't have a negative effect on your overall financial picture.

Moving Accounts

Home Accountz comes with a default basic accounts structure that includes Assets as an account group, which contains further accounts (such as Bank) and account groups (such as Investments and Major Items). If you have a particular preference for how your accounts should be structured or ordered, or you want to manage them in different ways (such as grouping certain types of accounts together), Home Accountz allows you to move accounts around in the Account Manager window.

Moving accounts from one group to another

You have a great deal of control over the makeup and structure of accounts:

- ✔ Add more groups and accounts.
- ✔ Move accounts between groups (if they're compatible — for example, you can't move an Income account into an Expense group).
- ✔ Rename accounts.
- ✔ Delete accounts (if they don't contain transactions).

You can move any account to a different group by following these steps:

1. **Click the Accounts, Balances & Budgeting button in the toolbar.**

   This button displays an image of three gold coins.

   The Accounts, Balances & Budgeting page opens, displaying the Accounts pane and the Accounts, Balances & Budgeting table.

2. **Click the Create/Edit Your Accounts button in the Accounts pane toolbar.**

   This button looks like a pencil.

   The Account Manager dialog box appears (shown in Figure 8-1).

   TIP

   The account structure tree appears quite narrow in this dialog box. If a group has a long name or you've expanded a group to see the accounts contained within, the information may not fit. In this case, use the scroll bar at the bottom of the dialog box to view all the information.

3. **In the Account Manager, select the account that you want to move.**

4. **Locate the group to which you want to move your selected account.**

   This group needs to be the same type of account (for example, an Expense account or an Asset account).

5. **Drag the account that you want to move to the new group.**

6. **Release the mouse button to drop the selected account into the group.**

   Your selected account is moved from its original location to its new group.

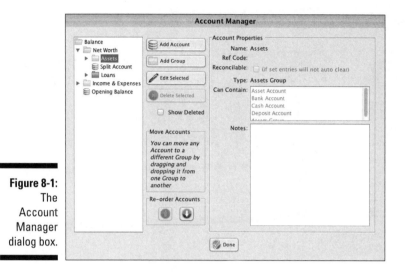

Figure 8-1:
The
Account
Manager
dialog box.

Knowing the restrictions of moving accounts between groups

Each account has a corresponding account type, which represents what sort of transaction each account can contain. For example, accounts in the Income group have an Income account type, and accounts in the Expenses group have an Expense account type.

The Account Manager dialog box displays a selected account's account type in the Type field of the Account Properties section of the dialog box (see Figure 8-2).

When an account moves from one group to another, Home Accountz may need to alter the account's account type to one that's compatible with the new group into which you're moving it. Home Accountz warns you about this in the right panel of the Accounts Manager window before you drop the account into its new group, as shown in Figure 8-3.

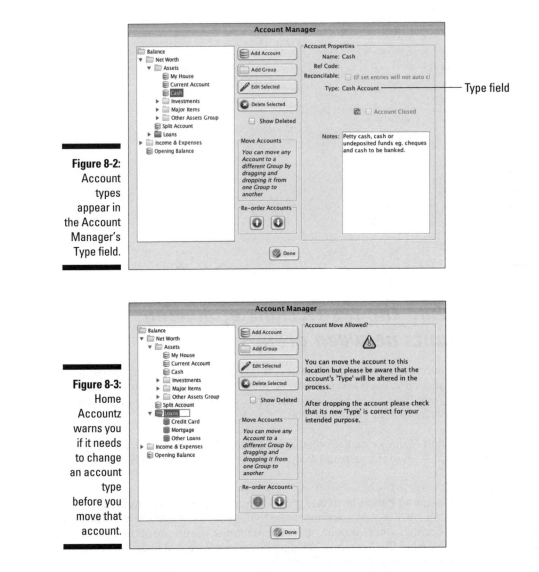

Figure 8-2:
Account
types
appear in
the Account
Manager's
Type field.

Type field

Figure 8-3:
Home
Accountz
warns you
if it needs
to change
an account
type
before you
move that
account.

The Accounts Manager tree also has restrictions as to what can be moved where. If you attempt to perform one of these restricted moves, a message appears in the far-right panel of the Accounts Manager window, explaining why the operation you're attempting isn't allowed.

Here are some example operations that aren't allowed:

✔ **Dragging a group to a new position:** Only accounts can be moved in the tree structure, not groups.

✔ **Dropping an account to its current group:** You're not actually moving the account, so nothing would be achieved by re-dropping it to its current group. A message appears in the far-right panel of the Accounts Manager window, warning you if you accidentally try to re-drop a group.

✔ **Dropping an account into another account:** An account can't contain another account; only groups can contain accounts. Groups are like folders, and accounts are like files. If you're trying to alter the order of accounts within a group by dragging the account within the group, you just drop the account on another account, which isn't allowed (a message appears in the far-right panel of the Accounts Manager window, explaining this). If you want to reorder the group, use the Reorder Accounts controls (see the following section).

Reordering accounts within a group

To reorder your accounts within a group (for example, to put your Bank account at the top of the group), follow these steps:

1. **Click the Create/Edit Your Accounts button (which displays a pencil) in the Accounts pane.**

   The Account Manager dialog box appears.

2. **Select the account that you want to move from the account structure tree.**

3. **Click either of the Reorder Accounts buttons to move the selected account within the group.**

   These buttons, which look like green circles that contain an up- or down-pointing arrow, move the account up or down within the group list, respectively.

   One click moves the selected account one position up or down within the list.

4. **Click the appropriate button until the selected account is in the position you want.**

5. **After you're happy with the position of the account, click the Done button.**

   The Account Manager dialog box closes, and you return to the Accounts, Balances & Budgeting page.

Hiding (Deleting) Accounts

If you no longer use an account or you've added an account by mistake, you may want to hide it from view. To hide an account in Home Accountz, you simply delete it. *Deleting* in Home Accountz isn't as drastic as it sounds — the account isn't actually removed from the application, it's just hidden from view. To hide an account, follow these steps:

1. **Click the Create/Edit Your Accounts button to open the Account Manager dialog box.**

   This button in the Accounts pane toolbar displays a pencil.

2. **Select the account that you want to hide.**

3. **Click the Delete Selected button.**

   This button appears in the center of the Account Manager dialog box; it displays a red circle with a white X.

   If this button is grayed out, it's not activated. Before you can delete an account, you need to remove any transactions from it. If an account has a transaction, the Delete Selected button is disabled to protect these existing transactions in the selected account. We cover deleting transactions in Chapter 7.

   The selected account is now removed from the list of accounts.

4. **Click the Done button to close the Account Manager dialog box and return to the Accounts, Balances & Budgeting page.**

Deleted accounts remain in your file, so you can recover them later, if necessary. They're only deleted from view. This setup is common in accounting software and makes it easy to recover accidentally deleted files. If you want to permanently delete any data, you need to create a new data file and start from scratch.

We explain the process of recovering deleted data in the following section.

If you want to remove a group, you first need to remove the accounts within that group. Double-click the group that you want to remove to open it; click each account within that group and click Delete Selected, and then click the empty group and click Deleted Selected to remove it.

Recovering a Deleted Account

You may need to recover an account you've deleted. Maybe you want to view a report of transactions that included that account, perhaps that account has become active again, or you may have simply deleted the account in error.

To recover an account you've previously deleted, follow these steps:

1. **Click the Create/Edit Your Accounts button (which looks like a pencil) in the Accounts pane to open the Account Manager dialog box.**

2. **In the center of the Account Manager dialog box, select the Show Deleted check box.**

   All deleted accounts now appear in the Accounts list on the left of the dialog box. The deleted accounts appear grayed out (meaning they're inactive).

3. **Select the account that you want to undelete.**

   You want this account to appear in the view.

4. **Click the Edit Selected button.**

   This button displays an image of a blue pen.

   The account properties for the deleted account now appear on the right of the dialog box.

5. **In the Accounts Properties section of the Account Manager dialog box, select the Deleted check box to remove the check.**

   This step brings the account back to life for you. The account is restored where it was originally placed and can be used as normal again.

6. **Click the Done button.**

   The Account Manager dialog box closes, and you return to the Accounts, Balances & Budgeting page, with the restored account appearing as a component of the Accounts, Balances & Budgeting tree.

Closing Accounts

If you no longer use an account, then you may want to close it to prevent accidentally adding more transactions to it. For example, if you move your current account to a new bank, you need to set up a new account for the new bank; however, you don't want to remove the old account because it holds vital historical data useful for budgets and forecasts. To prevent accidentally adding a transaction to the old account when you mean to add it to the live account, you can close the account you no longer use.

Closed accounts are still stored within Home Accountz, and you can view them in both the Accounts, Balances & Budgeting table and the Account Manager dialog box. Each locked account has a little padlock icon to distinguish it from the open accounts (see Figure 8-4). You can't edit a locked account or add a transaction to that account because all the buttons that allow you to do so are disabled.

Padlock icon

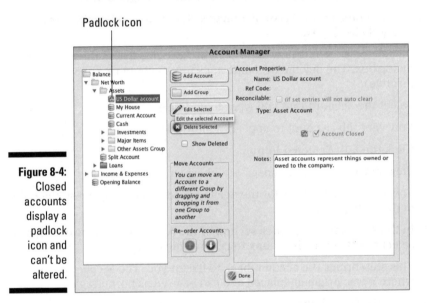

Figure 8-4:
Closed
accounts
display a
padlock
icon and
can't be
altered.

To close an account, follow these steps:

1. **Click the Create/Edit Your Accounts button in the Accounts pane.**

   The Account Manager dialog box appears.

2. **In the Account Manager, select the account that you want to lock.**

3. **Click the Edit Selected button.**

   This button displays an image that looks like a blue pen.

   The account properties for the account appear on the right side of the dialog box.

4. **In the Accounts Properties section of the dialog box, select the Account Closed check box.**

   This step locks the account, meaning you can't apply any more changes to that account.

5. **Click the Done button to close the Account Manager dialog box.**

   You return to the Accounts, Balances & Budgeting page.

Chapter 9

Importing from Other Programs

*N*ot everybody who buys a copy of Home Accountz is new to managing their money on their computers. So, the application includes support to import files in a number of different formats, including Quicken, Microsoft Money, and various statement formats. It also includes support for CSV import (allowing you to import from spreadsheets) and OFX (which allows you to import details from your bank statements).

In this chapter, we show you how to go about importing data from a number of different programs.

Working with Home Accountz's Import Wizards

Home Accountz has a range of different import wizards, depending on what you're trying to import. You can access these wizards by choosing File⇨Import and selecting the wizard from the submenu that appears (see Figure 9-1).

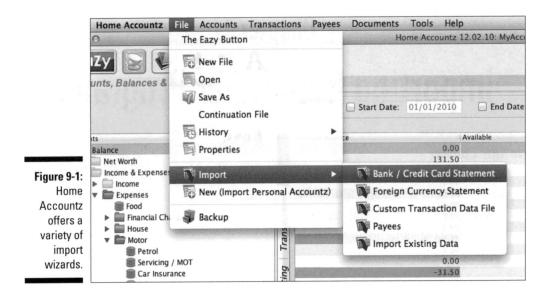

The import wizards available are

- **Bank/Credit Card Statement:** If you can download statements from your online bank or credit card provider, you can import them into Home Accountz by using the Bank/Credit Card Statement Import Wizard. This wizard supports importing statements for your *base currency* only — meaning the currency you use in your home country. In this book, we assume your base currency is pounds sterling. If you have a statement from a foreign bank or credit card, you should use the Foreign Currency Statement Import Wizard.

- **Foreign Currency Statement:** If you have bank accounts held in a foreign currency and want to import statements from those accounts, you can do so by using the Foreign Currency Statement Import Wizard.

- **Custom Transaction Data File:** If you have some transaction data in CSV, QIF, or OFX format, you can import that data into Home Accountz by using this wizard. If you want to import legacy data from an old accounting app (such as Quicken or MS Money), use the Import Existing Data option, instead.

- **Payees:** If you have some payee data in CSV format, you can import it into Home Accountz by using the Payees Import Wizard option.

- **Import Existing Data:** If you previously used a different accounting application (such as Quicken or MS Money) and want to import your accounting data from that application, you can use this import wizard.

Mapping is used extensively in the import wizards. When you *map* data, you tell Home Accountz where to place certain columns within Home Accountz.

Usually, Home Accountz needs confirmation rather than guidance: If what appears on the screen looks correct, allow Home Accountz to run with it.

Importing Bank, Credit Card, and Foreign Currency Statements

To use the Home Accountz import wizards for CSV-format bank, credit card, or foreign currency statements, follow these steps:

1. **Choose File⇨Import, and then select either Bank/Credit Card Statement or Foreign Currency Statement.**

   The wizard you selected opens.

2. **In the Choose the Data File You Wish to Import screen, locate and select the file on your hard drive that you want to import.**

   If you have multiple personal accounts, you can specify an alternative account in the Specify the Account the Statement Is For screen.

3. **In the Specify Options window, start typing the name of the account into which the statement should be imported.**

   If, for instance, you've downloaded a current account bank statement, start typing **Current Account** in the column Default Value field.

4. **Click Next.**

5. **In the Labels the Columns of Your Import File screen that appears, click within the header immediately at the top of each column.**

   You're presented with a drop-down list allowing you to choose to which column within Home Accountz the detail in that column should be applied (as shown in Figure 9-2). These columns can include the date, amount paid in, amount withdrawn, and so on.

6. **Select the option from the drop-down list that best represents that column's data.**

   If no equivalent value appears in the drop-down list (meaning Home Accountz doesn't have such a value), click Ignore, and that column won't be imported into the software.

   This process tells Home Accountz into which fields it should import your data. Make sure you do this correctly because otherwise, the data could be imported into the incorrect locations within the program.

7. **Click the Next button.**

   The Preview Data to Be Imported screen appears, displaying how the data will look when it's imported.

8. **Edit or correct any of the values by clicking within the appropriate fields and editing the content.**

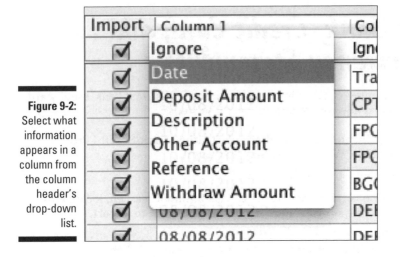

Figure 9-2:
Select what information appears in a column from the column header's drop-down list.

9. **Delete any rows that you don't want to import by selecting the rows' check boxes and then clicking the Delete button (marked with an X).**

10. **When you're happy with all the data, click the Done button to finish the import.**

QIF/OFX users, check out the section "Using the Mapping Tools and Table," later in this chapter.

Importing a Custom Transaction Data File

You can import transaction data in CSV, QIF, or OFX format by using the Custom Transaction Data File Import Wizard. As a minimum, the data that you want to import by using this wizard must have the following columns defined:

- Date
- Account From
- Account To
- Total Amount

To use the Custom Transaction Data File Import Wizard for a CSV file, follow these steps:

1. **Choose File⟹Import⟹Custom Transaction Data File.**

   The Custom Transaction Data File Import Wizard opens.

2. **In the navigation window of the Choose the Data File You Wish to Import screen, select the file on your hard drive that you want to import into Home Accountz.**

   The Label the Columns of Your Import File window opens.

3. **Click in the header of each column and, from the drop-down lists that appear, select which fields within Home Accountz should be used to contain each particular data element.**

   If you can't relate a field to an equivalent within Home Accountz, choose Ignore.

4. **When you finish assigning columns, click Next.**

   In the Specify Default Values screen that appears (shown in Figure 9-3), you can specify default values for fields that haven't already been mapped in the Label the Columns of Your Import File window, as described in Step 3.

5. **Add any values you want in the fields provided, as explained in Chapter 7.**

   The default values that can be set include

   - Reference
   - Description
   - Notes
   - Date
   - Project
   - Cleared (From)
   - Cleared (To)
   - Account From
   - Other Account
   - Account
   - Currency
   - Currency Rate

If you want, you can alter the Currency Rate value for individual transactions in the preview screen or after import (just as you would when editing data added into Home Accountz manually, which we describe in Chapters 7 and 8).

6. **Click Next to open the Preview Data to Be Imported window, which allows you to preview how the data will look when it's imported.**

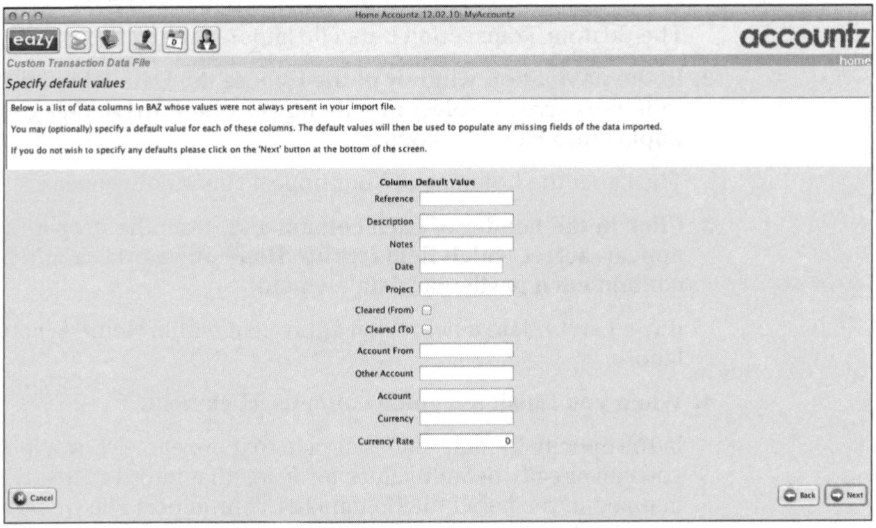

Figure 9-3:
Specifying
a default
value
ensures that
your data
is placed in
the correct
accounts.

7. **To edit or correct a value, select the item and enter your changes.**

8. **Delete any rows that you don't want to import by selecting the rows' check boxes and then clicking the Delete button (marked with an X).**

9. **After you make any necessary changes, click the Done button to finish the import.**

QIF/OFX users, see the "Using the Mapping Tools and Table" section, later in this chapter.

Importing Existing Data

To be able to import legacy data from a different accounting application, you first need to export it from your old accounting application:

✔ **Exporting from Microsoft Money:** Export your data from Microsoft Money by using the QIF format. You need to export each account into a separate QIF file. Save all these files to a single directory to make it easier to import them later.

✔ **Exporting from Intuit Quicken:** Export your data by using the QIF format. In Quicken, choose Export➪All Accounts.

After you export your data, you can import it into Home Accountz by follow-ing these steps:

1. **Choose File⇨Import⇨Import Existing Data.**

   The Import Existing Data Import Wizard opens.

2. **In the Selecting Which Application You Are Importing From screen, select the legacy application from the list provided (Microsoft Money, Intuit Quicken, or Misc), and then click Next.**

   The Choose the Data File You Wish to Import screen appears.

3. **In the navigation window, locate the file on your hard drive that you want to import into Home Accountz.**

   In the Map Your Old Accounts Structure to Your New Accounts Structure screen that appears, Home Accountz presents its own default accounts structure, which you can customize.

   The Mapping table on the left of the screen (see Figure 9-4) contains two columns:

   - *Old Accounts in File:* All the Accounts and Categories in your exported data file(s). The Categories are indented to match their structure as found in your legacy application.

   - *Maps To:* A series of Home Accountz account check boxes.

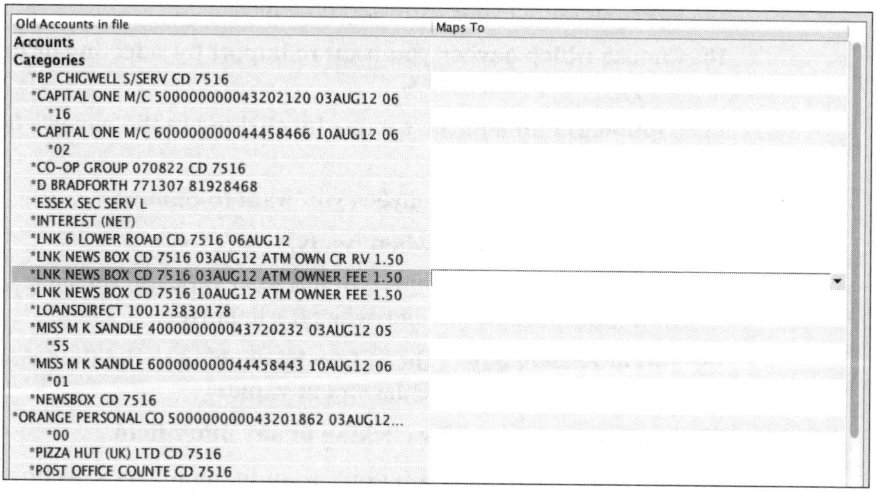

Figure 9-4:
The
Mapping
table in
Home
Accountz.

Old Accounts in file	Maps To
Accounts	
Categories	
*BP CHIGWELL S/SERV CD 7516	
*CAPITAL ONE M/C 500000000043202120 03AUG12 06	
*16	
*CAPITAL ONE M/C 600000000044458466 10AUG12 06	
*02	
*CO-OP GROUP 070822 CD 7516	
*D BRADFORTH 771307 81928468	
*ESSEX SEC SERV L	
*INTEREST (NET)	
*LNK 6 LOWER ROAD CD 7516 06AUG12	
*LNK NEWS BOX CD 7516 03AUG12 ATM OWN CR RV 1.50	
*LNK NEWS BOX CD 7516 03AUG12 ATM OWNER FEE 1.50	
*LNK NEWS BOX CD 7516 10AUG12 ATM OWNER FEE 1.50	
*LOANSDIRECT 100123830178	
*MISS M K SANDLE 400000000043720232 03AUG12 05	
*55	
*MISS M K SANDLE 600000000044458443 10AUG12 06	
*01	
*NEWSBOX CD 7516	
*ORANGE PERSONAL CO 500000000043201862 03AUG12...	
*00	
*PIZZA HUT (UK) LTD CD 7516	
*POST OFFICE COUNTE CD 7516	

4. **Start typing the name of the Home Accountz account in the Maps To column, and then select the account from the drop-down list that appears.**

   You want to enter the account name that corresponds to the legacy account that appears in the Old Accounts in File column.

5. **Repeat Step 4 for all entries.**

6. **(Optional) Create a new account to use in your Home Accountz file by dragging a row from the Mapping table and dropping it in the desired position in the New Accounts Structure tree.**

   If you select a row in the Mapping table that has already been mapped, the tree automatically selects the same account to show you where it appears in the account tree structure.

7. **(Optional) Click and drag an account from the tree and drop it onto one of the account check boxes in the Mapping table to set that account as the mapping for that particular row.**

8. **(Optional) Click the Add/Edit Accounts button at the top of the tree to open the Accounts Manager dialog box, and then edit the account tree structure.**

   In this dialog box, you can edit all aspects of the tree structure.

9. **Click the Next button when finished.**

   The Payees to Import screen that appears shows you a list of all the payees found in your exported data files.

10. **Choose which payees you want to import by selecting or deselecting the payees' check boxes.**

11. **(Optional) Edit a payee's name by clicking in the payee's field and entering a new name.**

12. **Repeat Step 11 for all payees you want to rename.**

13. **Click the Next button when ready.**

    The Preview Data to Be Imported screen appears, allowing you to preview how the data will look when it's imported.

14. **Edit or correct any of the values by clicking in the field you want to edit and then typing replacement values.**

15. **Confirm the change by clicking in any other field.**

16. **Delete any rows that you don't want to import by selecting that row and then clicking the Delete button.**

17. **When you finish previewing the data, click the Done button to complete the import.**

Using the Mapping Tools and Table

For QIF/OFX files, in the Bank/Credit Card Statement, Foreign Currency Statement, and Custom Transaction Data File import wizards, you make your main changes in the Define From/To/Other Account Values screen, which consists of a Mapping Tools widget and a Mapping table.

Mapping tools

The Mapping Tools widget on the left of the Define From/To/Other Account Values screen provides tools that can help you to complete the mapping process more quickly:

- **Deselect All/Select All:** Unchecks or checks all the check boxes of the Mapping table.

- **Set All Missing to X:** Allows you to map all the values that are currently missing to a chosen default value in one go. Clicking this button opens the Select Default Other Account value. Start to type the name of the default value in the Value text box, and then select the value from the list of values that appears; click the Done button. The chosen default value is populated in any mapping field that previously had no mapping.

- **Clear All:** Clear out any mappings currently made.

- **Strip Numbers from Values:** Remove all characters after the first number from the values found in your import file. You can click the button again to revert to the previous unstripped values.

This option is designed for situations in which you have an otherwise unique value that's repeated in the Mapping table because it's post-fixed with a date/time string. For example, if you have three values for Fuel on different dates, after clicking the Strip Numbers from Values toggle button, you're left with the single value of Fuel.

You may find this feature is useful for a number of values, but not all the values in your import file. However, you can save time mapping by temporarily enabling this feature, mapping the correctly consolidated values, and then disabling the feature again. After you disable the feature, the mappings you made still remain, so you don't have to individually map those values.

Mapping table

The Mapping table appears in the main part of the Account From/Account To/Payee Values screen. This table contains all the unique transaction values in your import file. So, if a value appears twice in your import file, it appears only once in this table.

The Mapping table is made up of three columns, which provide this information:

- ✔ **Map:** Deselect a value's check box in this column to ignore that value so that you don't have to map it to continue.

- ✔ **Value:** The value found in the file that you're importing.

- ✔ **Account From/Account To/Payee:** The system account or payee that you've mapped to the given value.

Part III
Exploring Transactions

The 5th Wave   By Rich Tennant

"It's really quite an entertaining piece of software. There's roller coaster action, suspense and drama, where skill and strategy are matched against winning and losing. And I thought managing our budget would be dull."

In this part . . .

Part III is all about transactions. We explore the different ways in which you can manage your transactions within the Home Accountz software, including recording transactions, dealing with foreign currencies, working with your data, and handling the different kinds of transactions.

Chapter 10

Recording Transactions with Templates

In This Chapter

▶ Using templates to record your purchases

▶ Creating, editing, deleting, and undeleting templates

▶ Creating a new filter

*T*emplate transactions are intended to make it easier and faster to insert similar or repeated transactions into Home Accountz. For example, if you buy a newspaper each morning, you can add these transactions by using a template transaction. The template allows you to insert a transaction easily by removing the need for you to type in the full information.

If you're familiar with using macros in applications such as Microsoft Word or Excel, then you'll be right at home with templates. By using a template in Home Accountz, you can specify and preset how you normally pay for an item; how you want the transaction — for example, the daily newspaper — allocated to an account for payment and an account for expenditure; how much you're paying for that item; a description of the item purchased; and so on. By allocating a transaction to an account, you're tracking that transaction — a payment from your Cash account that goes towards purchasing an item (for example, a newspaper).

After you set up a template, you can use that template at any time to fill in a transaction automatically, so templates are a great timesaver.

Creating Transaction Templates for Buying

A Transaction template is a template for a regular transaction — for example, buying a daily paper or a certain amount of fuel. In the following sections, we explore how to set them up and use them.

Setting up a template is quite straightforward. These templates are stored in the Template Transaction table. This table shows all the fields that you need to create a new template in its columns, and each template you create appears in a row in the table. Each column represents a field that appears in the templates and has a predefined heading that represents the content in that field.

Creating a template

To set up a new template, follow these steps:

1. **Click the Template Transactions button.**

   This button, which looks like a rubber stamp, is the sixth button from the left in the toolbar at the top of the Home Accountz window.

   The Template Transactions window opens.

2. **Click the Add button (which looks like a plus sign [+] in a green circle), shown in Figure 10-1.**

   A new row appears in the table.

Template Transactions button   Add button

Figure 10-1: The Template Transactions window.

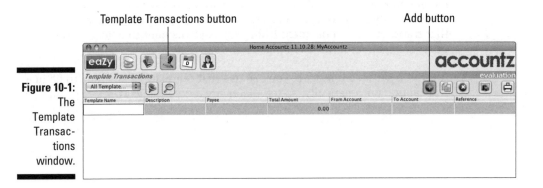

3. **In the field below the Template Name heading, enter a brief title for your template.**

   For example, we entered **Daily Mirror** to create a template for purchasing that newspaper.

4. **In the field below the Description heading, enter a specific description for that template.**

   In our example, we entered **Daily Tabloid Newspaper**.

5. **(Optional) To the right of the field below the Payee heading, click the button and select New from the drop-down list that appears.**

   The Add New Payee dialog box opens.

6. **(Optional) Enter the first few characters of the name of the company or shop where you pay for the item you purchase.**

   If the Payee is already within Home Accountz, the application suggests a list of whom you may want to use. If a suggestion is correct, select it in the list.

   This field simply reminds you where you bought the item. If we purchase the *Daily Mirror* regularly, we'd enter **The Local Newsagents**. If you go into a little more detail by naming the newsagents, you have a record of where exactly you buy that newspaper.

7. **In the Total Amount field, enter the price of the item you're buying.**

   This field contains the unit price or the cost of your purchase.

8. **Click in the From Account field, click the button to the right of the field, and then select an account from the drop-down list that appears.**

   The account you choose depends on how you pay for your item. If you're buying a newspaper from the corner shop with cash, then select Cash. If you have an account with the shop or pay by direct debit, select the Current Account option.

   We cover creating accounts in Chapter 8. You're likely to have a couple of main accounts: a Cash account from which cash payments are made, a Bank account for debit card and direct debit transactions, and perhaps a Savings account.

9. **To the right of the To Account field, click the button and select an account from the drop-down list that appears.**

   In our example, magazines and newspapers could fit in the catch-all account of Other Expenses.

   You can create a new account by selecting New Account at the bottom of the To Account drop-down list, which opens the Select An Account dialog box. Flip back to Chapter 8 for more on creating accounts.

10. **(Optional) If you want to add more templates, repeat Steps 2 through 9.**

   After you create a number of transaction templates, the list of templates looks like Figure 10-2.

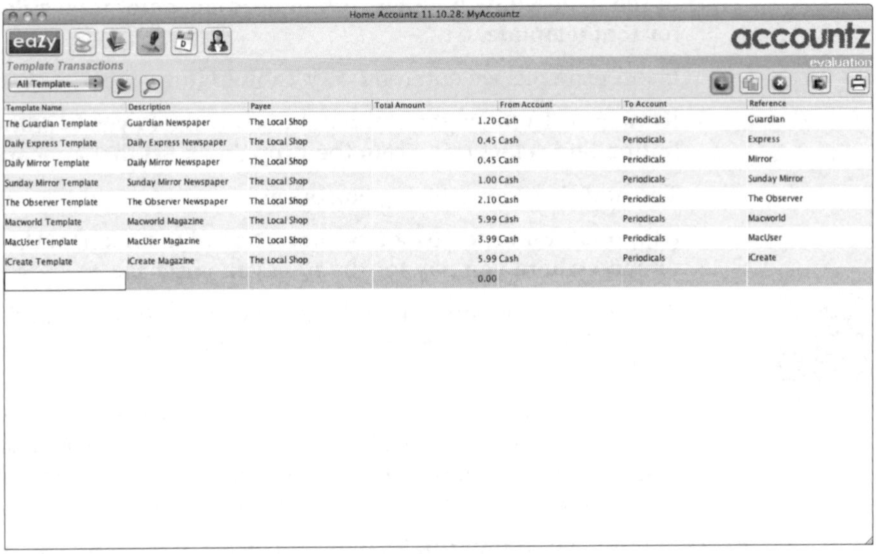

Figure 10-2:
A list of
template
transac-
tions.

Testing a template

To test your new template, follow these steps:

1. **Click the All Transactions button.**

   This button looks like a group of green books and is the fifth button from the left on the toolbar at the top of the Home Accountz window.

   The main Transaction table opens.

2. **Click the Create Transaction Using a Template button, which appears on the toolbar.**

   The button looks like a rubber stamp and is the third button in a group of four at the top-right of the window.

   A drop-down list of all defined template transactions appears.

3. **Select a template transaction from the list.**

   Your selection appears in the All Transactions table. A new Date column appears at the start of the All Transactions table, and until you enter a date, a red exclamation mark highlights the fact that nothing has been entered.

4. **Click the Date field and start to type in a date.**

   You can either finish typing in the date by using your keyboard or select the date from the calendar that appears.

   The transaction is now entered into Home Accountz. It appears as a new row in the All Transactions table.

5. **(Optional) Add transactions by repeating Steps 2 through 4.**

A Transaction template is used to enter transactions that have similar data. After you enter a transaction into the All Transactions table, you aren't constrained to the data supplied by the template. You can edit each of the fields.

If the price of an item stored in your template transaction changes for a limited period of time, you can manually adjust the price: Click in the Total Amount field on the newly created transaction, and then enter the new price. When you click outside the field or hit the Return or Enter key, the running balances change to reflect the new price. Any changes you make in the All Transactions table aren't transferred to your original template price, which is ready to use again whenever you need it.

Editing Templates

Transactions rarely remain constant over a period of time. For example, a permanent increase in price would mean you need to update the Transaction template. But you can easily make a change to an already defined template.

You can edit templates at any time, and any changes you make to a template merely update that template: The changes aren't transferred to previous transactions that you've made by using that template.

You may need to edit a template if, for example, the price of an item has changed or you decide to use a different account to pay for that item.

To edit a template transaction, follow these steps:

1. **Click the Template Transactions button.**

   This is the sixth button on the toolbar at the top-left of the Home Accountz window.

   The Template Transactions window appears. This window displays a table that contains any templates you've already created.

2. **Locate the transaction template that requires updating, double-click in the field that you want to change, and then enter the new information.**

   If, for instance, the price of a product has increased, double-click in the Total Amount field and enter the new price, as shown in Figure 10-3.

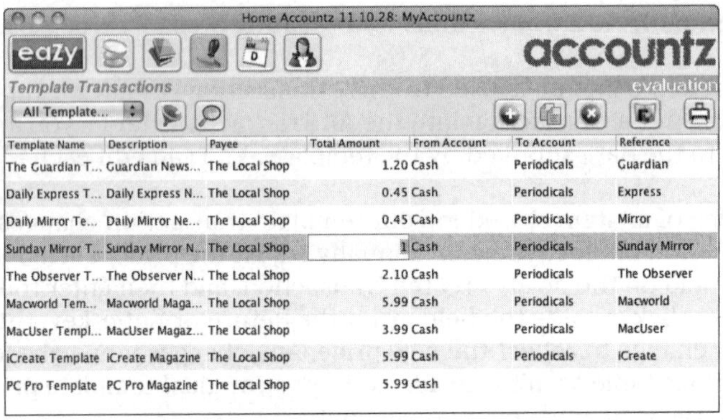

Figure 10-3: The price of the *Sunday Mirror* has risen, so we need to alter the template.

3. **Press the Return or Enter key to confirm the new price.**

   The edited field is now updated with the new price. This change is included in any new transaction added to Home Accountz by using your updated transaction template.

Deleting Templates

At some point, you may decide that you no longer want to use a template. For example, maybe you decide to stop getting the newspaper and so want to delete that template.

To delete a template transaction, follow these steps:

1. **Click the Template Transactions button (the sixth button on the toolbar at the top of the Home Accountz window).**

   The Template Transactions window opens.

2. **Click the check box to the left of the template transaction that you want to delete.**

   A check appears in the check box, and your selected template transaction is highlighted.

3. **Click the Delete Selected Transactions button.**

   This button looks like an X in a red circle and can be found in the tool-bar at the top-right of the window.

   A warning dialog box appears (as shown in Figure 10-4), prompting you to confirm the deletion.

4. **Click Delete to remove the template transaction from the Template Transaction table.**

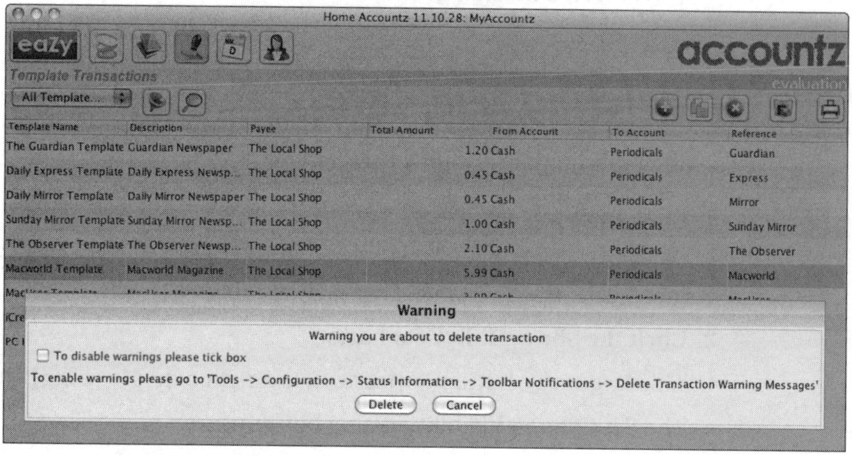

Figure 10-4: Are you sure you want to delete the selected transaction?

Undeleting Templates

If you delete a template by accident or find that you need to reuse a deleted template, Home Accountz lets you undelete templates by using the Filter view. The default is to view only non-deleted transactions, but by using a filter on the current view of a table, you can also view deleted templates.

Displaying deleted templates

To create a new view to display deleted templates, follow these steps:

1. **Select the Open/Close the View Editor panel button.**

   This button has an icon that looks like a funnel and appears in any trans-action table below the Table Name on the left side of the screen.

   A series of tabs appear, which you can click to access their associated panels.

2. **Click the Filter tab.**

This tab is one of three on the left of the screen; these tabs include View, Filter, and Chart.

The Template Transaction table switches to Filter view. This view allows you to filter (and consolidate) the data displayed in the table.

We explain filters in Chapter 14.

3. **Click the Include Deleted check box to place a check in it.**

The table's data changes to display any deleted templates.

Undeleting templates

To undelete a template, follow these steps:

1. **Click the View tab.**

The View panel appears. You can use this panel to add and remove columns from the Template Transaction table.

2. **Click the Show/Hide Cols button.**

This large gray button appears on the right side of the screen.

The Set Column Visibility dialog box appears.

3. **Click Deleted in the Hidden list.**

The Deleted column is selected.

4. **Click the Show button in the center of the dialog box.**

The Deleted column is moved to the Visible list.

5. **Click the Close Button at the bottom of the dialog box.**

The Deleted column now appears on the far-right of the table. Each deleted template has a check in the Deleted column's check box.

6. **Click the check box for the template that you want to undelete.**

The check is removed, and the template transaction is restored.

Hiding deleted templates

To return the Template Transactions table to its original state, with any deleted templates hidden, follow these steps:

1. **Click the Filter tab.**

The Template Transaction table is switched to Filter view.

2. **Click the Include Deleted check box to remove the check.**

   When you click the check box, deleted templates no longer appear in the table.

3. **To return the table to its original view, select the Open/Close the View Editor panel button.**

   This button has an icon that looks like a funnel.

   The Template Transactions table returns to its original state.

Reusing Templates

Over time, you may find that many of your templates follow a similar structure. If so, you can start reusing older templates to create new ones.

To reuse a template, follow these steps:

1. **If the template you want to reuse has been deleted, restore the deleted Template.**

   The section "Undeleting Templates," earlier in this chapter, describes how to restore a template.

2. **In the Template Transaction table, select the template that you want to reuse.**

3. **Click within a field that contains data you want to change, and then enter the new data.**

4. **Work through the fields, changing each item you want by repeating Step 3.**

5. **Confirm your changes by moving into a different line within the Template Transactions window.**

   To move into a different line, click any of the content on that line.

Chapter 11

Going International with Foreign Currencies

*B*y using Home Accountz, you can quickly and easily manage foreign-currency transactions by setting up a new account specifically for those transactions. This account deals with the conversion of money from one currency to another — from U.S. dollars to pounds sterling, for example.

This chapter explains how to handle foreign currencies within the Home Accountz software, from adding the account to recording transactions through to transferring money between currencies.

Setting Up a Foreign-Currency Account

Before you can work with a foreign currency, you need to add a new account to deal with that currency. For example, if you want to add an Australian-dollar account, you need to create an account called Australian Dollar, which you add to your Assets group by using the Account Manager menu. (See Chapter 3 for more about creating an account.)

Dealing with exchange rates

You can set an exchange rate for a transaction, which reflects the exchange rate for the date and time of the transaction. Home Accountz uses this exchange rate to do the conversion.

Home Accountz doesn't use a fixed exchange rate because, by their very nature, exchange rates are fluid, and they change on a daily or hourly basis.

Creating a foreign-currency account

After you add an account, you need to add some columns that deal with currency. You can also remove some irrelevant columns for the sake of clarity.

Follow these steps to set up a currency account in the Assets group of accounts:

1. **Click the Accounts button.**

   This button at the top-left of the screen displays gold coins.

   The Accounts, Balances & Budgeting window appears (see Figure 11-1).

Figure 11-1:
The
Accounts,
Balances &
Budgeting
window
contains
your current
financial
standing at
a glance.

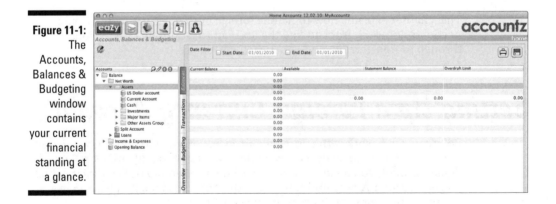

2. **Click the plus sign (+) button to the left of the Net Worth group to expand that group.**

   This group appears in the Accounts pane on the left side of the window.

3. **Click the plus sign (+) button to the left of the Assets group to open that group.**

4. **Select the Assets group.**

5. **Click the Create/Edit Your Accounts button, which appears in the Accounts pane toolbar.**

   This button looks like a green pencil.

   The Account Manager dialog box opens.

6. **Click the Add New Account button in the dialog box.**

   The Account Properties dialog box opens, which includes options to add a name and reference code, and to select whether the account is reconcilable.

7. **To give this new account a name, click in the Name text box, and then type the name that you want to use.**

   For example, you could enter **Australian Dollar** for an account that uses that currency.

8. **(Optional) Click in the Ref Code text box and enter a reference code.**

9. **Set the account type to Bank Account.**

10. **Click the Done button at the bottom of the menu.**

    You now have your foreign-currency account.

Setting up a foreign-currency view

For most tables, you can set up multiple views and define a view for your foreign-currency account. A *view* is a particular configuration of a table. You can use a view to control which columns are visible and the order in which those visible columns appear.

Follow these steps to create a new view that you can use to see the account in its native currency:

1. **Click the Open/Close the View Editor Panel button, which looks like a small blue funnel.**

   This button appears above the column headings on the left side of the table.

   The View Editor panel opens, as shown in Figure 11-2.

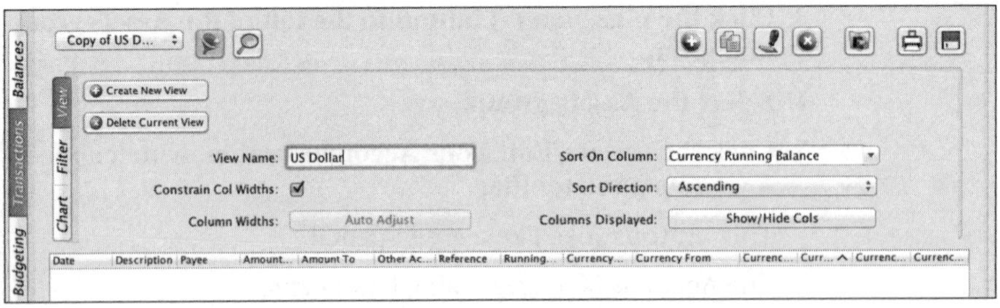

Figure 11-2:
The View
Editor panel.

2. **Click the Create New View button.**

This button displays a green circle with a white plus sign (+).

You can now edit the view details, including View Name, Constrain Column Widths, Column Widths (which you can set to Auto-Adjust), the column by which you want to sort, the direction in which you want to sort columns, and the columns that you want to display.

3. **Click in the View Name text box and type the name you want to use for the view.**

4. **Select Columns: Show/Hide Cols to open the Set Column Visibility dialog box.**

You can use this dialog box, shown in Figure 11-3, to add or remove columns from any table. It contains a Visible and a Hidden column. You can move column headers from one column to the other, depending on which columns you want to appear in your table.

Five columns are available to record multi-currency income and purchases:

- *Currency Code:* Currency codes are an international standard — ISO 4217; for example, EUR for Euro, USD for US dollar, and AUD for Australian dollar. You can find a full list of currency codes at www.xe.com/iso4217.php.

- *Currency Rate:* The conversion rate at the time of the transaction.

- *Currency Amount From:* The amount of money to be withdrawn from the account, in the base currency. (For example, if you're from the U.K., your base currency is pounds sterling.)

- *Currency Amount To:* The total amount of money to be deposited in the account, in the converted currency (for example, U.S. dollars if that's where you have the alternative currency account).

- *Currency Running Balance:* The *running balance* (the running total for the foreign currency within that account) and *current balance* (the total after any money has been spent) of the account.

- *Current Unit Price:* The cost of the foreign currency translation — or the exchange rate value.

5. **Select Currency Code in the Hidden column.**

6. **Click the Show button, which appears between the two columns.**

   Currency Code moves to the Visible column.

7. **Repeat Steps 5 and 6 for all the currency columns that you want to add.**

8. **To remove any columns that you don't need in this view, click a header in the Visible column, and then click the Hide button.**

   The selected header moves from the Visible column to the Hidden column.

   For example, you might want to remove the Running Balance, Amount To, and Amount From columns from your table if they don't apply to the task at hand.

9. **Repeat Step 8 to remove all the columns that you want to hide.**

10. **Click the Open/Close the View Editor Panel button to close the View Editor panel and return to the Transactions tab.**

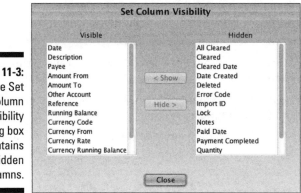

Figure 11-3:
The Set Column Visibility dialog box contains the hidden columns.

You can rearrange the order of the column headings in the table itself. Click the heading that you want to move and drag the column to its new position within the table; release the mouse button to drop the column heading in its new position.

You can view a foreign currency account just as you would a base currency account within the Accounts, Balances & Budgeting window. Just click your foreign currency account — for example, your U.S. Dollar account — and then click Transactions to view your foreign currency transactions within that account.

Entering Foreign-Currency Transactions

After you create a foreign-currency account and view (see the section "Setting Up a Foreign-Currency Account," earlier in this chapter), you're ready to add a foreign-currency transaction in the Transactions table.

To add a transaction by using your foreign-currency account (in our example, adding a transaction that uses Australian dollars as its currency), follow these steps:

1. **Click the Create a New Transaction button.**

   This button appears in the toolbar at the top-right of the screen and looks like a green circle with a white plus sign (+) in the middle.

   A new transaction line is added to your table.

2. **Add some basic information to the fields in the new transaction line.**

   For example, if you're entering a record of making a payment in Australian dollars, you'd enter this info:

   - *Date:* The date of the transaction

   - *Currency Code:* The currency code **AUD**

   - *Currency From:* The amount of currency you're transferring from your base currency

   - *Other Account:* The payment or income account relevant to the transaction (for example, Food)

   - *Currency Rate:* The exchange rate at the time of the transaction

Transferring between Foreign-Currency Accounts

When working with foreign-currency accounts, you may need to transfer funds across two countries or more — for example, from the U.S. to the U.K. If you're transferring money between two different currency accounts, you need to manually edit the conversion rate because Home Accountz doesn't have access to up-to-the-minute conversion rates (not to mention that very few institutions agree on the same rate at any given point in time).

To transfer money from your base-currency bank account to the foreign-currency equivalent, follow these steps:

1. **Create a transaction in the base currency for the amount sent in that unit (for example, $100) by entering 100 in the Amount From field.**

2. **Set the Other Account field to the foreign-currency bank account.**

3. **Select the foreign-currency account (such as Australian Dollars) in the Accounts window and the View relevant to this currency, and then locate the transaction entered.**

4. **Enter the foreign currency's code in the Currency Code field, and edit the Currency Rate to reflect the exact exchange rate for the transaction.**

   The Currency To field should now match the transaction on your foreign account's bank statement.

The Currency Running Balance is mainly to keep track of foreign-currency bank accounts. You can set two separate currency accounts (such as Euro & USD) in the Accounts, Balances & Budgeting window. As we discuss in the section "Setting Up a Foreign-Currency View," earlier in this chapter, you have to turn on the columns such as Currency Code, Currency From, Currency To, Currency Rate, and Currency Running Balance on the right side of the particular account in the Transactions tab.

 Make sure that all the currency columns (Currency Code, Currency From, Currency To, Currency Rate, and Currency Running Balance) are visible. If you don't include the Currency Code (such as USD or EUR) and Currency Rate (the value of the currency when compared to your base currency) columns when you select the others, the Currency Running Balance doesn't appear correctly in the last column.

When you click the Balances tab in the Accounts, Balances & Budgeting section (available by clicking the icon that looks like gold coins), the Current Balance field appears in the base currency. (So, if you have everything set up for pounds sterling, the current balance appears as a pounds-sterling value for your foreign-currency balances).

You can find the video tutorial link about how to deal with multiple-currency transactions in Home Accountz at `www.accountz.com/accountz/multi-currency`.

Chapter 12

Working with Your Data

*I*n this chapter, we talk about different ways of looking at your data. Most tables in Home Accountz support multiple *views,* which are particular configurations of a table. You can define these views and tailor them to suit your needs:

✔ Use a view to control different aspects of a table. For example, specify which columns are visible and set the order in which those visible columns appear.

✔ Define the individual widths of the visible columns, as well as whether your table has horizontal scroll bars (so that you don't have to restrict the combined width of all the columns to the width onscreen).

✔ Control which column the table's data is sorted by and in what way it's sorted (ascending or descending).

✔ Control how you want to filter the table's data (for example, selectively excluding transactions that match a particular condition).

✔ Specify the type of chart that's generated from the table's data (for instance, a bar or pie chart).

Views let you create very detailed reports and graphs of your data, as we describe in this chapter.

Looking at Your Data

The Accounts view allows you to see the whole structure of your home accounts as a navigable tree.

In the past, you may have kept track of your home finances by checking your bank account statement. The data presented in a bank account statement is manageable because it's a snapshot in time and doesn't contain anywhere near the amount of detail that can be stored in Home Accountz. You can use Home Accountz to look at you home finances in the same way that you look at a bank statement — just look at the data in list form on the All Transactions page by clicking the All Transactions button (which displays an image of two green books). However, the comprehensive information in this view can be daunting.

Home Accountz allows you to apply filters, which let you view only the information you need. You can also create reports that present account information from the past, present, and future.

Organizing your data

To help you effectively view you accounts, you need to organize your data. Home Accountz helps you keep things organized by using a structure made up of accounts and groups of accounts.

For example, you can collect all accounts related to your home in a group called My House. Each group is just like a folder, and that folder contains accounts. Also, a group might contain other groups, such as Furniture, Jewelry, and so on. And you can organize the groups however you want. Your My House group could contain accounts that represent each room, rather than types of items, for example.

When you first open the Accounts, Balances & Budgeting page by clicking the button that looks like a pile of coins, the basic structure of your home accounts consists of a couple of main groups:

- ✔ **Net Worth:** All those accounts that make up your net worth are placed in the Net Worth group. Your *net worth* is the amount left over after you take away what you owe from the things you own and earn.

- ✔ **Income & Expenses:** All the accounts that record your income and expenditure are collected into the Income & Expenses group.

Creating accounts groups

To keep track of all accounts that relate to all your possessions in your house, follow these steps:

1. **In the Accounts tree (on the left in the Accounts, Balances & Budgeting window), click the Assets folder to select the Assets group.**

   By adding a group for house items in the Assets group, you collect together an inventory that you can use for insurance purposes.

2. **Click the Edit button.**

   This button displays a pencil.

   The Accounts Manager dialog box appears. You can add, delete, rename, move, and create new groups through this dialog box.

3. **Click Add Account.**

4. **Click in the Name text box and type** My House.

5. **Click Done to close the dialog box.**

   A new account appears directly below Assets within the Accounts tree.

 At this point, you may want to create an Expenses group for your house. If so, repeat the preceding steps, except in Step 1, select the Expenses folder below Income & Budgeting, rather than the Assets folder.

After you create groups and accounts, you can navigate them by using the controls in the left panel. See Chapter 7 for information on controlling the Accounts tree.

Viewing Your Transactions

In Home Accountz, you can view transactions in three ways:

✔ **All Transactions:** Accessible by clicking the button that looks like a pile of books. All Transactions presents each of the transactions within your Home Accountz data in a list, with no real distinction between each transaction.

✔ **Accounts, Balances & Budgeting:** To access, click the button that looks like a pile of coins, select an account in the list at left, and click the Transactions tab. This tab shows the transactions for the selected account only. To view transactions for an account group, select the Entries tab.

✔ **Payees:** Accessible by clicking the button that looks like a woman. The right panel of this component shows only the transactions for the selected Payee.

✔ **Template Transactions:** Accessible by clicking the button that looks like a rubber stamp. Template Transactions includes only those transactions based on a predefined template (such as buying the daily paper).

✔ **Automated Transactions:** Accessible by clicking the button that looks like a calendar. Automated Transactions are those that are inserted automatically based on a common payment received or paid out: for example your mortgage, council tax, and so on.

Each view displays the following items on the far-left of its toolbar (shown in Figure 12-1):

✔ **View drop-down list:** Contains the presently defined views.

By default, the application defines a few views for you. Most of these predefined views are fully editable, but some predefined views do restrict what you can edit about them (for instance, you can't rename some views or alter their filters).

✔ **Open/Close the View Editor Panel button:** This button shows or hides the View Editor panel, depending on whether it's currently displayed.

✔ **Search button:** Allows you to search within your Transaction list for a particular transaction.

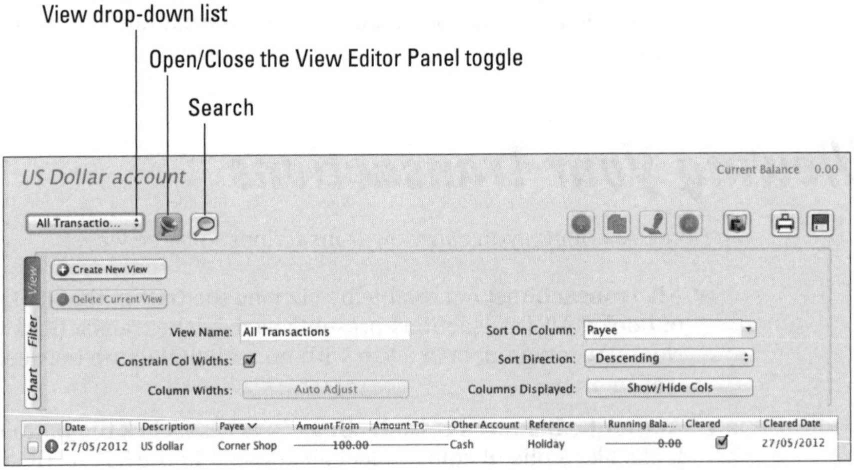

Figure 12-1:
These items
appear on
the far-left
of every
view's
toolbar.

Home Accountz supplies a number of predefined views that allow you to see certain aspects of your financial position. These views include

- **All Transactions:** See every transaction within your database.

- **Cleared:** See only cleared transactions.

- **In Error:** See transactions that are currently in error.

- **Include Deleted:** Bring Deleted Transactions back into the transaction view.

- **Last 7 Days:** View only transactions from the last seven days.

- **Next Month:** View transactions for coming month.

- **Uncleared:** View only uncleared transactions.

- **Template Transactions:** For the Template Transactions section. View transactions created by means of a template.

- **Automated Transactions:** For the Automated Transactions section. View transactions inserted automatically into your data.

Select a view from the View drop-down list (shown in Figure 12-2) to apply any of the views in the preceding list to the account you're working with. For example, you could select Last 7 Days to see all the transactions listed from the previous seven days. The table changes to reflect the settings for your selected view.

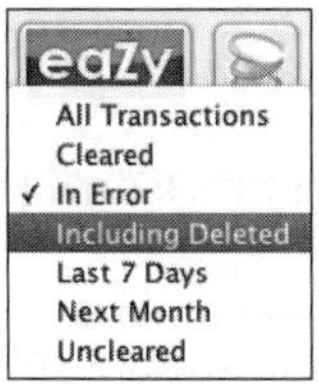

Figure 12-2:
Select an alternative view.

Using the View Editor

The View Editor panel (see Figure 12-3) allows you to edit all aspects of the currently selected view or create a new view based on the currently selected view. You can customize views to suit your needs and also create your own views.

Clicking the Open/Close the View Editor Panel toggle button (which looks like a blue funnel) shows or hides the View Editor panel, depending on whether it's already displayed. The View Editor panel appears between the column headers and the toolbar for the table.

The View Editor panel is made up of three tabs:

- ✔ **View tab:** Edit all aspects of a view, apart from the view's filter and chart.

- ✔ **Filter tab:** Construct new and modify existing filter conditions to control what rows appear in the table.

- ✔ **Chart tab:** Modify all aspects of the chart that you can construct from the data that appears in the table. Your data is presented in a chart showing the financial implications of the currently selected view. You can alter the chart by clicking a button for a different type of chart — for example, a pie chart, bar chart, scatter chart, and so on. By setting the horizontal axis values in a drop-down list, you can alter the data being represented on the chart.

Creating a new view

Clicking the Create New View button allows you to create a new view for the given table. Follow these steps to create a new view:

1. **Click the Open/Close View Editor Panel toggle button if the View Editor panel isn't visible.**

   The View Editor panel appears.

2. **Select a view from the View drop-down list.**

3. **Click the Create New View button.**

   This button displays a green circle with a white plus sign (+) inside.

   The new view is created in place of the previously chosen view. All settings of the new view (apart from the name) are copied from the view that you selected in Step 2 (so the existing view is effectively cloned).

4. **Enter a name in the View Name text box.**

   Home Accountz also suggests a new name for the view, so you can simply stick with that name by skipping this step.

5. **To confirm the view, click the Filter tab, and then click the View tab.**

Deleting a view

The Delete Current View button allows you to delete the currently selected view. Follow these steps to delete a view:

1. **From the View drop-down list, select the view that you want to delete.**

   This button is disabled for certain system default views — for example, the All Transactions view — because you can't delete those views.

   If you select a view that can be deleted, the Delete Current View button remains active.

2. **Before you click the Delete Current View button, make sure that you've selected the correct view.**

3. **Click the Delete Current View button.**

   It's the button that displays a red circle containing a white X.

   The currently selected view is deleted.

Customizing views

You can customize each of the views that you define so that they present data in a form that's most useful to your needs.

Specifying column widths

By default, all tables adjust the width of every visible column onscreen so that you don't need horizontal scroll bars. However, if a table has a lot of visible columns, it can get very crowded, forcing each column to be quite narrow (sometimes too narrow to read). Deselecting the Constrain Col Widths check box (located immediately below the View Name text box in the View tab) solves this problem.

After the constraint is removed, the table doesn't need to force all columns to fit onscreen at the same time; the columns are allowed to overflow horizontally to the right. So, you can set the column widths to whatever size you want — for example, you can set them generously for readability.

Click the scrollbar buttons at the bottom of the screen to scroll through any columns that don't currently appear on the screen.

If the Constrain Col Widths check box is deselected, the Column Widths: Auto Adjust button becomes available to use. Clicking this button, which is available only when the Constrain Col Widths check box isn't selected, automatically resizes the widths of all visible columns so that they're equal to the maximum width of their content (they resize to fit the size of the longest entry).This button is immediately below the Constrain Col Widths check box.

Sorting by column

The Sort on Column drop-down list (shown in Figure 12-4) and the Sort Direction drop-down list allow you to pick which (if any) table columns you want to sort the table contents by, and in what direction. Follow these steps:

1. **Make a selection from the Sort on Column drop-down list, which appears near the right of the View Editor screen.**

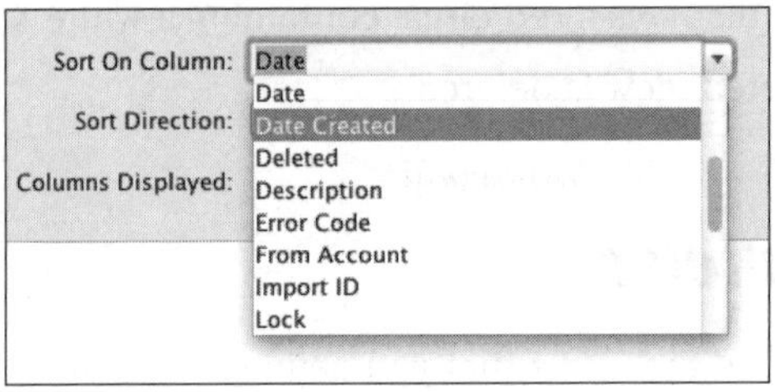

Figure 12-4:
Use the Sort on Column drop-down list to change the order in which transactions appear.

Sort On Column:	Date
Sort Direction:	Date
	Date Created
Columns Displayed:	Deleted
	Description
	Error Code
	From Account
	Import ID
	Lock

The table refreshes and reconfigures to display the contents sorted by your column choice.

2. **Select an option from the Sort Direction drop-down list.**

This drop-down list is located immediately below the Sort on Column drop-down list. It allows you to pick which (if any) direction you want to sort the chosen in the Sort on Column option in Step 1. Click the small down-pointing arrow to open the Sort Direction drop-down list, which contains these options:

   • Ascending (for example, from A to Z)

   • Descending (from Z to A)

   • None (no sorting is applied)

The table changes immediately when you select a Sort Direction.

Alternatively, you can control what direction a column is sorted by (and what column is being sorted) by clicking the column's heading in the table.

Displaying (and hiding) columns

You have control over which columns appear in your table and which don't. Follow these steps to add or remove columns from the table:

1. **Click the Columns Displayed: Show/Hide Cols button, which appears below the Sort Direction drop-down list.**

   The Set Column Visibility dialog box appears (see Figure 12-5). This dialog box allows you to control which table columns appear onscreen and which are hidden.

Set Column Visibility

Visible	Hidden
Date	Cleared (From)
Description	Cleared (To)
Payee	Cleared Date (From)
Total Amount	Cleared Date (To)
From Account	Currency Amount
To Account	Currency Code
Reference	Currency Rate
	Currency Unit Price
	Date Created
	Deleted
	Error Code
	Import ID

< Show

Hide >

Close

Figure 12-5: The Set Column Visibility dialog box.

2. **To hide columns, select one or more columns in the Visible column list, and then click the Hide button to move those columns into the Hidden column list.**

3. **To show hidden columns, select the column or columns in the Hidden column list that you want to display, and then click the Show button.**

   Those columns move into the Visible column list.

The columns that you move from one list to the other appear or disappear in the table under the dialog box while you move them.

Using the Chart tab

You can view your data in the form of a chart. The Chart tab lets you create and customize a chart for the currently selected view.

When you click the Chart tab, the chart automatically appears on top of the main table area.

You can show or hide a table's chart at any time simply by clicking the Show/ Hide Chart button, which appears on the table's toolbar at the top-right of the screen.

 When you display the chart, all the other toolbar buttons become disabled. You can't edit a table while viewing its chart (see Chapter 16 for a full guide to charting your data).

Evaluating Your Current Finances

When you look at your current financial position, you need to know your current balances. You may also need to see how you're doing against your current budget. In the following sections, we discuss ways in which you can view balances, get a financial overview, and manage your current financial position.

Viewing account balances

To view account balances, follow these steps:

1. **Click the Accounts, Balances & Budgeting button.**

   This green button displays an image of gold coins.

   Your accounts appear in the pane on the left side of the screen (see Figure 12-6).

2. **Click the Balances tab.**

   The tab is located to the top-right of the Accounts tree. We discuss the five other tabs — Transactions, Budgeting, Overview, Monthly, and Entries — throughout this book.

3. **To view individual account balances, double-click an account group (which looks like a computer directory folder) to expand the tree structure, and then select the relevant account.**

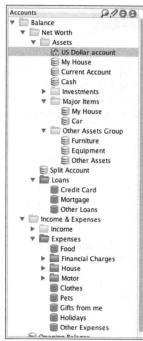

Figure 12-6:
View the
Accounts
tree on the
left of the
Accounts,
Balances &
Budgeting
screen.

Using the Overview tab

The Overview tab lets you compare your budgets with your actual balances for a selected period, for the year to date, and for the full year.

In the Overview tab, you need to select the period for which you want to report. Follow these steps:

1. **Click the Report on Period drop-down list.**

   This drop-down list contains the months of the year.

2. **Click a month to select the period for which you want the report.**

   The table is updated to reflect your choice.

3. **To compare the figures for your chosen period against a set budget, make a selection from the For Budget drop-down list.**

   This list displays all your defined budgets.

   The table is updated with the appropriate budget information.

Seeing Where You're Headed

You can use views (described in the section "Viewing Your Transactions," earlier in this chapter) to forecast where your bank balance will be at the end of the month. Can you afford any luxuries this month — or indeed, in six months? You can also use the tabs in the Accounts view — such as Budget and Monthly — to see how your financial position will probably look.

Home Accountz can forecast any account by looking at an account's automated transactions (discussed in Chapter 13) and applying them to views.

To forecast any account, make sure you've entered all the direct debits and credits, standing orders, and any other automated transactions. Then, follow these steps:

1. **In the Accounts pane on the left side of the screen, click the Accounts component for which you want to create a forecast.**

   For example, select Current Account if you want to get an idea about the potential future position of your current account.

   After you select an account, the table on the right side of the screen is updated and populated with the data from the selected account.

2. **Click the Transactions tab.**

   In the right panel, click to open the View drop-down list.

3. **Select the Next Month option from the drop-down list.**

   A forecast for the coming month appears in the account table on the right.

You don't have to forecast by month: by manipulating the view and creating your own, you can forecast by quarter, half year, or year.

Chapter 13

Working with Automated Transactions

In This Chapter

▶ Finding your way around the Automated Transactions window

▶ Creating transactions that recur automatically

▶ Editing and deleting automated transactions

*W*ith automated transactions in Home Accountz, you can create future and recurring entries that will be automatically inserted into the All Transactions table, which you can access by clicking the All Transactions button (which looks like a stack of green books) in the toolbar at the top of the Home Accountz window; this is useful if you make regular payments — such as paying off your credit card.

You can use automated transactions to create direct debits, direct credits, and regularly occurring transactions such as salaries, pensions, and child tax credits. Automated transactions are also great for standing orders.

Navigating the Automated Transactions Window

Open the Automated Transactions window by clicking the Automated Transactions button at the top of the main Home Accountz window.

The toolbars at the top-left and top-right of the table in the Automated Transactions window feature the following tools (from left to right):

- ✔ **Select Current View:** Allows you to change the view that's currently in use by the table

- ✔ **Toggle View Editor Panel:** Shows or hides the View Editor panel, which allows you to edit the current view, or create or delete a view

- ✔ **Search:** Shows or hides the table's Search panel, which allows you to search for keywords (or amounts) in the current table

- ✔ **Create Transaction:** Creates a new empty transaction

- ✔ **Copy Transaction:** Makes a copy of the currently selected transaction

- ✔ **Delete Transaction:** Hides the currently selected transaction from view (use the Filter Selector drop-down list to show all deleted transactions again — you can also undelete them, if you want)

- ✔ **Holiday Rules Configuration:** Gives you control over whether to include weekends and bank holidays in the schedule; also lets you set the country, which then displays the scheduled bank holidays for that country

- ✔ **Show/Hide Chart:** Displays or hides the chart for the currently selected view

- ✔ **Print This Table:** Prints the table

The different flavors of automated transactions

You set up automated transactions for direct debits, credits, and standing orders in slightly different ways — standing orders have a fixed amount, whereas direct debits and direct credits can vary in amount.

Direct debit and direct credit amounts can change. If you agree to a varying direct debit — for instance, for a mobile phone — no advice is required, but for larger payments, suppliers usually inform you in writing before altering the direct debit amount. Home Accountz makes this change very simple — you just have to edit your automated transaction. We discuss editing automated transactions in the section "Editing Automated Transactions," in this chapter.

Home Accountz also has the ability to reschedule automated transactions if they occur outside of banking hours — for example, due to a weekend or bank holiday. In these cases, payments are automatically deferred to the next working day, and income is pushed to the first working day prior to the scheduled date.

For example, a payment scheduled to happen on a Saturday would be pushed to the following Monday (and if the Monday is a bank holiday, then it will be pushed to Tuesday). An automated credit (or income) is pushed to the previous Friday (or Thursday if the Friday happens to be a bank holiday).

Visible columns

The Automated Transactions table is just like all the other tables in Home Accountz: You can change the way the table is organized and how it appears by making a selection from the Select Current View drop-down list at the top-left of the table.

The table contains a complete automated transaction template on each row. The settings of these transactions determine when they're inserted automatically into the All Transactions table — which you can access by clicking the All Transactions button (which looks like a stack of green books) in the toolbar at the top of the Home Accountz window. The All Transactions button is available from most windows within Home Accountz.

The Automated Transactions table displays a number of columns by default:

- ✔ **Start Date:** The date from which this transaction will start to be automatically inserted into your books.

- ✔ **Period:** The frequency with which this transaction will automatically be inserted into your books. Pressing the space bar on your keyboard will bring up a list of available period options.

- ✔ **Total Insertions:** The maximum number of times this transaction should automatically be inserted into your books.

  Setting this column's value to 0 (zero) effectively disables the automated transaction.

- ✔ **Insertions Done:** The number of times this transaction has already been inserted. When the number in this column equals the number in the Total Insertions column, the application will stop automatically inserting this transaction into your books.

- ✔ **Next Date Due:** The date of the next automatic insertion of this transaction. This column isn't editable: Home Accountz calculates its value based on the values in the Start Date, Period, Total Number of Insertions, Insertions Done, and Weekend/Bank Holiday settings.

- ✔ **Description:** Any descriptive text to help you identify this transaction after it's placed in the All Transactions table. For example, if you're creating a car loan payment, you may want to enter the car make and model in this column.

- ✔ **Payee:** Choose the payee involved with this transaction. You can create any payees that aren't yet within Home Accountz by selecting the New option from the drop-down list to the right of the Payee field and entering the name of the new payee. To confirm the payee, click OK. If this is a new automated transaction to a new payee, you can use the New option to create the transaction right in the table, instead of having to open the Payee window.

- ✔ **Total Amount:** The full total of the transaction.
- ✔ **From Account:** Where the money came from (for example, an income account for an income or expense).
- ✔ **To Account:** Where the money went (for example, the bank if an income or an expense account if a purchase).
- ✔ **Reference:** A reference value for the current transaction entry. For example, if the transaction is a direct debit, you might enter **DD** as a reference. If it's a loan, you may want to enter the loan account number.
- ✔ **Active:** If checked, the transactions will be inserted as defined. If unchecked, transactions won't be inserted but can still be used for forecasting.

Hidden columns

Every table has a large selection of columns. You can display or hide columns within the View Editor panel by clicking the Show/Hide Cols button:

- ✔ **To bring a column into the current table:** Click the column title, and then select Show from the pop-up menu that appears. The column title moves into the Visible column.
- ✔ **To hide a column from the table:** Click the column header, and then select Hide from the pop-up menu that appears. That column title is moved into the Hidden column.

Here's a list of columns that are hidden by default but which you can add:

- ✔ **Cleared (From):** Represents whether the From side of the transaction (the account from which the money is withdrawn) has cleared.

  A *cleared* transaction is one that has appeared on your bank statement and shows the same information as your transaction in Home Accountz. When your bank statement and Home Accountz entry are in agreement, you can set the Cleared (From) field in any transaction to verify you have checked it.

- ✔ **Cleared (To):** Represents whether the To side of the transaction (the account into which the money goes) has cleared.
- ✔ **Cleared Date (From):** Gives the date that the payment cleared out of the source account.
- ✔ **Cleared Date (To):** Gives the date that the payment cleared in the destination account.

✔ **Currency Amount:** The equivalent to the figure in the Total Amount column, converted to the chosen foreign currency (as defined in the Currency Code column).

✔ **Currency Code:** The three-character currency code of the chosen foreign currency.

To choose the currency, start typing part of its currency code (normally three letters, such as USD for U.S. dollars and GBP for pounds) in the Currency Code column, and then select the currency from the pop-up menu that appears.

✔ **Currency Rate:** The exchange rate to use when converting between the native and chosen foreign currency (as defined in the Currency Code column).

✔ **Date Created:** The actual creation date of this transaction. The contents of this column are created automatically every time you add a transaction, and you can't edit them.

✔ **Deleted:** Signifies whether this transaction has been deleted. By default, you see only non-deleted transactions, but you can modify the Current filter to show deleted transactions, as well.

✔ **Error Code:** If the transaction is in error (has a red background), this column displays a description of the error.

You can also view the description of the error by hovering your mouse anywhere on the transaction's row.

✔ **Notes:** A place to record any additional notes about this transaction. For example, if you bought a car, you may want to include details of the warranty or perhaps any other details of the car you want to record for future reference.

✔ **Quantity:** Used when a transaction line contains multiples of the same item. You can use this column in conjunction with the Unit Price.

The fields in the preceding list, when added to your Home Accountz data, can help expand the depth of the information available. The use of Notes, for instance, is entirely optional.

Setting Up Automated Transactions

Whenever you sign a new direct debit, direct credit, or standing order with your bank, you want to replicate that transaction in Home Accountz so that you keep your books up to date with the bank.

Follow these steps to set up an automated transaction:

1. **Click the Automated Transactions button located at the top of the Home Accountz window.**

   The button displays a D on a diary page.

   Clicking this button opens the Automated Transactions window.

2. **To add an automated transaction, click the green plus sign (+) button, as shown in Figure 13-1.**

Figure 13-1:
Creating an
automated
transaction.

   In the new row that appears in the table, you can start adding in the detail of the automated transaction.

3. **In the Start Date field, enter the first date on which you want to make that payment.**

4. **In the Period field, enter the frequency of the payment.**

   Enter the first few letters of the frequency — for example, entering **dai** will bring up Daily; **we** will bring up Every 1 Week, Every 2 Weeks and so on; **mon** will bring up Monthly; and **yea** will bring up Every Year (annually), Every 2 Years (biannually) and Every 6 Months (half-yearly).

5. **In the Total Insertions field, enter the total number of times you want to make the payment.**

   For example, if you were entering a brand new 25-year monthly mortgage, then enter 300 (25 years × 12 monthly payments = 300 total payments).

   Home Accountz automatically updates the figure in the Insertions Done field for the number of payments already made and records the payments until the final payment is made.

6. **In the Description field, record details of what you're paying for.**

   For example, if you're making a loan payment, you can record details of the loan in this column. For example, you could record the make and model of some camera equipment you bought.

7. **Enter the name of the person or company you're making payment to or receiving payment from in the Payee field.**

8. **In the Total Amount field, enter the amount to be paid for each installment.**

9. **In the From Account field, indicate where you want the money to be taken from.**

   In most cases, it'll be your Current Account because automated payments such as direct debits and standing orders are usually associated with bank accounts.

10. **In the To Account field, begin to enter where the money is going, and then select the account name from the pop-up menu that appears.**

    If you're paying your mortgage, for example, choose the name of your mortgage company account.

    If you don't have an account set up, select the New Account option from the pop-up menu, and then create a new account (which we describe in Chapter 7).

11. **In the Reference field, enter an account reference, if you have one.**

    For example, enter your mortgage account number if you're creating a transaction for your mortgage.

12. **Make sure the Active check box is selected.**

    You can make your automated transaction template inactive by deselecting this option. You may want to do this if, for example, your mortgage company defers your monthly payments for a few months.

Editing Automated Transactions

You may need to edit an automated transaction template for many reasons, including changing the amount of a direct debit or direct credit. You may also want to change a reference or other field.

Any changes you make to an automated transaction template affect only new transactions created from that template. Transactions already created from the changed template remain unchanged.

To edit a template transaction, follow these steps:

1. **Click the Automated Transactions button that appears at the top of the Home Accountz window.**

   This step takes you to the Automated Transactions window.

2. **Locate the automated transaction you want to alter from the list, double-click in the field, and then enter the new value (see Figure 13-2).**

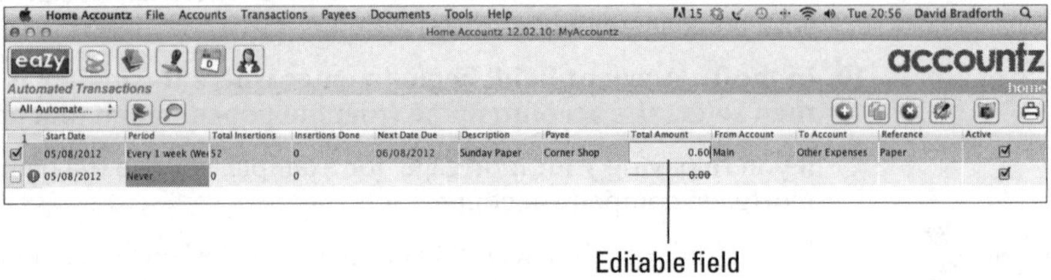

Figure 13-2:
Double-
click in the
automated
transaction
field that
you want to
change.

Editable field

If the price of that product has increased, for instance, double-click in the Total Amount field and enter the new price.

3. **Press Return or Enter to confirm the new value.**

From that point forward, whenever you use that template, the new value will be put into place.

Deleting Automated Transactions

After an automated transaction has ended, you may want to delete it to ensure that you're not distracted by automated transaction templates that are no longer relevant.

Deleting an automated transaction template doesn't affect any existing transactions that have been created by that template.

To delete a template transaction, follow these steps:

1. **Click the Automated Transactions button that appears at the top of the Home Accountz window.**

   The Automated Transactions window opens.

2. **Click anywhere within the row for the automated transaction you want to delete.**

3. **Click the Delete button (which looks like a red circle with a white X).**

   You're prompted to confirm the deletion (as shown in Figure 13-3).

4. **Click Delete to confirm the deletion.**

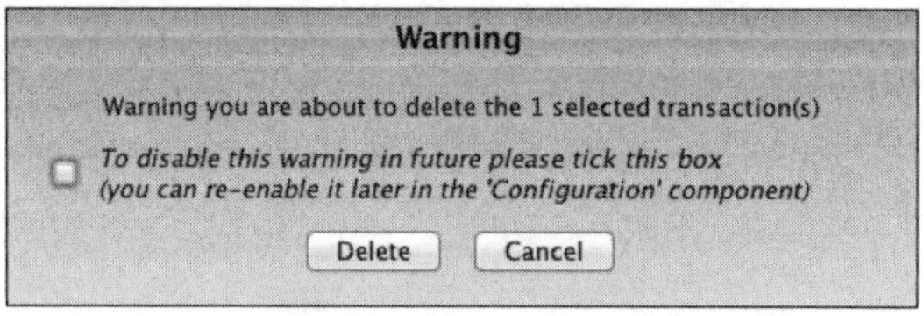

Figure 13-3:
You're
asked to
confirm the
automated-
transaction
deletion.

Warning

Warning you are about to delete the 1 selected transaction(s)

☐ *To disable this warning in future please tick this box (you can re-enable it later in the 'Configuration' component)*

[Delete]   [Cancel]

Undeleting Automated Transactions

If you decide you need to recover a deleted transaction template, you can do so with little complication. To recover a template transaction, follow these steps:

1. **Click the View Editor Panel button, which looks like a funnel.**

   The View Editor panel opens.

2. **Click the Create New View button.**

   A carbon copy of the current view is created, which you need to do because you can't alter the filter values on the default view.

3. **Click the Show/Hide Cols button.**

   The Set Column Visibility window opens.

4. **Select Deleted in the Hidden list, and then click the Show button.**

5. **Click Close.**

   The Deleted check boxes now appear at the end of the column list.

6. **Click the Filter button, and then select the Include Deleted check box.**

   Deleted transactions appear in the list.

7. **Deselect the Deleted check box from the end of the row relating to the transaction you want to recover (see Figure 13-4).**

   This will undelete the automated transaction and make it active again.

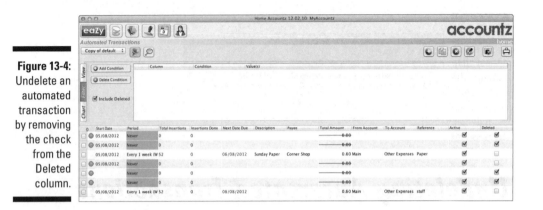

Figure 13-4:
Undelete an
automated
transaction
by removing
the check
from the
Deleted
column.

Holiday Rules Configuration

Home Accountz recognizes bank holidays for ten different countries:

- ✔ England
- ✔ Wales
- ✔ Scotland
- ✔ Northern Ireland
- ✔ France
- ✔ Germany
- ✔ Ireland
- ✔ Italy
- ✔ Spain
- ✔ United States

Bank transactions, such as direct debits or direct credits, which would normally fall on a bank holiday, are instead moved the next working day. By setting up the Holiday Rules, you can ensure that the transactions are entered correctly. Follow these steps:

1. Click the Holiday Rules button.

This button, which displays a cog and screwdriver, is immediately to the right of the Delete button.

The Configure Holiday Rules dialog box opens (see Figure 13-5).

2. **Make the appropriate selections from the options displayed.**

   The options are

   - *Do Not Insert Transactions on Weekends:* Select this option to pre-vent automated transactions from being entered on days that fall on weekends.

   - *Do Not Insert Transactions on Holidays:* Select to prevent automated transactions from being entered on bank/public holidays.

   - *Country:* Select the country from this drop-down list to ensure that the correct bank/public holiday list is used.

3. **When you're happy with your choices, click the Done button to con-firm them.**

Figure 13-5:
The
Configure
Holiday
Rules dialog
box.

Configure Holiday Rules

☑ Do not insert transactions on weekends

☑ Do not insert transactions on holidays

Country: England ▲▼

Name	Date
New Year	2 January
Easter Monday	9 April
Early May Bank Holiday	7 May
Spring Bank Holiday	4 June
Queen´s Diamond Jubilee	5 June
Summer Bank Holiday	27 August
Christmas	25 December
Boxing Day	26 December

Done

Part IV
Managing Your Money

The 5th Wave   By Rich Tennant

"I bought a software program that should help
us monitor and control our spending habits, and
while I was there, I picked up a few new games,
a couple of screensavers, four new mousepads,
this nifty pullout keyboard cradle..."

In this part . . .

Part IV is about creating and using reports. We explore the ways in which you can present your data using the facilities available within the Home Accountz software. You can find out how to use views and tables, as well as how to present your information in a graph or chart. We talk about how to sift through your data, and we explain the Home Accountz Document Designer, which you can use to create document templates.

This part also explores budgeting itself with Home Accountz. You can find out how to create budgets within Home Accountz and how to compare current and previous periods to get an idea of your future financial state.

Chapter 14

Using Views and Tables

*H*ome Accountz is, as an application, based around a series of tables. These tables can be manipulated to present the data in a number of different ways, called *alternative views*. In this chapter, we look at the different ways you can alter the views of each table to best present the data contained within those tables.

Figuring Out the Table Basics

In the following sections, we explore the basics of manipulating the views available within Home Accountz. We discuss how to select a view, create a view, and work with transactions.

Selecting a view

A view is a way of looking at your data. Each view contains all data that meets a particular set of criteria, which you can set up via a filter. (See the section "Filtering the columns in your view," later in this chapter, for more about filters.)

Some of the views available include

✔ All Transactions

✔ Cleared Transactions

✔ In Error

✔ Including Deleted

✔ Last 7 Days

✔ Next Month

✔ Uncleared

Click the Views button to display the Views drop-down list (as shown in Figure 14-1). Views let you filter your data in many different ways. For example, to reconcile a bank account, select the Uncleared Transactions view. After you reconcile (or clear) your transactions, select the Cleared Transactions view to get a look-alike statement, complete with running balance, so that you can visually see whether your data contains any mistakes.

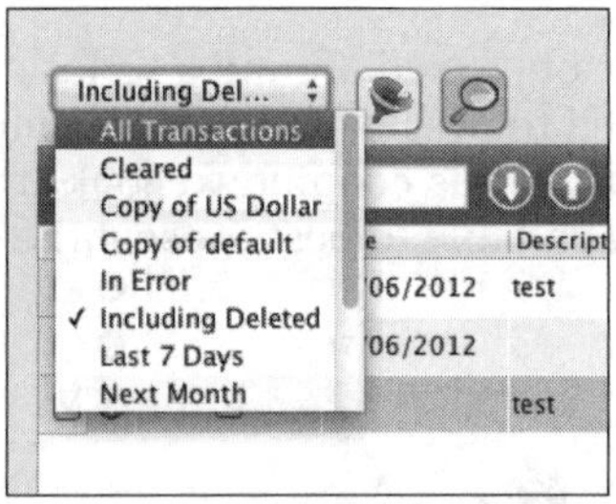

Figure 14-1:
Access
the views
available
within Home
Accountz in
the Views
drop-down
list.

Creating a view

A view provides a particular way to look at the data you have available within Home Accountz. The default views cover common periods of time, such as the last seven days, or common requirements, such as uncleared transactions. Follow these steps to create your own view:

1. **Click the Open/Close the View Editor Panel button to open the View Editor panel (see Figure 14-2).**

   This button looks like a funnel and appears at the top of any Transaction table.

2. **Click the Create New View button.**

   A new view appears in the same window, allowing you to create a new view template based on the filter conditions of the current view — so if your present view shows the previous year's data, your new view shows the exact same data.

View Editor Panel button

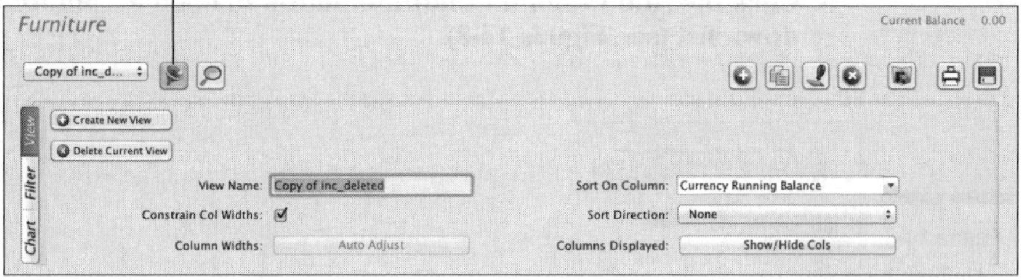

Figure 14-2:
The View
Editor panel
at the top
of the main
window.

3. **In the View Name field, enter an appropriate name for the new view.**

   For example, you might enter Bank Account.

4. **(Optional) Prevent the alteration of the column widths by selecting the Constrain Col Widths check box.**

   If you deselect this check box, you can manually set the column widths for your data by clicking and dragging the column edges left or right.

5. **(Optional) Set the view to always sort on a certain column by selecting a data field from the Sort on Column drop-down list.**

   More commonly that not, you want to look at your finances for a particular time so that you can get a better understanding of your financial situation.

6. **(Optional) Select Ascending or Descending from the Sort Direction drop-down list to change how the data is sorted.**

   The default value for Sort Direction is None. We recommend setting this value to Descending so that the current date appears closest to the top of the list.

7. **(Optional) Set what columns appear in the view by clicking the Show/Hide Cols button, and then selecting the appropriate fields.**

   How you set the columns depends on what you want to do with them:

   • *Hide a field.* Click that field, and then select Hide.

   • *Make a field visible.* Click that field, and then select Show.

Filtering the columns in your view

You can set which columns appear in your created view, as well as the column widths. Follow these steps:

1. **Click the Filter tab on the left of the View panel.**

   The Filter view opens.

2. **Select a column in the Filter table (to the right of the Filter tab).**

3. **Click the Add Column Condition button to open a Condition drop-down list (see Figure 14-3).**

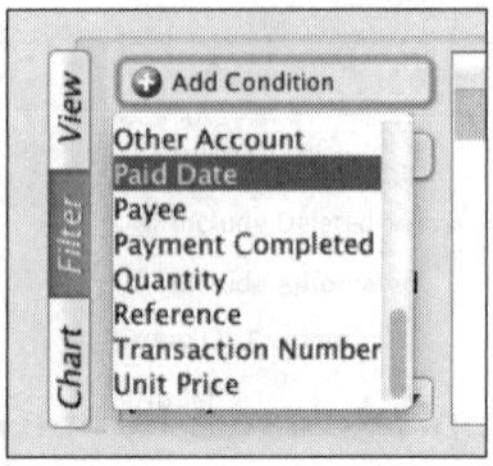

Figure 14-3:
Filter your
data quickly
and easily.

Add Condition
Other Account
Paid Date
Payee
Payment Completed
Quantity
Reference
Transaction Number
Unit Price

The column conditions available are

- Account Involved
- Cleared (From)
- Cleared (To)
- Cleared Date (From)
- Cleared Date (To)
- Currency Amount
- Currency Code
- Currency Rate
- Currency Unit Price
- Date Created
- Date
- Description
- Error Code

- From Account
- Import ID
- Lock
- Notes
- Paid Date
- Payee
- Payment Completed
- Quantity
- Reference
- To Account
- Total Amount
- Transaction Number
- Unit Price

4. **Select the appropriate options from the Condition drop-down list.**

   The conditions vary, depending on the column condition. For example, if you want to filter to all events in the past month, select Date, and then select Occurred in the Last. The view then changes to reflect only those transactions that occurred in the last month.

5. **Repeat Steps 2 through 4 to add additional columns with conditions.**

   In our example, you can add another column condition, set the To side to be cleared, and make sure the two columns have the AND symbol in the left side of the column containing the condition to create a copy of the Cleared view.

The Cleared view reflects any transactions in which their financial components have fully cleared — for example, a check tends to be cleared at your bank five working days after you deposit it.

Creating a chart

Follow these steps to work in the Chart tab (which appears below the Filter tab):

1. **Click the Chart tab.**

   The Chart view (shown in Figure 14-4) opens.

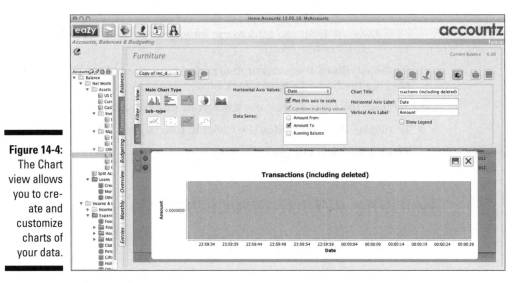

Figure 14-4: The Chart view allows you to create and customize charts of your data.

2. **Select the style of chart by clicking any of the Main Chart Type buttons.**

3. **Select a Sub Type from the options that appear.**

   These options allow you to customize the look of the chart type you selected in Step 2.

4. **From the Category Labels drop-down list (to the right of the chart type), select the column that you want to use.**

   Typically, people use the Date column for this axis because it's a useful tracker when keeping an eye on your finances, allowing you to track the account balance over time.

5. **Below the Category Labels drop-down list, select the check box for the data series that you want to use.**

   The *data series* is the data that you want to use in this graph. For a bank-style chart, you may want to chart the Running Balance.

6. **(Optional) Add labels to the chart for the horizontal and vertical axes, as well as the chart title.**

   You can make these changes by following these steps:

   a. *Enter the title you want to use in the Chart Title text box on the right of the Chart window.*

   b. *Set the horizontal axis label by entering it in the Horizontal Axis Label text box.*

   c. *Enter the label you want to use for the vertical axis in the Vertical Axis Label text box.*

7. **(Optional) Show the column names that you selected for the chart by clicking the Show Legend check box.**

8. **To close the View Editor, click the View Editor button.**

9. **To display the chart, click the Chart button in the toolbar.**

   To turn off the chart, click the button again.

Working with transactions

You can work with transactions in a variety of ways, and the following list outlines the features available when you do so:

- **Searching transactions:** Click the Magnifying Glass button to open the Search text box, which appears at the top of the Account Information panel. Type in any part of what you're looking for — for example, enter an amount or description. Then, press the Enter key. All transactions that contain the text you entered are highlighted. Click the red-arrow button that appears at the top of the Account Information panel to move from one match to the next.

  If you want to make the search case-sensitive, click the Match Case button.

- **Adding a new transaction:** Click the green plus sign (+) button (located at the top-right of the Account Information panel) to add a new transaction.

- ✔ **Copying a transaction:** Select a transaction, and then click the Copy button (located to the right of the Add New Transaction button) that appears to make a copy of a transaction. The copy appears at the bottom of the transaction list.

- ✔ **Inserting a template transaction:** Click the Insert Template button (which looks like a stamp) to insert a template transaction. You create a template for commonly occurring transactions (such as cash withdrawals, food, or fuel) so that you can preset the transaction and then access it by selecting it from the drop-down list that appears directly below this button.

- ✔ **Deleting a transaction:** Select a transaction, and then click the Delete button. Another transaction becomes highlighted after the delete, so take care not to press the button again.

You can turn on the Lock column to manually lock transactions that you don't want to change. Even after you lock a transaction, you can still clear that transaction when you reconcile an account.

- ✔ **Undeleting a transaction:** Select the Include Deleted view from the Views drop-down list to display all the deleted transactions, and then deselect the Deleted check box to undelete them.

- ✔ **Displaying or hiding a chart:** To see a chart of your current view, click the Chart button. The chart is constructed by using the relevant data entered into Home Accountz and reflects your financial situation at that point in time. Click the button again to turn off the chart.

- ✔ **Printing:** To print the current view, click the Print button.

- ✔ **Exporting to CSV:** To export the current view to a file on your hard drive, click the Export to CSV button. You can then import your data into any spreadsheet — or e-mail it to friends or family who want to help with your financial planning.

Chapter 15

Visualizing Your Information with Graphs and Charts

In This Chapter

▶ Getting Home Accountz into Charts view

▶ Creating and customizing charts

*A*fter you input your financial data (which we describe in Chapter 3), you can more easily analyze — and hence use — the data when it's presented in a form other than as a list of numbers, suppliers, and dates. That's where graphs and charts can come in handy.

In this chapter, we explore how you can present your data in graphs and charts.

Switching to Charts View

Creating a template isn't as complicated as you might think. You can create simple charts quickly by using the Home Accountz Charts view, and then you can customize those charts to meet your needs.

To switch to the Charts view and create a simple chart, follow these steps:

1. **Click the All Transactions button to switch to All Transactions view.**

   This button, which displays an image of green books, is fifth from the left on the toolbar at the top-left of the Home Accountz window.

2. **Click the Show/Hide the Chart for This View button.**

   This button looks like a small 3D bar chart and is at the top-right of the view.

   A chart created by using the data stored in the All Transactions view now appears on top of the All Transactions view (see Figure 15-1), which you can still see grayed out in the background. This chart shows transactions over time in a simple bar chart with basic axis labels and chart title.

Charts View tab

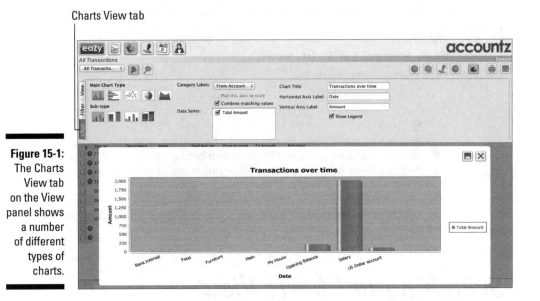

3. **Open the Editor panel by selecting the Open/Close the View Editor Panel button.**

   This button displays an image that looks like a funnel; it appears below a table's Name on the left side of the window.

   The View Editor panel appears above the chart. The panel contains a series of tabs that allow you to access their associated panels.

4. **Click the Chart tab.**

   The Chart Filter view opens.

   You can change the both the chart type and chart subtype, as well as adjusting category labels, data series, and the chart title. You can also edit both the horizontal and vertical axis titles. (We talk about how to make these changes in the following section.)

You can show or hide a table's chart at any time simply by clicking the Show/Hide Chart button on the table's toolbar. When the chart is being displayed, all the other toolbar buttons become disabled because you can't edit a table while viewing its chart.

Working with Charts

You can select from five main chart types (each chart type has a button in the Main Chart Type section of the View Editor panel). This table shows both the chart type and its button.

Chart Type	*Button*
Vertical bar chart	
Horizontal bar chart	
Line chart	
Pie chart	
Area chart	

You use the different types of charts to plots various kinds of data:

- **Bar charts and pie charts:** Often used to plot categorical data. Each row in the table represents a category, and one column from the table provides labels used to identify the categories.

- **Line graphs and area charts:** Can also be used to plot categorical data but are typically used to plot values on a scaled horizontal axis. One column in the table provides the specific values along this horizontal axis.

Table 15-1 shows the different types of vertical and horizontal bar charts available in Home Accountz.

Table 15-1	Vertical and Horizontal Bar Charts	
Icon	*Chart Name*	*Chart Description*
	2D Bar Chart	The selected data series are plotted in separate bars.
	Stacked 2D Bar Chart	The selected data series are positioned on top of each other, illustrating their combined values.
	3D Bar Chart	Like the 2D Bar Chart, but the bars are depicted in 3D.
	Stacked 3D Bar Chart	Like the Stacked 2D Bar Chart, but the bars are depicted in 3D.

In Table 15-2, you can see the different types of line charts you can use.

Table 15-2	Line Charts	
Icon	*Chart Name*	*Chart Description*
	Lines Only	The selected data series are plotted by using straight lines between values.
	Points Only	Just the data values themselves are plotted, like a scatter diagram.
	Lines & Points	A combination of the Lines Only and Points Only chart types.
	Stepped Line Chart	The selected data series are plotted in a group of steps. One data point steps up or down to the next.

Table 15-3 gives you information about the types of pie and area charts you can create.

Table 15-3		Pie and Area Charts
Icon	*Chart Name*	*Chart Description*
	2D Pie Chart	A simple two-dimensional pie chart, which presents data in the form slices of a circle. Larger values form the larger pieces of the pie.
	3D Pie Chart	A pie chart depicted in 3D that presents data as different-sized pie pieces.
	Transparent Layers Area Chart	Each data series is plotted as a shaded area. The shaded areas are semi-transparent so that the area from each data series is visible beneath the others.
	Stacked Area Chart	The shaded areas from each selected data series are stacked to show their combined values.

Selecting a chart type

Decide which chart best allows you to analyze or present your data, and then click the button for that chart type in the Main Chart Type section. Below the Main Chart Type section, the Sub-Type section appears. The buttons displayed in this section depend on which Main Chart type you select. When you click one of the subtype buttons, the graph or chart displayed changes immediately to reflect the new selection.

Adding data to your chart

After you select the chart type, you need to select the data to be used in the chart. You choose data by selecting columns from the All Transactions table. Just follow these steps:

1. **Click the Category Labels or Horizontal Axis Values button.**

   Which button appears depends on the type of chart that you selected.

2. **In the drop-down list that appears (see Figure 15-2 for an example of the Category Labels drop-down list), select the label or value you want to use as the basis for this chart.**

The selected data is used to identify the labels for categorical data (or the horizontal axis values for scaled data).

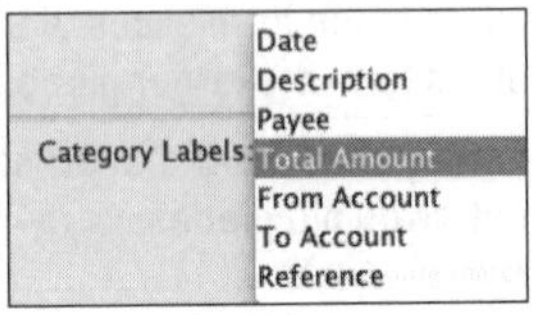

Figure 15-2:
The
Category
Labels drop-
down list for
a chart.

Category Labels:	Date
	Description
	Payee
	Total Amount
	From Account
	To Account
	Reference

3. **Add further data series to the chart by selecting the corresponding columns' check boxes in the Data Series section.**

This section appears below the Category Labels or Horizontal Axis Values button.

Only columns that contain numerical data appear in the Data Series section because only numerical data can be represented on a chart. You need to select at least one data series to produce a chart.

Pie charts can represent only one data series. If you select more than one data series, Home Accountz uses the first data series in the chart and ignores the other selections.

In all charts other than pie charts, each data series is represented on the chart by a separate color. Because a pie chart has only one data series, different colors distinguish between the categories.

Combining matching values

If the column that represents the category labels has the same value in more than one row, the data can be interpreted in two ways:

✔ Each row is treated as a distinct category, despite the duplicated label(s).

✔ Rows that have matching category labels are considered the same category, and their respective values are combined into one value.

To switch between these options, click the Combine Matching Values check box, which appears below the Category Labels button. If this check box is selected, then rows that have matching category labels are considered one category — if it's not selected, each row is distinct.

Plotting the horizontal axis to scale

You can use line charts and area charts to plot different parts of your finances against a horizontal axis. If the column selected as the horizontal axis is a date or a numerical column, then you have the option to plot the horizontal axis to scale. *Plotting to scale* means that instead of plotting the values on the chart at regular intervals along the horizontal axis, the values can be placed according to their numerical or chronological value (so figures are placed in order of their relative size).

To plot the horizontal axis to scale, click either the Line Chart or Area Chart button. To switch between these two modes, select the line chart or area chart that you want to switch, and then click Plot This Axis to Scale check box to either remove or insert the check in the check box.

Customizing your chart

Several options allow you to customize your chart. You can add your own chart title and label to both the horizontal and vertical axes, as well as choose whether to show a *legend* (which is a representation of what each component of the chart symbolizes). You can also add value labels to a pie chart (see Figure 15-3).

Figure 15-3:
Add labels to a pie chart and choose whether to include a legend.

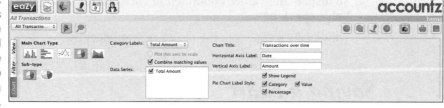

You can change these items by clicking in the appropriate text box, deleting the information already there and entering new information:

- ✔ Chart title
- ✔ Horizontal axis label
- ✔ Vertical axis label

You can add legends by selecting the Show Legend check box. The legend can't be customized: It reflects the type and quantity of data being displayed within the currently selected chart.

To add value labels to a pie chart, follow these steps:

1. **Click the Pie Chart button.**

   This button appears fourth from the left in the Main Chart Type section.

   A pie chart opens in the main view.

2. **Click the button for the pie chart you want to customize from the sub-type buttons.**

3. **From the Category Labels drop-down list, select the category of data you want to present in the chart.**

   After you make this selection, the chart updates itself.

   The pie chart labels are located at the bottom-right of the Chart panel. The options include

   - Show Legend
   - Category
   - Value
   - Percentage

4. **To display the values contained in each section of the pie, select the Value check box.**

   These values appear in the pie when you select them.

Saving a chart

After you create your chart, you can export it as a PNG graphics file for use in other programs or presentations.

Follow these steps:

1. **Within the Chart view, click the Save This Chart as a Graphics File button.**

   This button looks like a blue floppy disc and appears in the top-right corner of the chart window.

   The Save dialog box appears.

2. **(Optional) Navigate to the folder where you want to save the chart file.**

   By default, your chart is saved in your Documents folder.

3. **Type the filename that you want to use into the File Name text box.**

4. **Click the Save button.**

   The chart file is saved.

5. **To close the chart, click the gray X button at the top-right of the Chart window.**

Chapter 16

Exporting and Printing Reports and Charts

· ·

In This Chapter

▶ Exporting a Home Accountz table

▶ Preparing your reports

· ·

*A*fter you set up your accounts and input your data, you may find it difficult and time-consuming to analyze the raw data so that you can get some meaningful information from your accounts. Home Accountz saves you the trouble, providing the tools you need to quickly and easily produce both reports and charts, which can help you make sense of your data.

In this chapter, we cover the ways you can get data out of Home Accountz: You can export data as a CSV file, which can be opened in a spreadsheet program, such as Microsoft Excel.

Exporting Your Data

After you create your accounts and input your data, you're not locked into using Home Accountz to work with and analyze that information. Home Accountz allows you to export data in CSV format, which can be read by any spreadsheet or database program. Because it's a plain-text file, it can also be read by word processor or notepad programs. In practice, you'll probably use a CSV file exported from Home Accountz to create a spreadsheet in Excel.

In a number of the tables in Home Accountz, you can export data by following these steps:

1. **Click the Export as CSV File button.**

   This button appears on the far-right of the screen and looks like a blue disk. For example, you can click this button in Transactions view. (We talk about Transactions view in Chapter 14.)

   A Save dialog box opens (as shown in Figure 16-1).

2. **Select the folder on your computer's hard drive in which you want to create a CSV file.**

3. **Click Save to save the new file.**

   This file contains the exported contents of the selected table (in our example, the Transactions table). The table is formatted as a series of lines of text; each column value is separated by a comma from the next column's value, and each row starts a new line.

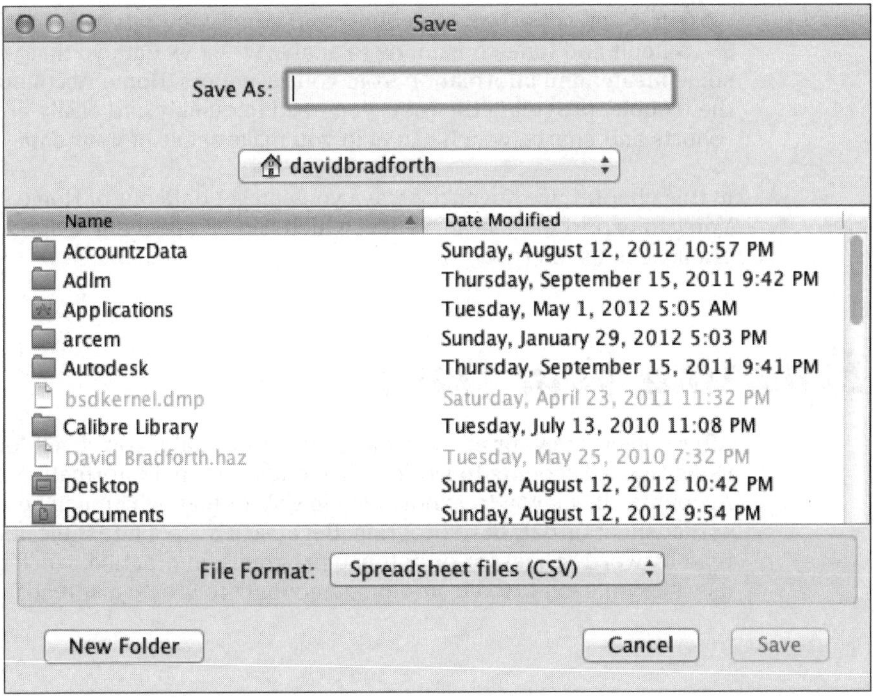

Figure 16-1:
In the Save dialog box, specify where you want to export data.

Name	Date Modified
AccountzData	Sunday, August 12, 2012 10:57 PM
Adlm	Thursday, September 15, 2011 9:42 PM
Applications	Tuesday, May 1, 2012 5:05 AM
arcem	Sunday, January 29, 2012 5:03 PM
Autodesk	Thursday, September 15, 2011 9:41 PM
bsdkernel.dmp	Saturday, April 23, 2011 11:32 PM
Calibre Library	Tuesday, July 13, 2010 11:08 PM
David Bradforth.haz	Tuesday, May 25, 2010 7:32 PM
Desktop	Sunday, August 12, 2012 10:42 PM
Documents	Sunday, August 12, 2012 9:54 PM

Save

Save As:

davidbradforth

File Format: Spreadsheet files (CSV)

New Folder   Cancel   Save

4. **Locate the file you just created and double-click it to open it in the default program for your operating system.**

   Alternatively, open the program you want to use, and then choose File⇨Open and select the file on your computer.

   For example, if you open a CSV file exported from Home Accountz by using Excel, Excel creates a new, properly laid-out worksheet that contains the data stored in the Home Accountz Transactions table.

Accessing Your Reports

With Home Accountz, the eaZy button provides one-click access to a number of reports and charts. Follow these simple steps:

1. **Click the eaZy button.**

   The eaZy button appears below the menu bar at the top of the screen.

2. **In the eaZy Button screen that appears, click the Set Up/Report tab at the top-right (see Figure 16-2).**

   This tab provides access to a number of types of reports. The eaZy button is discussed in detail in Chapter 3.

The Set Up/Report tab offers seven reports located in the bottom half of the panel. These reports draw on information you've previously entered into Home Accountz.

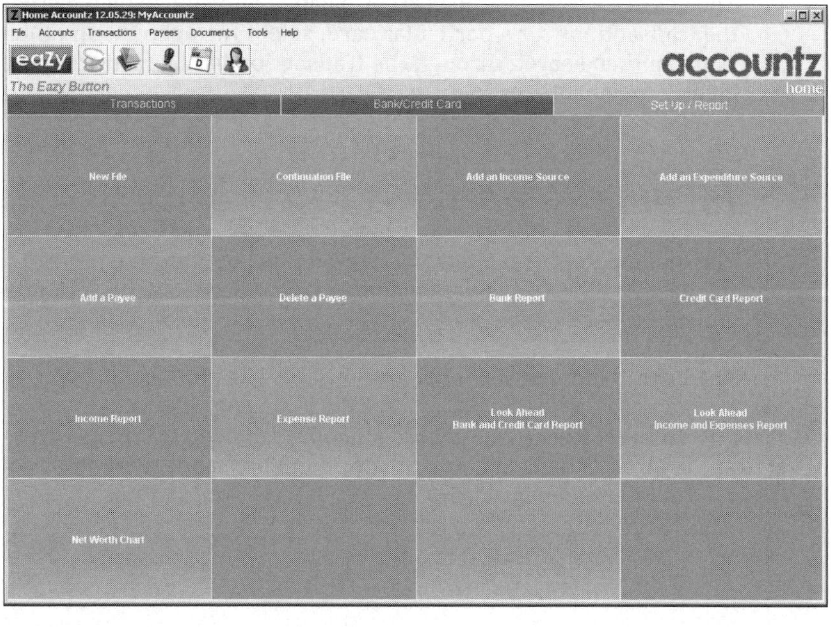

Figure 16-2: The eaZy button's Report tab contains seven different types of reports.

Bank Report

In the Bank Report tab, you can view recent transactions within any of your bank accounts. Follow these steps:

1. **Click the Bank Report button to display a list of your bank accounts.**

   If you have just the one account, it's probably called Current Account, and the current balance of your account, as well as any credit available, appears next to the name (this information could be useful if you have an overdraft on your account, for example).

2. **Select the account that you want to view, and then click Next.**

   A full list of the transactions within your account appears, giving the date of each transaction, a description, the payee, the amount of money, and where it came from or where it went.

3. **(Optional) Search through the transactions by entering text in the Search field and then clicking the up- or down-arrow button.**

Credit Card Report

The Credit Card Report tab allows you to view recent transactions within any of your credit card accounts.

Clicking the Credit Card report button opens a list of your credit card accounts. If you have any store cards, they likely appear in this list, as well. The list of cards gives the current balance and any available credit. To see the transactions for a particular card, select the account and then click Next. You can then search through the transaction list by using the Search field to identify payments made on your card.

Income Report

The Income Report tab lets you view details of your most recent income (for the past 30 days). This data includes your salary, any bank interest received, and any other income.

The default income accounts are

 ✔ **Interest Received:** Records income received by virtue of interest, such as from a bank account. If your bank has made a credit to your account of interest against your savings, it's recorded in this account.

✔ **Other Income:** Records income into your account other than your salary. If, for example, you won the U.K. National Lottery, it's recorded in this account.

✔ **Salary:** The income from your employment. If you work for a company, you probably receive your salary either weekly or monthly. If you work for yourself, the payments may be somewhat more infrequent and reflect your business state of affairs at that particular time.

Expenses Report

The Expenses Report tab shows you details of the money you've paid over the past 30 days. Expense reports are available to cover any expense accounts set up within the software, including

✔ **Bank Interest:** Any charges the bank makes for overdrafts, loans, and so on. Viewing this report gives you a breakdown of charges for that last month.

✔ **Credit Card Interest:** Any interest charges applied to your credit card.

✔ **Electricity:** Any payments you make to your electricity supplier.

It's worth reviewing how you make payments to your electricity supplier — some companies offer significant discounts for paying via direct debit, for example.

✔ **Food:** Payments made for food, perhaps including the supermarket or restaurants — it depends on whether you want to separate eating out rather than eating at home.

✔ **Gas:** Either a monthly direct debit or a quarterly charge from the gas company. You may also pay by meter, in which case, the gas charges may be £20 a week, for instance.

✔ **Gifts from Me:** Payment you make for presents for others, such as any payments you make for birthdays, holiday presents, engagement rings, and so on.

✔ **Mortgage Interest:** The interest charges applied to your mortgage.

You can use this account to track the actual cost of your mortgage with a view to getting a better rate. Taking a copy of the data generated by this report to your mortgage advisor could help get a rate improvement.

✔ **Other Expenses:** Expenses that can't be classified elsewhere. If you have a personal classification for an expense, you probably want to create an expense account of your own, which we explain in Chapter 8.

✔ **Telephone:** Charges for your telephone service — you can use this to keep track on the usage of your phone line and, perhaps, apply restrictions to the service to reduce call costs.

Look Ahead Bank and Credit Card Report

The Look Ahead Bank and Credit Card Report tab shows the automated transactions for the next 30 days, allowing you to see the up-and-coming transactions for the Bank and Credit Card accounts.

Viewing this report presents the list of accounts that contain automated transactions. Select the account whose transactions you want to view and then click Next to see the list of automated transactions being applied to that account.

Look Ahead Income and Expenses Report

In the Look Ahead Income and Expenses Report tab, you can see the automated transactions that will be applied to the Income and Expense accounts over the next 30 days.

Viewing this report presents the list of accounts that have automated transactions applying to the Income and Expense accounts. You can view a list of the automated transactions being applied to an account by selecting that account and clicking Next.

Net Worth Chart

Clicking the Net Worth Chart tab automatically creates a bar chart that shows your net worth, with each account as a bar, assets plotted on the X-axis and amount plotted on the Y-axis.

Running a Report

To run a report, you first need to view the report by navigating to the eaZy button Report tab (as described in the section "Accessing Your Reports," earlier in this chapter), and then follow these steps:

1. **Click the appropriate report button.**

   For example, if you click the Bank Report button, a dialog box appears that contains a list of bank accounts that you have set up in Home Accountz, as shown in Figure 16-3.

2. **Select an account from this list.**

   For example, you select House if you have a separate bank account for your house finances. At the bottom of the dialog box, the balance of the currently selected account appears.

3. **Click the Next button.**

   Alternatively, double-click the account for which you want to create a report.

   The screen lists all recent transactions recorded in that account. The following detail is given for each entry:

   - *Date:* The date recorded for the transaction

   - *Description:* Any description you entered (for example, **Wages**)

   - *Payee:* The person or company who made the payment to you

   - *Total Amount:* The value of the payment

   - *From Account:* Where the money came from (for example, the Salary account)

   - *To Account:* The account into which it was paid (for example, the Bank/Current account)

   - *Reference:* Any reference — normally a number or code — that you made about the payment

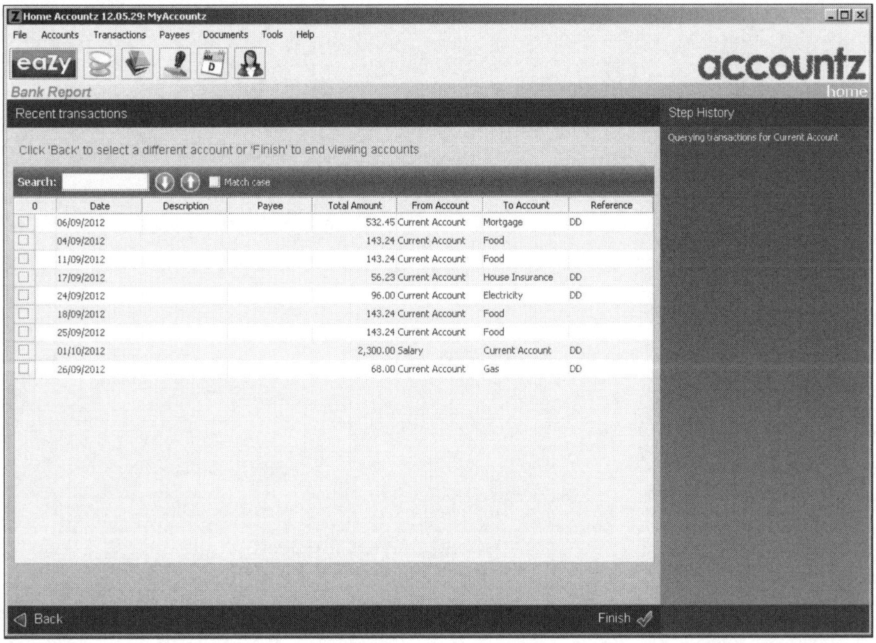

Figure 16-3:
View recent Bank Report transactions.

4. **To search this data, in the Search text box above the list, type in part of the information you're looking for.**

   For example, you can enter the Payee name or part of that name.

   Alternatively, you can browse the information by using the up and down arrows next to the Search text box.

Home Accountz presently doesn't offer you a means to print data from these reports, but a future release should include this capability. In the meantime, you can print the reports by opening them in Excel, styling them to suit your needs, and then choosing File➪Print.

Chapter 17

Creating Report Designs with the Documents Component

- -

In This Chapter

▶ Creating new template designs and using the template wizard

▶ Using your new templates to create documents

- -

The Documents component allows you to customize the design and structure of the document templates available within Home Accountz. In this chapter, we take a look at how you can customize document templates within Home Accountz, and then show you how to choose your own templates when you go to print your document. *Note:* You can also e-mail, save, and generate your document as a PDF.

Whenever you click the Print icon above any Transaction table in the software, the current view becomes a printable document in the Document Editor. The design and layout of the document is determined by the document template. Home Accountz automatically creates a set of default templates when you run the software for the first time.

You can create new designs or edit an existing one. After you create it, the new template can be selected for use within the Document Editor.

Home Accountz 2012 offers two ways to create new document template designs. You can either use the Templates Builder Wizard to create a completely new set of templates, or use the Templates Editor to edit individual templates.

Using the Templates Builder Wizard

The Templates Builder is a step-by-step wizard that allows you to create a set of templates for all, or selected, document types, applying your own values to settings such as table color, font, and page layout.

It also offers a preview screen where you can further refine your template by using the Templates Editor tools (see the following sections). After you finish the wizard, the new templates are available for selection in the software.

To run the Templates Builder, follow these steps:

1. **Choose Documents⇨Templates Builder.**

   The Templates Builder Wizard launches.

2. **In the Document Types screen, select or deselect the check boxes to specify which document types you want to apply the wizard to.**

   You can select whether you want to apply the wizard to all document types or to certain types, including Balance, Budgeting, and Transactions.

3. **Click Next to continue.**

   The Document Templates Name screen appears.

   From this point on, all user-defined settings are listed in the right panel.

4. **Enter a unique name for the templates being created in the Document Template Name field.**

   This name appears in the Templates section and in the Document Editor Template Picker list.

5. **Click Next.**

6. **In the Page Format screen, select whether you want your templates to be in A4 Portrait or Landscape orientation, and then click Next.**

   The Global Font screen appears.

7. **Click the icon next to Font Name, and then select a font from the drop-down list that appears, then click OK to confirm.**

8. **Click Next to open the Table Colours screen.**

   This screen allows you to set colors for the following table values:

   - Header Background
   - Header Text
   - Lines

9. **Click the color bar to reveal a color picker, select a new color, and then click OK to confirm your choice.**

10. **Click Next.**

11. **In the Date Format screen that appears, choose your preferred date format.**

    This format is how dates outside of Transaction tables appear (meaning how dates look when printed or exported).

    If you previously defined this format manually, click User Defined to retain this setting.

12. **Click Next to proceed to the Preview Intro screen.**

    This screen notifies you that when you click Next, the following screen will display an editable document preview that encompasses the values you've set so far.

13. **Click Next.**

14. **The Preview launches.**

    In this screen, you can preview how your settings actually look.

15. **(Optional) Edit the template further, if necessary, by using the tools described in the following sections.**

16. **Click Next when you're happy with the changes.**

    The Action screen that appears offers you a final chance to review your changes (listed in the right panel, as shown in Figure 17-1).

17. **Click Finish to complete the wizard.**

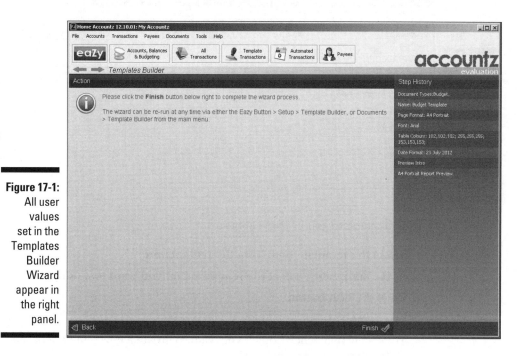

Figure 17-1: All user values set in the Templates Builder Wizard appear in the right panel.

Editing Individual Templates

You can edit document templates individually by using the Templates Editor. Access the Templates Editor by clicking the Edit Template button (which looks like a yellow pencil) in either the Templates screen or the Document Editor.

To open the Templates screen, choose Documents⇨Templates. The Templates screen allows you to view and edit all existing document templates and offers a number of predesigned document templates.

The templates are divided into six types, detailed in the left column (see Figure 17-2). Each type of template covers a different part of your data:

- ✔ **Balances:** Gives the balances of your accounts
- ✔ **Budget:** Reports on the current year's budget
- ✔ **Transactions:** Shows transfer transactions
- ✔ **Automated Transactions:** Details all automated transactions
- ✔ **Template Transactions:** Details all template transactions
- ✔ **Entries:** Shows account group transactions

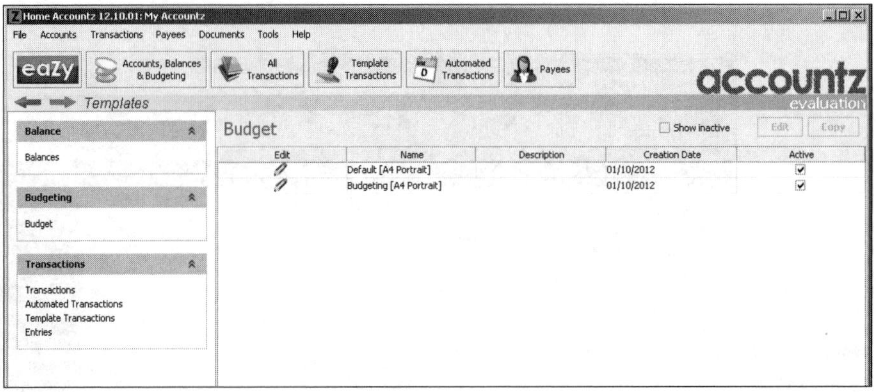

Figure 17-2: The six template types are listed in the Templates screen's left panel.

To edit a template, follow these steps:

1. **Select the template type from the left column.**

2. **In the main table, select the template that you want to modify.**

3. **Click the Edit button.**

   The Templates Editor launches.

   You can instead click Copy if you want to create a new template based on the one you select in Step 2.

The Templates Editor (see Figure 17-3) enables you to set the size of the table; adjust column widths; and add extra text, graphics, and other design elements. All the changes you make in the Template Editor are reflected in every document you print that uses this template.

You can edit various aspects of the current template by using these options:

- ✔ **Canvas:** Edit selected elements in the Canvas screen itself
- ✔ **Left toolbar:** Edit shapes, text, and images
- ✔ **Properties panel:** Edit the selected element's attributes
- ✔ **Top toolbar:** Lets you preview the template
- ✔ **Bottom toolbar:** Further preview the template by using zoom and resize tools

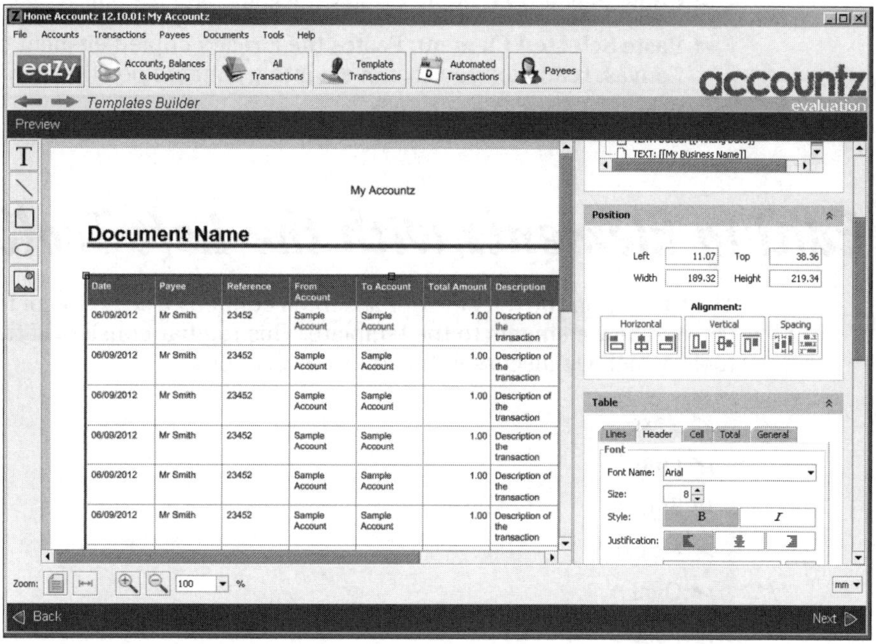

Figure 17-3: The Templates Editor lets you redesign your template.

The following sections go into detail about each of these editing options.

Canvasing Your Template

The Canvas area of the Templates Builder appears in the center of the screen. It contains a preview of the document template itself, where you can use a number of commonly recognized mouse and keyboard options to modify the template. You can click and drag items around the Canvas and Ctrl-click (⌘-click on the Mac) to select more than one item at a time. To resize an element, click and drag its handles.

Right-clicking in the Canvas opens a pop-up menu that contains the following options:

- **Move to Front:** Moves the selected element to the top layer

- **Move Forwards:** Moves the selected element up a layer

- **Move Backwards:** Moves the selected element down a layer

- **Move to Back:** Moves the selected element to the lowest layer

- **Move in/out of Table Area:** Moves the selected element in or out of the Transaction table

- **Copy Selected Element:** Copies the selected element

- **Paste Selected Element:** Pastes the already copied element onto the Canvas, ready for you to move it into a suitable position if you need to

- **Delete:** Deletes the selected element

Editing Elements with the Left Toolbar

The toolbar on the left side of the screen contains a selection of tools that let you add new elements to the template. This toolbar consists of the following tools, which we discuss in the following sections:

- Text
- Line
- Square
- Ellipse
- Oval
- Image

Editable properties for these elements appear in the Properties panel, described in the section "Looking at the Properties Panel," later in this chapter.

Text

The Text tool allows you to insert text into the document. To use the text tool, follow these steps:

1. Click the Text Tool button in the left toolbar.

2. **Click where you want to position the text in the document.**

   The Add New Text Area field appears.

3. **Enter the text that you want to add, and then click Done.**

Line

The Line tool allows you to draw lines on the document. To draw a line, click the Line tool icon, and then click and drag from a point on the document page where you want the line to begin to the point where you want the line to end.

Square and Ellipse

The Square tool allows you to create a square or rectangle on the document, and the Ellipse tool lets you create an ellipse or circle. To use either tool, simply click the appropriate tool icon, and then click and drag from the position you want the rectangle or ellipse to start to where you want to locate the opposite corner. Release the mouse button to create the rectangle or ellipse.

Image

You can use the Image tool to place images on your document page by following these steps:

1. **Click the Image tool icon.**

2. **Click in the position where you want the image to appear in the document.**

   The point you click becomes the top-left corner of the image.

3. **Click to open the File Chooser dialog box.**

4. **Select Import New Image, locate the image file, and then click Select to close the dialog box and insert the image in the document.**

You can import images in one of three file formats:

- **GIF:** Graphic Interchange Format; frequently used for Internet graphics
- **JPG/JPEG:** Joint Photographic Experts Group; frequently used for photographs
- **PNG:** Portable Network Graphics; a vector format used on the Internet

Looking at the Properties Panel

If you select an element, either within the canvas itself or within the Page Elements window described in the following section, the editable options for that element appear in the Properties panel.

Located on the right of the screen, this area lets you adjust the individual elements on the canvas. *Note:* The editable properties area changes according to which page element is selected.

The Properties Panel comprises the following items:

- Page Elements
- Position
- Table
- Image
- Column Visibility
- Text
- Line
- Fill
- Formats

We talk about each of these items in the following sections.

Page Elements

The Page Elements window displays all the elements currently within the document template. Selecting an element in this window reveals the property boxes relevant to that element in the panel below the window. You can move elements within the window (and therefore the template) by using the buttons discussed in the section "Canvasing Your Template," earlier in this chapter.

Position

The Position option allows you to move the selected element by editing the values for the element's horizontal start position (Left), vertical start position (Top), Width, and Height.

The Position window also offers the following alignment options:

- **Horizontal:** Horizontally (left/center/right) align multiple selected elements.
- **Vertical:** Vertically (bottom/center/top) align multiple selected elements.
- **Spacing:** Evenly space (either vertically or horizontally) three or more selected elements.

When you use a Position option, the elements are aligned to the item first selected.

Table

With the Table option, the user can edit various settings for the Transaction table within the template. It comprises five tabs reflecting different aspects of the table, as outlined in the following sections.

Lines

In the Lines tab, you can edit the values for the various lines that make up the table (Border, Horizontal, and Vertical):

- **Width:** Use the up and down arrows, or click in the text box and enter a value to manually set the line width.
- **Unit Picker:** Select the line-width type from this drop-down list.
- **Line Picker:** Select the line width from this drop-down list.
- **Transparency:** Use the slider to set the line transparency.

Header, Cell, and Total

The Header tab allows you to set an assortment of table header values, and the Cell tab lets you set those same values for certain table cells. In the Total tab, you can also specify these values for the Total field. The Font options for the table header and cells, as well as the Total field, include

- **Font Name:** Set the Font type.
- **Size:** Set the font size.

✔ **Style:** Italicize or embolden the text.

✔ **Justification:** Select whether the text is left-, center-, or right-aligned.

✔ **Padding:** Set the amount of padding around the text.

✔ **Padding Unit:** Set the unit type for padding.

Set the text color by clicking the Text Color color bar. You can also set the text transparency by using the Text Transparency slider.

Set the background color with the Background Color option and specify the transparency of the background by using the Background Transparency slider.

General

In the General tab, you can adjust the number of rows in the table by changing the No of Rows value. Also, selecting the Fill Available Height check box causes the table to remain the same (full) size as set on the template; deselecting the check box causes the table to resize to fit the number of rows of data in the individual document.

Image

The Image option allows you to edit and review the selected image element in the following ways:

✔ **Image:** Displays the current image filename.

✔ **Image Picker:** Click here to select a different image.

✔ **Fixed Aspect Ratio:** If you resize the image, selecting this check box ensures the image retains its aspect ratio.

You can also edit the following Image Border properties:

✔ **Width:** Use the up and down arrows to set the line width.

✔ **Unit Picker:** Set the line width unit type.

✔ **Line Picker:** Select a line width from the drop-down list.

✔ **Line Pattern Picker:** Select the line pattern from the drop-down list.

✔ **Colour:** Set the line color.

✔ **Transparency:** Set the line transparency by using the slider.

Column Visibility

The Column Visibility panel allows you to adjust certain column visibility values within the transaction table:

- ✔ **Show:** Select or deselect the check boxes to add and remove columns from the table.
- ✔ **Order:** Click the up arrow to move the selected column left and the down arrow to move it right in the table.
- ✔ **Heading Text:** Edit this text box to change the header text for the selected column.
- ✔ **Display Total:** Displays the total for the selected Amount column at the bottom of the table.
- ✔ **Width:** Edit the width of the selected column by clicking the up or down arrow, or manually editing the figure.
- ✔ **Sample Data:** Edit the sample data for this column, as displayed in the Templates Editor preview.
- ✔ **Alignment:** Set the text alignment (left/center/right) for the selected column's data.

Text

In the Text option, you can edit various aspects of the selected text field, including many of the specifications available in other options (see the section "Header, Cell, and Total," earlier in this chapter).

Also, you can click in the Edit Text field to edit the text, as required. And the Insert New Custom Field allows you to add a Custom Field (such as Date or Page Number) to the text field. Select from the drop-down list and click Okay to complete the insertion.

Line

The Line option allows you to adjust a number of line values:

- ✔ **Width:** Edit the line's width using the arrows or by manually editing the value.
- ✔ **Width Unit:** Set the preferred width unit type, such as PT or MM.

- **Width Picker:** As an alternative to the Width option, you can select the line width from a drop-down list
- **Pattern:** Select a number of line patterns (dotted, unbroken, and so on) from the drop-down list.
- **Colour:** Set the line color by clicking the color bar and selecting an alternative from the picker that appears.
- **Transparency:** Drag the slider to set line transparency.

Fill

The Fill option enables you to set the color and transparency for any shape (such as a square or ellipse) entered in the template. You can pick a color from the selection of colors in the color bar and drag the Transparency slider to adjust the shape's transparency (the higher the value, the more transparent the object).

Formats

The Formats option allows you to edit the following formats for the selected element:

- Date Format
- Date Time Format
- Time Format
- Amount Format

To edit a format, click Edit next to the relevant option, enter the desired format into the Format field, and click Okay to confirm the changes.

Looking Up to the Top Toolbar

The top toolbar appears (surprise) at the top of the window, just above the Properties panel. In this toolbar, you can view and edit different pages within the template (if the template is made up of more than one page) by clicking the left- and right-arrow buttons. Also, clicking the PDF button launches the template as a PDF (for print-previewing purposes).

Digging Down to the Bottom Toolbar

In the bottom toolbar, you can use various zoom settings to preview the Canvas more easily. The toolbar contains the following buttons and tools (as shown in Figure 17-4):

- ✔ **Show Whole Page:** Clicking the leftmost button zooms the Canvas out to show the whole page.

- ✔ **Fill Whole Available Canvas Width:** Click the button to the right of the Show Whole Page button to resize the Canvas width to fill the whole Canvas area.

- ✔ **Increase Magnification of Whole Page:** Click this button, which resembles a magnifying glass with a plus sign (+), to zoom in on the Canvas.

- ✔ **Decrease Magnification of Whole Page:** Clicking this button, which resembles a magnifying glass with a minus sign (–), zooms the Canvas out.

- ✔ **Set Zoom %:** Set the Canvas zoom percentage manually by selecting from the drop-down list.

- ✔ **Mouse Coordinates:** Displays the horizontal and vertical mouse coordinates.

- ✔ **Mouse Coordinate Units:** Change the coordinates unit type by selecting from the drop-down list.

Using Your New Templates

After you create or edit the templates to your satisfaction, they're immediately available for you to use — you can access them via the Document Editor.

Press the Print icon above any Transaction table to launch the Document Editor. This window displays a preview of a printable report (see Figure 7-4). The report is composed of the actual data based on the currently selected view and with a design or layout based on the selected template. In the Document Editor, you can print, e-mail, and save your document, or even generate your document as a PDF file.

Previewing a document

You can use a variety of tools to preview the current document. The bottom toolbar offers the same buttons as the Templates Editor for resizing and zooming purposes (see the section "Digging Down to the Bottom Toolbar," earlier in this chapter).

If the document comprises multiple pages, you can click the page arrows at the top-right of the screen to switch between pages.

Switching templates

You can change the template upon which the displayed document is based. Just click the Template Picker drop-down list (see Figure 17-4) in the top-left of the screen to reveal a list of all available templates for the document type. Click the desired template to select it.

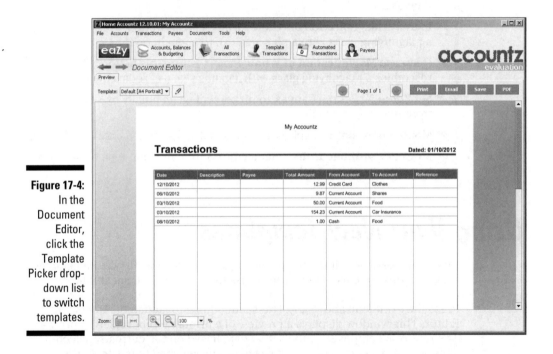

Figure 17-4:
In the
Document
Editor,
click the
Template
Picker drop-
down list
to switch
templates.

Editing templates

If you want to edit the currently selected template, click the Edit button (shaped like a yellow pencil) to launch the template for editing in the Templates Editor, discussed in the section "Editing Individual Templates," earlier in this chapter. After you're satisfied with your changes, click the left-arrow button at the top-left of the screen to go back to the Document Editor. Your changes are automatically saved.

After you preview the document and make any changes necessary, you have several options at your disposal:

- ✓ **Print the document.** Click the Print button in the top-right to send the document to your printer.

- ✓ **E-mail the document.** Click the Email button to launch a new e-mail in your e-mail client. You just need to attach the document file to the e-mail.

- ✓ **Save the document.** This option allows you to save the document to your computer. Click the Save button, select the desired folder or file path, and then click Save.

- ✓ **Generate a PDF.** Click the PDF button to create a PDF file of the document and launch it in Adobe Reader.

Resetting templates

You can reset all your templates by choosing Documents⇨Reset Templates. The Templates Builder launches (see the section "Using the Templates Builder Wizard," earlier in this chapter). The wizard prompts you to create a new set of document templates.

After the wizard is complete, the new templates are available for selection in the Templates screen (which you access by choosing Documents⇨Templates).

Any old templates are hidden from view; if you want to access the hidden templates, select the Show Inactive check box in the Templates window.

Chapter 18

Keeping Track of Your Finances

- -

- -

When it comes to home accounting, you need to do more than just enter data: You need to use that data to influence the way you manage your money in the future. Home Accountz can help you keep your finances in order.

This chapter explains how you can compare your budgets against your actual balances. If the two are essentially the same, then superb — if they aren't, then you need to use the budgets to influence your future spending.

Also, you can find out how to look towards future spending after you enter a period's worth of data: direct debits, standing orders, and expenses such as your average weekly shopping trip.

Comparing Actual Balances to Budgets

Comparing the actual balances in your accounts versus your budgets, called *variance analysis,* can help you manage your accounts. You can make predictions by estimating future financial data (obviously influenced by factors such as varying costs, such as the price of fuel).

 Information in the Actual vs. Budget table can help you plan out your finances for the coming year and see how well you're actually doing financially, as opposed to how you thought you'd be doing. You can then use this information to take corrective action to get your finances in order if needed or your circumstances change.

Using the Overview tab

The Overview tab, which appears in the Accounts, Balances & Budgeting table (see Chapter 14), lets you compare your budgets with your actual balances for a selected period, for the year to date, and for the full year.

The Overview table (shown in Figure 18-1) includes the following columns, which reflect the different time periods being analyzed — month, year to date, and full year:

- ✔ **Period:** From the first to the last date of the selected period
- ✔ **Year to Date:** From the start of the calendar year to the current date
- ✔ **Full Year:** The full and current calendar year

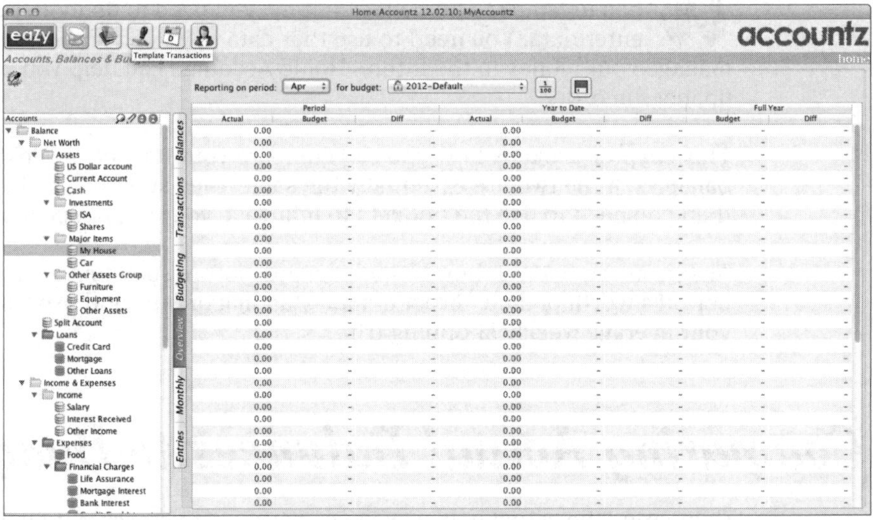

Figure 18-1:
The Overview table before any data has been entered.

When forecasting, you make plans for future spending. In the Accounts, Balances & Budgeting table, you can consolidate your budgets and actual balances to determine how close they are:

- ✔ **Actual:** The current actual value, which comes from the data you've entered in Home Accountz.
- ✔ **Budget:** The budgeted value. These figures come from the Budgeting tab.
- ✔ **Diff:** The difference between the Actual value and the Budget value.

Comparing budgets with actual balances

You can analyze your spending by comparing your budget's amounts with the actual spending figures. Just follow these steps:

1. **Click the Accounts, Balances & Budgeting button.**

   This toolbar button displays an image of three gold coins.

2. **Click the Overview tab.**

   This tab appears between the Accounts window and the Account Report form.

3. **To select which period you want to create a report for, click the Reporting on Period button.**

   A drop-down list appears.

4. **Select which period's actual figures you want to compare against their Budget and Diff values.**

5. **Click the For Budget button, and then select a budget from the drop-down list that appears.**

6. **(Optional) Click the Control whether Pence Are Displayed toggle button if you want to hide (or display) pence in the report.**

   This button appears on the control bar above the Report window. It looks like a square displaying ⅟₁₀₀.

   The report updates onscreen when you select each option, so you don't need to create or confirm the settings of the report.

After you create your report, you can export it for use in other programs. Just click the Export Budget to CSV button (which appears on the control bar above the Report window and looks like a floppy disk). The File Save dialog box appears (shown in Figure 18-2), asking you to specify the name and location of the CSV file you want to create.

The CSV file contains all the data in the active Home Accountz table in a very simple database format. You can import the CSV file into either a database or a spreadsheet.

Figure 18-2:
Export
your report
from Home
Accountz in
CSV format.

Forecasting

One of the major features of Home Accountz is its ability to make predictions, or *forecasts,* about any account. It takes into account any automated trans-actions that you may have set up and applies them by using Creating and Customizing Views to forecast the future balance of a particular account (see Chapter 12).

To forecast any account, make sure you enter all the direct debits and cred-its, standing orders, and any other automated transactions.

Producing a forecast can help you manage your accounts, but don't confuse a forecast with a budget. A *budget* is a financial plan and a list of all planned bills and income, but a *forecast* is a prediction of your future financial position. A forecast is typically based on prior experience — for example, you can fore-cast your spending on food for the next 12 months, but that forecast doesn't take into account the rise in cost of food. Within a budget, you can typically allow for price changes.

Applying forecasting to an account

Follow these steps to apply forecasting to one of your accounts:

1. **Click the Accounts, Balances & Budgeting button.**

   This button in the toolbar displays three gold coins.

   The Accounts, Balances & Budgeting window opens.

2. **To open all account groups, click the Expand All Account Groups button.**

   This green button displays two white arrows, one pointing up and one pointing down.

   A new panel in the right pane opens, displaying all groups.

3. **Click the account to which you want to apply a forecast.**

   The account is highlighted.

4. **Click the Transactions tab.**

   You can find this tab on the separation bar to the right of the Accounts section.

   The Transactions list appears, displaying all the previous and upcoming transactions in your accounts.

5. **Click the All Transactions button, which appears in the right panel.**

   The All Transactions drop-down list opens.

6. **Select Next Month from the drop-down list.**

   Next Month is the only option in this drop-down list. When you select it, a view of transactions forecast for the next month appears.

Setting the forecast time period

If you want to adjust how far in the future the forecast predicts, then you need to create a new view based on the one you created (which we describe in the preceding sections) in the View tab of the View Editor panel (shown in Figure 18-3). To create the new view, follow these steps:

1. **Click the Open/Close View Editor Panel button.**

   The button displays a blue funnel and appears on the left side of the Transaction Form toolbar. This toolbar appears at the top of any Transaction window, immediately to the right of the current view option (such as All Transactions, Next Month, or Last 7 Days).

   A new set of controls appears above the form.

View tab   View Editor panel button

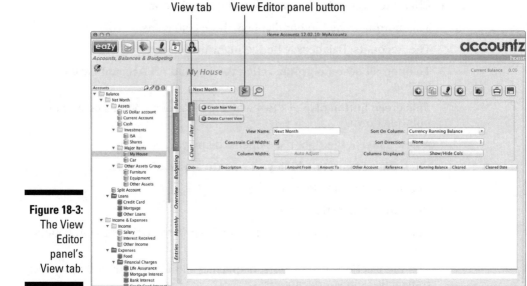

Figure 18-3:
The View
Editor
panel's
View tab.

2. **If required, click the View tab.**

The tabs appear immediately to the left of the Create New View button, located at the top of the screen. You may not need to click the View tab because it's the default for the View Editor panel.

The View tab contains the options that allow you to create and customize a view within Home Accountz, including

- View Name
- Constrain Col Widths
- Column Widths
- Sort on Column
- Sort Direction
- Columns Displayed

3. **Click the Create New View button (the green button displaying a white plus sign [+] and the words Create New View).**

This button appears at the top-left side of the View Editor panel.

4. **Click in the View Name text box and type in a new name for the view.**

For example, if you want to create a forecast that covers the next three months, you can enter Next 3 Months.

5. Click the Filter tab.

A series of columns are added to the top of the table, titled Column, Condition, and Value.

6. Add a condition by clicking the Add Condition button and selecting a condition from the drop-down list that appears (shown in Figure 18-4).

The available condition options include (but aren't limited to) information about

- Amount

- Date

- Currency

- Descriptions or notes

- Quantity or price

A new row is created in the table, and the condition you selected appears in the first cell of the first column.

For our example, you select Date, and Date appears in the table.

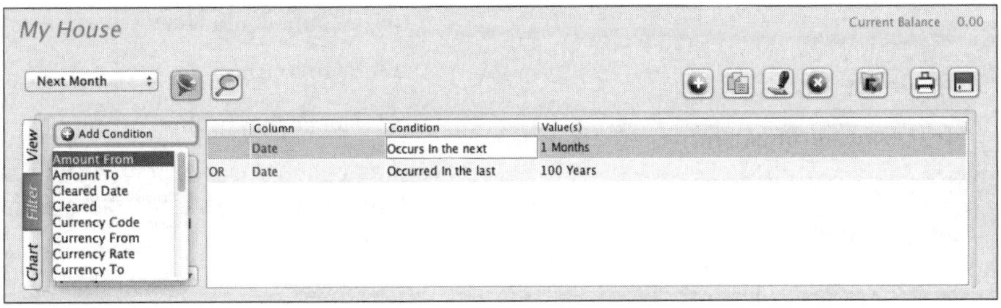

Figure 18-4:
Applying a condition to a new view.

7. Click in the Condition cell in the Filter table, and then select Occurs in the Next from the drop-down list that appears (shown in Figure 18-5).

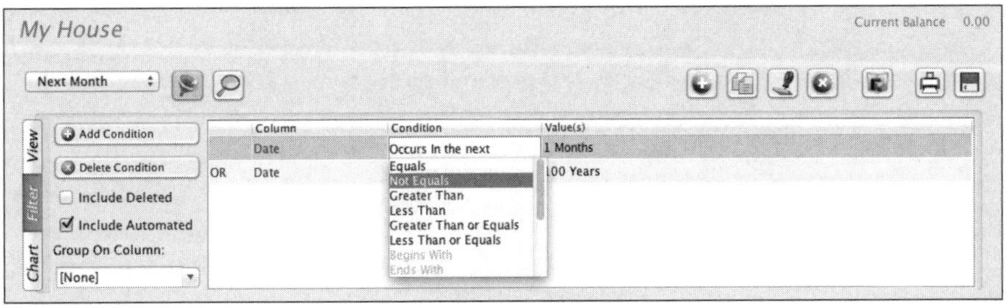

Figure 18-5:
Filters available to apply to a condition in the view you're creating.

8. **Click in the Values text box, and then type in the amount of time over which you want to forecast.**

   You can create a forecast covering any range of time — anything from a day to many years.

9. **(Optional) Click in the Value field to open a drop-down list, and then change the filter by selecting an option.**

   If you're filtering by the date, you can select Years, Months, Weeks, or Days. The Values available change depending on the column selected and the condition(s) applied.

Setting your filter conditions

The Condition drop-down list in the Filter table offers a number of filters that you can add to a condition in the view that you create, including

- Not Equals
- Greater Than
- Less Than
- Greater Than or Equals
- Less Than or Equals
- Begins With
- Ends With
- Contains
- Occurs Between
- Does Not Occur Between
- Occurred in the Last
- Occurs in the Next
- Within Group
- Not Within Group

If an option appears grayed out in the list, that filter isn't available for the condition you've selected.

Part V
The Part of Tens

The 5th Wave   By Rich Tennant

"So... did you find the money that was missing from the bottom line?"

In this part . . .

*P*art V covers the most confusing accounting terms
you're likely to encounter and explains their meaning
as they apply to personal finances. You can also find the
answer to the most common problems you may encounter while setting up your home finances and explanation
of the rapid data entry system so that you can become a
Home Accountz power user. Finally, we give you tips for
setting up and sticking to your budgets.

Chapter 19

Ten Most Confusing Home Accounting Terms

. . . .

In This Chapter

▶ Understanding terms related to your money

▶ Knowing how to define financial processes

. . . .

*W*hen managing your home finances, you need to understand a number of accounting terms if you're reliably to get control. These terms cover all sorts of issues, from financial to taxation, and really understanding them (and being able to apply them) can help you track, plan, and forecast your finances.

In this chapter, we take a look at a number of these terms, explaining what they mean and putting them into the context of managing your home finances. None of these terms are specifically relevant to Home Accountz as a product, but they are relevant to accounting and home financial planning as a whole.

Accounts

As far as Home Accountz is concerned, an *account* is a container that holds a series of transactions. Accounts can fall into two main groups — Net Worth and Revenue. To find out more about adding and controlling accounts, see Chapters 3 and 8.

Transaction

A *transaction* is a pair of entries that make up a purchase or a sale. Every transaction needs at least two entries — one showing where the money is coming from and one showing what the money is paying for.

You add a transaction to Home Accountz by entering the required information across a single line in the Transactions table. Complete the minimal required data — Tax Date, From Account, To Account, Total Amount, and VAT Code (if you're VAT-registered) — and add in a description so that you can track the transaction. This procedure ensures that your personal finances always reflect both money out and new purchases. For more about transactions, please see Chapters 7 and 8.

Assets

An *asset* is something you own that can create revenue for you. You can use assets

- ✔ To add to your total worth
- ✔ As security or collateral for loans
- ✔ As payment for a loan if you can't pay it with cash

Assets can be tangible or intangible.

Tangible assets

Tangible assets are things you own that you can touch — for example, any properties, such as your home, or high-value assets, such as your car. Here are some examples of tangible assets:

- ✔ **Property or real-estate:** Your home, or any buildings or land that you own.
- ✔ **Expensive possessions:** Cars, boats, recreational vehicles, and jewelry are all examples. These items form a part of your personal inventory.
- ✔ **Cash:** This money can be in the form of savings or just working capital.
- ✔ **Fixtures and fittings:** This class of assets includes furniture, filing cabinets, display cases, shelving, and the like.

Intangible

Intangible assets are things that you own that can't be seen or touched because they lack physical substance. However, they still have monetary value. Intangible assets include

- ✔ **Intellectual property:** Basically, your ideas or a body of work that's uniquely yours (you thought of it, and you can prove it's yours) — such as an invention or a process that didn't exist until you had the idea or completed the process.

  You can protect your intellectual property (for example, with copyright laws), and then use it to create a revenue stream.

- ✔ **Internet assets:** Websites and blogs don't have a physical form; however, they have the potential to be very valuable — just look at Facebook!

- ✔ **Goodwill:** The reputation and trust you build up with the people with whom you do business. If this goodwill is attached to a company, it has a worth because it attracts new customers by word of mouth and keeps existing customers through good customer service. Goodwill is usually included if the business is to be sold as a going concern (which means that it essentially doesn't change).

Assets form an important part of your accounts: They are, at the very least, an item of value. We explain setting up accounts in Chapter 3.

Liability

A *liability* is a debt or loan that you owe to someone or some company. It's a legally binding agreement, an obligation to pay a debt. Liabilities can include a credit agreement, recurring bills, or service that you owe.

In Home Accountz, you can set up budgets to reduce liabilities effectively over a period of time. Chapter 3 shows how to set up an account, and Chapter 12 explores budgeting.

Equity

Equity is the net difference between your assets and your liabilities. Simply take the sum of what you own (your assets) and subtract everything you owe. The amount you have left is your equity. If this sum is negative, you have *negative equity* (you're in debt). You can determine the equity of portions of your assets and liabilities. For example, you can balance the equity in your house with the market value and unpaid mortgage balance.

Revenue

When a sale is made or a service is provided, a monetary reward — called *revenue* — is expected for that service. For example, when you go to work (meaning you provide a service to your employer or client), you either receive a salary or issue an invoice expecting payment.

Expense

When you spend money, that's an *expense,* meaning any purchases or payments that you make at any time. These expenses can be either fixed or variable:

- ✔ **Fixed expenses:** Amounts that you have to pay that remain similar from month to month. For example, if you have a home telephone line that includes all call charges, regardless of the kind of calls, your telephone bill is the same month in, month out. Further examples include monthly insurance payments, loan repayments, and tuition fees.

- ✔ **Variable expenses:** Amounts that may vary each time you pay them. For example, fuel for your car is a variable expense — the amount charged for fuel depends entirely on how far and how frequently you make trips.

We talk more about these important terms in Chapter 7.

Depreciation and Appreciation

Depreciation refers to the financial worth an item of value loses over time. A car bought for £20,000 may lose £5,000 in value over the next three years before significantly decreasing in value after that time. In many cases, you can mitigate the loss in value by carrying out work to enhance the lifespan of such items.

An example of *appreciation,* when the value of an item increases, occurs in the housing market. House prices, for instance, are affected by the environment and the buildings surrounding them. If you start with a two-bedroom house and convert one of the other rooms into another bedroom, you're materially increasing the value of the house because you have expanded the potential market for the property from a family with one child to a family with two children.

You need to know the depreciation (or appreciation) of an item when calculating the long term value of a fixed asset — such as your home. For example, you use this information when securing finance against your house or looking for a new property and hence working out the worth of your current home.

Interest

In financial terms, *interest* means any money paid or received as a premium on money lent. If you take out a loan, then you usually have to pay interest, on top of paying back the original loan amount. On the other hand, if you're lending money to someone else, you may want to charge him interest for the loan. Here are some examples:

- **Interest received:** When a bank, building society, or investment pays you interest on a saving or holding, depending on the size of that saving or holding. For instance, if you have a savings account that pays an annual interest rate of 5% and £1,000 in the account, you receive £50 of interest.

  If you leave those savings for five years, you don't end up with £1,250 (£50 each year); you end up with more than that because of *compound interest,* meaning interest you earn on interest you've already earned. You earned £50 in Year 1, so in Year 2 you have £1,050 to which the 5% interest rate is applied.

- **Interest charged:** The money a bank, building society, or company makes in return for providing credit. There's a significant difference between the interest a bank charges people for lending money and the interest it pays out to people who save money with them.

  Interest charged also experiences compound interest. For example, a balance of £1,000 at an annual percentage rate (APR) of 17.9%, with repayments of £200 a month, has the following components in its second month:

  - **Original amount:** £1,000
  - **Repayment:** £200
  - **Interest:** £143.20 (£800 × .179)
  - **Balance:** £943.20 (£800 + £143.20)

When building your budget, you need to consider interest payments.

Debit and Credit

You use debits and credits in a form of accounting known as double-entry bookkeeping, an accounting practice used to balance the books (your accounts). Every credit entered into the Credit or Equity side of the Accounts book must also be added to the Debit side. The terms debits and credits describe the flow of money from one account to another:

- ✔ **Debit:** A payment to one of your accounts. For example, when you make a payment of £40 to your local garage, that payment appears in your account as a debit to Joe Bloggs Garage.
- ✔ **Credit:** A payment into your account, such as your salary.

In Home Accountz, these terms are replaced with From and To (which makes the program intuitive to use):

- ✔ **Credit:** From
- ✔ **Debit:** To

Here are some examples:

- ✔ To enter a payment from your bank to buy some food, you enter a transaction from your Bank account in Home Accountz to your Food account.
- ✔ To enter a receipt of money — for example, a gift from a relation — enter a transaction from your Gifts account to your Bank account.
- ✔ To pay off your credit card balance at the end of a month, enter a transaction from your Bank account to your Credit Card account.

You need to enter debits and credits correctly in order to keep up to date with your financial position, which plays an important part when you're building your budget.

Chapter 20

Ten Solutions to Home Accountz Problems

In This Chapter

▶ Troubleshooting the Home Accountz software

▶ Using work files

▶ Finding your way around the Home Accountz windows

*H*ome accounting software answers many questions, not least of which is what your financial situation is like at any given point in time. You'll probably find, however, that it also presents a number of problems — problems that may not immediately be clear. The 10 (or 11) questions and answers in this chapter deal with a number of potential problems.

How Do I Use a USB Backup of My Home Accountz Data?

If your database becomes corrupted (perhaps due to a computer error), you may need to restore both your Home Accountz license and an earlier work file from a USB backup. (We describe creating a backup in Chapter 4.) Follow these steps:

1. **Open the BAK folder on your USB memory stick.**

   The BAK folder contains a number of automatic backups done by the software.

2. **Click Date Modified (which appears at the top of the BAK folder's window).**

   The backup files become organized by date.

3. **Select the backup file you want to work with, and then right-click (Ctrl-click on a Mac) and select Copy from the pop-up menu that appears.**

4. **Navigate to the location on your computer's hard drive where you want to paste the backup file.**

5. **In that folder, right-click (Ctrl-click on a Mac) and select Paste from the pop-up menu that appears.**

   This location may be the desktop or your user area on your computer.

6. **Select the filename.**

   The name becomes editable.

7. **Enter a new filename, and then press the Return (Enter) key.**

   You can change the name to something like My Accounts.

   In the BAK folder on your USB stick, you can find a file called `instal-info.ehaz`.

8. **Copy the `instal-info.ehaz` file by right-clicking (Ctrl-clicking on a Mac) and then selecting Copy from the pop-up menu that appears.**

9. **Navigate to the location where Home Accountz is installed on your computer, and then right-click (Ctrl-click on a Mac) and select Paste from the menu that appears to paste the `install-info.ehaz` file there.**

   For Windows users, the Home Accountz folder is located at `C:\Program Files\Home_Accountz`; for Mac users, it's located at `\Applications\Home_Accountz_2012`.

10. **In the folder where you've installed Home Accountz, select the file `app-config.haz`, and then press the Delete key on the keyboard.**

    The file is deleted.

11. **In the BAK folder of the new installation of Home Accountz, delete the App-Config folder by selecting it and then pressing the Delete key.**

12. **Double-click the Home Accountz icon to start Home Accountz.**

13. **Choose File➪Open.**

    The Open dialog box appears.

14. **Navigate to where you pasted your backup file in Step 5.**

15. **Select the file (as renamed in Step 7), and then click Open.**

    The backup file opens in Home Accountz.

You can now make this process simpler by choosing File➪Restore Backup.

How Do I Restore the Home Accountz Work File from the BAK Folder?

To restore data from the backup folder of Home Accountz, follow these steps:

1. **Navigate to the Installation folder.**

   This folder is located at `C:\Program Files\Home_Accountz\BAK` for Windows users; and for Mac users, it's located at `\Applications\ Home_Accountz\BAK`.

2. **Right-click the file that you want to restore (Last Recent Backup), and then select Copy from the pop-up menu that appears.**

3. **Navigate to the location where you want to paste the backup file, and then right-click (or Ctrl-click on a Mac) and select Paste from the pop-up menu that appears.**

4. **Click the filename.**

   It becomes editable.

5. **Rename the file by typing in a new one.**

   Name the file something like My Accountz Work File so that you can easily identify it.

6. **In the Home_Accountz folder, select the `app-config.haz` file, and then press the Delete key.**

   The file is deleted.

7. **In the BAK folder, delete the App-Config folder by selecting it and then pressing the Delete key.**

8. **Double-click the Home Accountz icon to start Home Accountz.**

9. **Choose File⇨Open.**

   An Open dialog box appears.

10. **Navigate to the location where you pasted the backup file (refer to Step 3).**

11. **Select the file, and then click open.**

    The backup file opens in Home Accountz.

You can also easily restore the file by choosing File⇨Restore Backup.

How Do I Open Work Files?

You have the ability within Home Accountz to open different work files so that one copy of Home Accountz could be used to look after the personal finances of many people within a household — mom may have a file, dad may have a file, and the son or daughter who's away at university may have a file.

By default, Home Accountz saves work files in the AccountzData folder:

- For Windows Vista and Windows 7 users, this folder is located at `C:\users\`*`your_username`*`\AccountzData`.

- Windows XP users can quickly locate the folder by searching through My Computer.

- For Mac users, use Spotlight and search for **AccountzData**. (The folder is located within the user folder for the currently selected Mac user. If you're not prompted to log in when you start your Mac, it appears in the folder for the user you created when setting up the computer).

To open files from the File menu, follow these steps:

1. **Choose File⇨Open.**

   The Open dialog box appears.

2. **Navigate to the location of the work file and select that file.**

3. **Click Open Existing File.**

   The file opens in Home Accountz.

If you've opened and saved a work file in Home Accountz previously, you can find a list of these files in the Home Accountz program's History. Just choose File⇨History, and then choose the file from the submenu that appears (see Figure 20-1). This submenu contains files that you've saved, as well as files that Home Accountz has automatically saved.

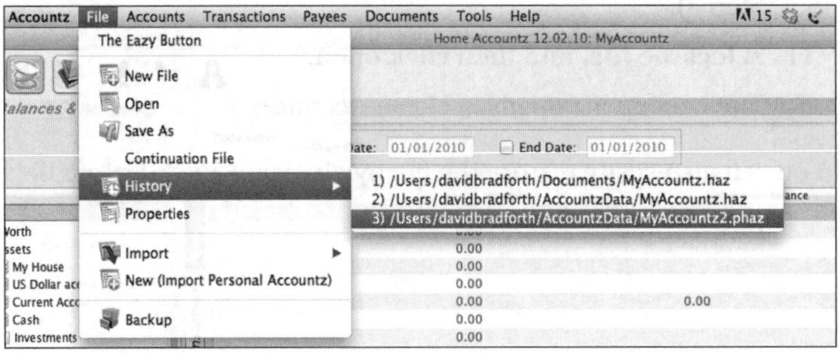

Figure 20-1: The History submenu displays work files, allowing you to quickly move between files.

How Do I View All Account Transactions?

If you want to view the all account transactions throughout your Home Accountz application in one place, follow these steps:

1. **In Home Accountz, click the Green Books button at the top of the window.**

2. **Select All Transactions from the drop-down list that appears.**

   All your account transactions are displayed in the main panel of the Home Accountz window.

How Do I View Individual Account Transactions?

To view individual account transactions from within your currently open data, follow these steps:

1. **Click the Accounts, Balances & Budgeting button at the top of the window.**

   This button displays three gold coins.

   The Accounts, Balances & Budgeting window opens.

2. **Click the Transactions tab to open it.**

3. **Click the plus sign (+) next to the main group that you want to view in the tree structure.**

   That group expands.

4. **Click plus sign (+) next to the subgroup that you want to see to expand that subgroup.**

5. **Select the relevant account (for example, Bank Account) in the subgroup.**

   All transactions for the selected account are displayed on the right side of the window.

How Do I Create a Budget in Home Accountz?

To create a budget in Home Accountz, follow these steps:

1. **Click the Accounts, Balances & Budgeting button (which looks like a pile of coins) at the top of the Home Accountz window.**

   The Accounts, Balances & Budgeting window opens.

2. **Click the Budgeting tab, which appears at the left of the main window.**

3. **Click the Add Budget button.**

   This button looks like a plus sign (+) in a green circle.

4. **Give the budget a name and add a start date by completing the fields that appear.**

   You can set a budget to start at any point.

5. **Click Create.**

   The new budget appears in the main window. At this stage, the budget is blank — a screen full of dashes.

6. **To add a budget figure to an account, click the account within the Accounts tree.**

   The line you're working with is highlighted in blue.

7. **Type in an annual budget figure to the applicable columns across the budget window (see Figure 20-2).**

   Alternatively, you can enter a monthly budget figure if it varies from month to month.

8. **To switch from one budget to another, select the alternative budget in the Budget drop-down list.**

   This list appears towards the top-left of the screen.

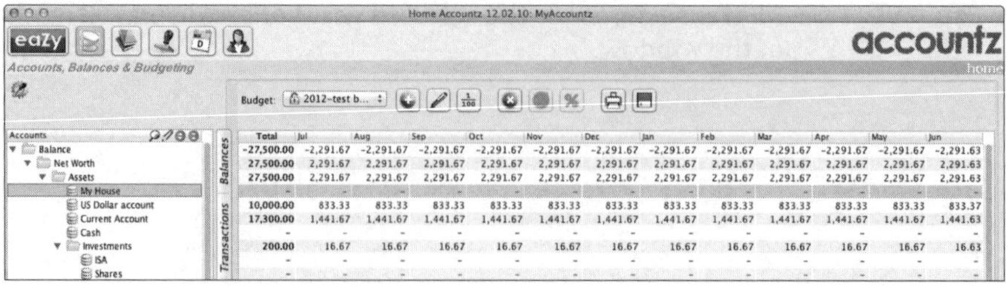

Figure 20-2: Base budgets on annual figures or individual monthly allocations.

How Do I View Account Balances in Home Accountz?

To view account balances, follow these steps:

1. **Click the Accounts, Balances & Budgeting button, which displays three gold coins, to open the Accounts, Balances & Budgeting window.**

2. **Select the Balances tab.**

   The balances for all your accounts now appear.

3. **To view an individual account balance, expand the tree structure by clicking the plus sign (+) next to the main group of accounts, and then select the relevant account from the list that appears.**

   The balance for the selected account appears in the window immediately to the right of the selected account, and the selection is highlighted in blue so that you can more easily read it.

How Do I Move Home Accountz from One Computer to Another?

To move your installation of Home Accountz from one computer to another, you first need to get a second key for the software. Call Accountz.com Limited at 01354 691650 and speak to their technical department.

To register the second installation (with the key you obtain from Accountz.com), follow these steps:

1. **Locate your work file.**

   If you don't know where this file is, choose File➪Properties — the location is listed alongside the specifications of the file.

2. **Transfer the work file via memory stick, e-mail, or a similar medium.**

3. **Copy and paste the file you've transferred onto the second computer.**

   It's entirely up to you where on the computer you want to put the file.

4. **Choose File➪Open on the new computer, and then navigate to where you've pasted the file in the Open dialog box that appears.**

5. **Click OK to open the file.**

How Do I Back Up My License?

You might want to back up your Home Accountz license because if your data becomes corrupted, you can't reactivate the software without contacting Accountz.com's technical support and answering a few questions.

First, install your Home Accountz software and go through the setup wizard (which we cover in Chapter 2). Then, follow these steps:

1. **At the end of the setup process, choose Home Accountz⇨Help⇨Set Licence Wizard.**

   The Set Licence Wizard opens.

2. **Click Next at the bottom-right of the screen.**

3. **Enter the license key in the appropriate field.**

   If you paid for a retail copy of Home Accountz, this key comes with the documentation. If you got a digital download, you receive the license key in an e-mail.

4. **Click Next.**

   The license is checked against the servers at Accountz.com.

5. **After the license validates, close the software, and then restart it.**

   This restart allows the license change to take effect.

6. **Close the software again.**

7. **Open the installation folder, and then right-click (Ctrl-click on a Mac) the BAK folder.**

   The default location of the BAK folder and the `install-info.ehaz` depends on your computer:

   - **Windows:** `C:\Program Files\Home_Accountz`
   - **Windows 64-bit:** `C:\Program Files (x86)\Home_Accountz`
   - **Mac:** `/Applications/Home_Accountz`

8. **Select Copy from the pop-up menu that appears.**

9. **Navigate to the folder where you want to store the backup.**

10. **Right-click (or Ctrl-click on a Mac), and then select Paste from the pop-up menu that appears.**

11. **Repeat Steps 7 through 10, copying over the `install-info.ehaz` file, rather than the BAK folder.**

You can use your key for only one copy of Home Accountz at a time. However, if you have to reinstall Home Accountz on the same computer, for whatever reason, then you can restore your license from the BAK folder and restore the `install-info.ehaz` file. The license is stored in your work files, so it's reapplied to the software when the data is restored.

How Do I Archive Data?

If you want to see only recent transactions in your Home Accountz tables, set up a new view that restricts what you see to the recent past. Follow these steps:

1. **In the Accounts panel of the Accounts, Balances & Budgeting window, select any account and click the Transactions tab.**

2. **Select the All Transactions default view, and then click the Views button (which looks like a funnel).**

3. **In the View tab that opens, click the Create New View button.**

   A new view is created based on the current view, and it's named initially Copy of *View*.

4. **Enter a name for the new view (something like Recent Transactions).**

5. **Select the Filter tab to open it, and then click the Add Condition button.**

   The list of available conditions opens.

6. **Select the Date option from the drop-down list.**

7. **In the row that appears to the right of the drop-down list, click the Condition column and select Occurred in the Last from the drop-down list that opens.**

   Occurred appears near the bottom of the list, below the grayed-out options.

8. **In the Value(s) column, select the Month option and, in the high-lighted field, enter a value to restrict the view (see Figure 20-3).**

   For example, you'd enter **6** if you want to restrict the view to the last six months.

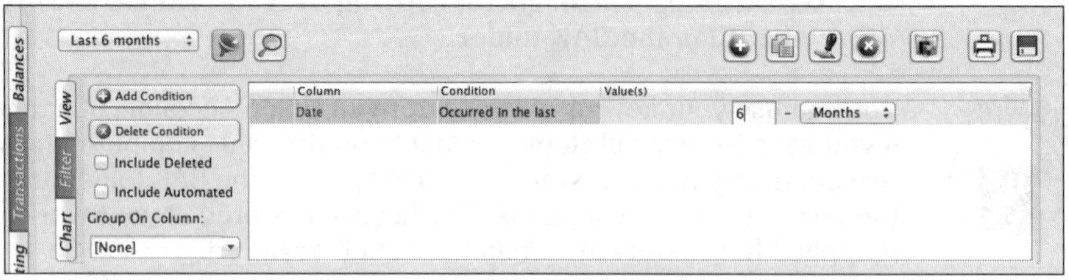
Last 6 months
Balances
Transactions
View
Filter
Chart
Add Condition
Delete Condition
Include Deleted
Include Automated
Group On Column:
[None]
Column
Condition
Value(s)
Date
Occurred in the last
6
Months

Figure 20-3: Amending a view so that only six months' transactions are visible.

You can watch a video that explains how to create new views at `www.accountz.com/accountz/views-and-powerful-aspects`.

Chapter 21

Ten (or So) Ways to Use Rapid Data Entry Effectively

Accounting is good for the brain. But you probably don't want to spend too much time doing it. So the rapid data entry system in Home Accountz comes in very handy. You can quickly enter dates, accounts, and other information directly into tables, and hence reduce the time you have to spend working on your accounts.

After you enter the data, you have the option of reusing payees, account names, and so on quickly and simply by typing in the first few letters of the element's name or reference, and then selecting the element from the drop-down list that appears.

Entering Dates

Home Accountz's Date Picker is interactive (see Figure 21-1): Start typing a date, and the calendar opens and reacts to everything you type. Press the Enter key when the date you want is selected.

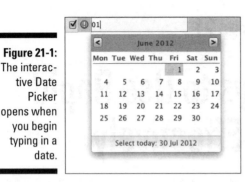

Figure 21-1:
The interactive Date Picker opens when you begin typing in a date.

Anywhere in Home Accountz where you can enter a date, you can make a small calendar pop up by pressing the spacebar or starting to type a date. You can use this calendar to select a date to be entered into the field.

You can enter the date by using the keyboard, and while you enter the date, the calendar jumps to that point. You can use any form of punctuation as a separator (for example, a space, a period, a forward or back slash, and so on), and you don't have to include zeroes for numbers less than 10 (so you can enter **9**, rather than **09**).

Press the Enter key if the calendar shows the date you want or double-click a particular day to select it with the mouse.

Working with Calculations

The Amount fields (Total Amount, Amount From, and Amount To) in any Transaction table has the capacity to handle calculations. Simply enter the equal sign (=) followed by the numbers you want to calculate (as shown in Figure 21-2), and then press Enter, and the software totals the calculation for you automatically.

Figure 21-2:
You can enter calculations into the amount fields within Home Accountz.

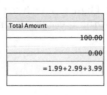

Selecting Items in Lookup Lists

Home Accountz displays some options in drop-down lists, which are called *lookup lists* (see Figure 21-3). You can access these drop-down lists in the Payee, Account From, and Account To fields in Transaction tables.

The lists are filtered automatically when you start typing in one of the relevant fields. For example, if you want to select a Payee for a particular transaction whose name is Big Food Company, then as soon as you start typing any part of the name, the drop-down list appears, displaying any matching names, immediately.

While you type more of the name, the list is reduced until you end up with only the selection you want. Typically, this narrowing-down process happens after only three key presses, so you don't need to type in the whole name. You can select the desired name from the list by either pressing the up- or down-arrow key or clicking the mouse on the name you want.

As soon as you make the selection, the selected account or payee is inserted in the relevant field in the Transaction table.

If you can't remember the payee or account you want to enter, pressing the spacebar before you type anything displays a list of all the options available. Use the scroll bar to find the payee or account that you want.

From Account
US Dollar account
Furniture
Furniture ▼
Furniture
Garden
Gas
Gifts from me
Holidays
House Insurance
Interest Received
ISA
New Account...

Figure 21-3:
A lookup list in action.

If you use these lists, you can keep your hands on the keyboard, which can help you enter numbers quickly. Also, you can click an item in the list by using the mouse, if you prefer.

Using Templates

The Templates feature enables you to enter near-complete transactions into any transaction table with a single mouse click, leaving just the Date and Amount fields for you to fill in to complete the transaction.

For a transaction that always involves the same amount, you can include that amount in the template, too.

For example, if you regularly take out £50 from a cash machine, then you can set up a template with all the fields filled in. When you use this template to enter your transaction, the only thing you need to enter to complete the transaction is the date, which speeds up your data entry significantly.

Sorting Tables

Click any column header to sort the table by that column. Click again to reverse the sort. Click a third time to turn sorting off. When sorting is off, the table re-sorts to the original order in which you entered your transactions.

You can see by which column the table is sorted based on a small up or down arrow to the right of the column name.

You can also right-click (or Ctrl-click on a Mac) any column header and choose the sort option that you want to use from the pop-up menu that appears (as shown in Figure 21-4).

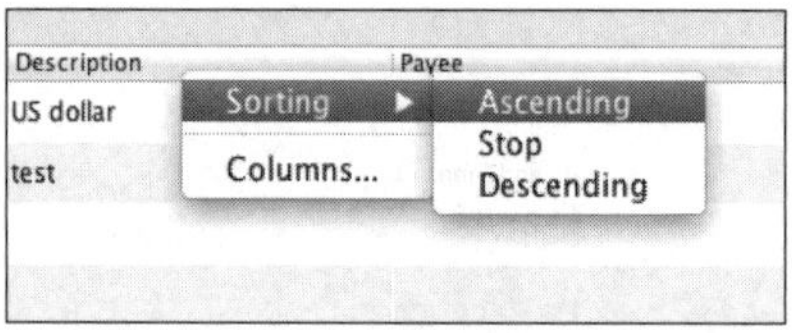

Figure 21-4:
Right-click
the header
of any table
to sort
the data.

Description		Payee	
US dollar	Sorting ▶	Ascending	
		Stop	
test	Columns...	Descending	

Sorting columns is a great way to find items quickly. For example, if you need to locate transactions of a certain value, sorting by the Total Amount column not only puts all the transactions of the same value together, but also enables you to see those transactions that are close to the value you're after.

Hiding or Showing Columns in Tables

You can speed up data input by hiding the columns you don't need or displaying columns you do need that are currently hidden. For example, you may have turned off the Transaction Number column but later decide that you want to turn it back on to check a certain transaction. Follow these steps:

1. **Right-click (Ctrl-click if you're using a Mac) any of the column headers within a table.**

2. **Choose Columns from the pop-up menu that appears.**

   The Set Column Visibility dialog box opens, as shown in Figure 21-5.

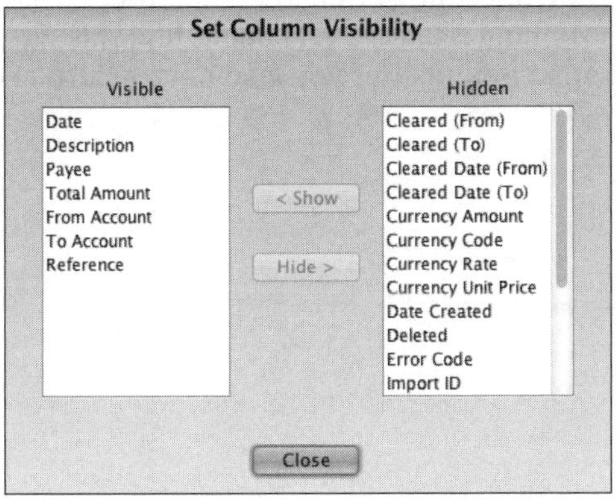

Figure 21-5:
In the Set Column Visibility dialog box, choose which columns appear in tables.

Set Column Visibility	
Visible	**Hidden**
Date	Cleared (From)
Description	Cleared (To)
Payee	Cleared Date (From)
Total Amount	Cleared Date (To)
From Account	Currency Amount
To Account	Currency Code
Reference	Currency Rate
	Currency Unit Price
	Date Created
	Deleted
	Error Code
	Import ID

< Show

Hide >

Close

3. **To make a hidden column visible in a table, select it in the Hidden Columns list and click the Show button.**

4. **To hide a column, select it from the Visible Columns list and click the Hide button.**

Swapping Columns in Tables

You can drag any columns left or right to switch the column order. So, for example, you can rearrange columns in Home Accountz so that you enter the Account From and Account To information before entering the Total Amount. Therefore, you can set up your accounts to suit the way you work, which can help speed up your use of the software.

Adjusting Column Width in Tables

You can increase or decrease the width of any of the columns within a table by clicking and dragging the column separators. If you have a lot of columns visible and a low resolution on your computer screen, adjusting column widths can keep the whole table in view (so you don't have to use scroll bars to see all your data).

Altering Your Table Views

You can filter most of the tables in any way you want. For example, you can create a new filter to show transactions that are in another currency, including the other currency's running balance. You might find this filter useful if your base currency is British pounds but you also have a Euro account.

Chapter 22

Ten Tips for Setting Up Your Budgets and Sticking to Them

*B*y now, you're probably all fired up and ready to manage your money. But how do you go about setting a budget that's workable? In fact, how do you go about setting a budget at all?

In this chapter, we offer ten essential aids for creating a budget and give suggestions about ways in which you can budget so as to make everything balance. A budget is a tool — it's not the be all and end all, so you do need to use it correctly if it it's to be of help to you.

Get Your Finances Organized

Just how organized are you, financially? Do you keep all your papers together? Do you know *exactly* where to find your credit card bill, mortgage statement, receipts for major purchases, and receipts for daily purchases (such as food)?

 If you have a scanner, there's actually a very simple way to bring all of this material together. Create for yourself a folder on your desktop called something like Budget. Within this folder, create subfolders, such as Mortgage, Credit Card, Fuel, Food, Electricity, TV/Broadband/Phone, and so on. Then, scan each of the documents you have. Save each document in the appropriate folder, with the date of the bill or receipt as the filename. You then have quick and easy access to your most recent bills, and you can find them simply via the date.

If you don't have a scanner, then you can keep your receipts in date order in a stationery box folder or lever arch file.

Your bank's online system can provide you with a quick indication of what you've spent and where you spent it. If you're not registered for online banking, it's worth considering — it gives you a simple way to check whether your bank balance agrees with what appears in Home Accountz and to check for fraudulent transactions.

With Home Accountz, you can download your online banking information and reconcile this against the figures within Home Accountz, which gives you another way to ensure that the information is all correct and tallies up.

Save for a Rainy Day

If only you had a crystal ball, you could plan for the day the car breaks down or the cat gets sick. You may not be psychic, but you can plan for these unexpected bumps on your financial road. You could take out insurance plans to cover every eventuality — and indeed, some forms of insurance are a must. For everything else, create a rainy day fund. By using the accounts system in Home Accountz, you can channel a regular sum of money into an account created specifically to remove some funds from your available pot of money.

You just need to create a Savings account in the Accounts Manager, into which you transfer any free money you have at the end of each month. You can then, across the year, predict the finances you have available to cater to those expenses you simply can't predict.

Plan for the Big Bills

Make sure you plan for the larger, less frequent payments, such as quarterly and yearly bills. You can take the pain away from these payments by dividing them up by month and allocating them to accounts. For example, if you know you have to insure your car, divide your last insurance premium by ten months. (You could divide by 12 to cover the entire year, but you can give yourself a little breathing space for unexpected or seasonal expenses, or to take into account a price rise in your premium, by not factoring in two months' payments.)

Create an account within the Account Manager (see Chapter 8) and allocate this amount to the account each month.

Create a Budget

After you're aware of your spending habits, you need to track the specifics of your income and outgoings to give yourself an at-a-glance view of how much money you have coming in, directly plotted against how much money you're spending.

If you find that you're spending more than you earn, it's worth looking at ways to reduce your spending. For example

✔ **Do you buy a cup of coffee each day on the way to work?** You could take a thermos of coffee from home and save yourself a considerable amount of money across the week.

✔ **Did the weekly lunchtime pub trip become daily some years back?** Take a look at cutting down to once a week again and save yourself perhaps £10 a day on lunch.

✔ **Do you buy lunch at work every day?** A lunch that costs you up to £10 a day could cost only £2 if you bring a packed lunch from home.

Obviously, you can't easily reduce your spending on some things: If you drive to work, you're going to need fuel — that's an aspect of spending that you can't avoid. However, if you don't actually *need* to drive to work because your office is ten minutes down the road, save yourself some money and get a little fitter by walking, rather than driving.

What's important is that you regularly review your proposed budget. Things change over time — that's a fact of life — and unless you regularly review these figures, you're likely to find the budget eventually bears little or no relation to your actual financial situation.

Shop Around

If you find that you're spending more money than you have but you feel that there's no real way to reduce the amount you're spending, shop around. Take the time to look around to see whether anybody has cheaper alternatives for the products you're buying.

Join the supermarket wars

A fairly average shopping trip (for two adults and one young child) can cost quite a lot. It doesn't have to feature anything particularly extravagant; simply food for the family for just over a week can add up.

You'll frequently notice stories in the press about store wars. Stores always have a fierce competition, and they often use the price of essential food items — bread, eggs, milk, cheese, and so on — as a loss leader to convince you to become a customer. Each strives to beat the others in terms of the average price of a weekly shop. So, the name of the game is to go where the bargains are — even if that means shopping in more than one store.

Reduce interest payments

If you have an active credit card, bank loan, or mortgage, you can reduce interest payments by shopping around for a better deal.

Your credit score is important. If you have less-than-perfect credit, you may find it difficult to get the best interest rate because the rate you pay is directly related to your credit score. Many of the lower rates offered tend to be only short term — you must keep an eye out for sudden sharp interest rate rises, in both loans and credit cards.

Note that if you get rejected by one credit card supplier, it's not worth working your way down the list applying to each in turn — if a number of companies reject you, you'll end up with a lot of black marks against you on your credit file.

If you're rejected, get yourself a credit report. You can find plenty of Internet-based companies that provide you with a cheap (or even free) report. Then, if you think the credit card supplier has no reason to reject you, ask them to review their decision and offer them the information that tells them why you feel you should receive an account.

Talk to the Retentions department

If you're at the end of your mobile phone contract, or your landline or broadband deal is coming to an end, it's worth giving your supplier's Retentions department a ring. Whichever way you look at it, you're an asset to your phone or broadband supplier — every time you renew your contract with them, they're guaranteed a fixed sum of money over the life of the contract. Attracting new customers costs the company money; retaining customers costs them nothing.

It's in their interests to keep you, but they don't make it obvious that they're willing to pass on some of those savings to you. So don't just renew your contract; ask for a deal. They'll usually make certain offers available to you to keep you as a customer.

If your current bill is higher than new promotional tariffs designed to get customers to join the network, then during your contract period, the company may be prepared to match or beat the offers available to new customers. Customer loyalty has value — if you've been a customer with a network for ten years, you may find that you have significant power to negotiate.

Cut Back

You can cut back so that you reduce the amount of money you spend in a number of ways:

- **Socializing:** Limit the amount you spend while out socializing. If you're going to have a drink, consider having one before you leave the house so that you can limit your spending in the pub or club. Of course, there's one excellent way to ensure you limit your spending while you're out — don't take your credit card with you and take a limited amount of cash instead.

- **Lunch:** You may face the temptation to pop in to your favorite sandwich shop each day, and perhaps pay a weekly visit to your favorite Thai restaurant. By making your own lunch, you can feed yourself for the week on what you may otherwise spend in a day or two.

- **Cash drains:** Uncompetitive credit cards and store cards that have high interest rates can drain a lot of cash from your account. Review your cards regularly and switch to take advantage of cards that offer better rates. Keep an eye on regular automatic payments, such as magazine subscriptions: Do you really need that magazine? If the answer is no, consider canceling your subscription and using the money for something else.

- **Gym subscriptions:** Do you actually go to the gym? Do you make the most of the gym membership that you pay for as regularly as clockwork by going to the gym regularly? No? We didn't think so. As soon as you can, cancel your gym membership. Visit eBay (www.ebay.com) and search for exercise equipment — many of the things you probably thought about using in the gym (such as weights, stationary bikes, and so on) are waiting to be bought there and usually aren't that expensive.

- **Home entertainment:** Don't pay for subscription TV if you never watch anything. Also, hard-drive–based personal video recorders (PVRs) now put you in control of what shows you watch. Why not ditch the TV subscription and create your own channel by using a PVR and recording your pick of Freeview TV?

Sell Things You Don't Need

Your clutter can end up costing you money. You may have cash locked away in the attic, or filling your shed or garage — some of your possessions may keep their value and some may even become antiques (but not all them, of course).

You can sell items you don't want in many ways:

- ✔ **eBay:** If you want instant access to a potential audience of millions, all looking for that item you're selling, consider using eBay (www.ebay.com). You need to remember that there are costs to this; for example, eBay charges for the listing (if the start price is above 99p), and it costs more to upgrade listings (including bold text, adding a bigger picture, and so on). eBay also encourages using PayPal for payments, which it charges you to use when selling items.

- ✔ **Personal ads:** If you have anything particularly special to sell, it may be worth taking a personal ad in a magazine or on a website relating to that subject. If you want to sell copies of the magazine *Model Engineer,* for instance, an advertisement in that magazine is targeted to a particular audience and will no doubt give you a better response than a more general audience, such as eBay.

- ✔ **Garage sales:** Most people have a garage sale just before they move, and you can have one to get rid of some of the clutter you've built up. Even if you're not moving, you may save money if you can reclaim your garage for the car, for example, protecting it from the elements, which saves you maintenance costs.

Reward Yourself

If you manage to keep to your budget for three months, why not allow yourself a small amount of money to go out and celebrate? Whether it's a night out at the cinema or a fancy dinner with your better half, make the reward something you'll genuinely look forward to — that way, you'll appreciate the reward if you get it and really feel the consequences of not getting it if you don't keep to your budget.

Be honest with yourself and do the best you can to achieve your goal — it makes the rewards themselves all the better when you do achieve the end result.

Be Realistic

If you leave out of your budget everything that you do for personal pleasure, the chances are that you'll never be able to stick with it. A budget should be about matching up your wants with your needs.

We know the basics: food, water, gas, electricity, council tax, rent or mortgage payments; but you also need to allow for entertainment. Without entertainment, you'll have little or no quality of life, which ultimately will cause more issues than it can ever resolve.

A budget is a tool, and it needs to be used appropriately.

Keep Your Budget Up to Date

Your budget — whether you prepare it in Home Accountz, by hand, or by using a computer program such as Excel — can only ever be as accurate as the information you put into it. Make sure to keep track of your receipts, bills, and income, and enter that information as and when it applies. Without continuous updating, a budget will never be worth anything.

Update it to reflect your current situation; make a point of ensuring that if your income changes, you take that change into consideration so that the end figure (the money you have left over after expenses) is correct.

Appendix

Glossary of Accounting Terms

· ·

above the line: This term can be applied to many aspects of accounting. It means transactions, assets, and so on, that are associated with the everyday running of a business. See also *below the line*.

account: A section in a ledger devoted to a single aspect of business or personal finances (for example, a bank account, wages account, or office expenses account).

accounting cycle: Everything from opening the books at the start of the year to closing them at the end of it. In other words, everything you need to do in one financial year, accounting-wise.

accounting equation: The formula used to prepare a balance sheet: assets = liability + equity. See also *assets, equity, liabilities*.

Accounts Payable: An account in the nominal ledger that contains the overall balance of the purchase ledger. See also *nominal ledger, purchase ledger*.

Accounts Payable ledger: A subsidiary ledger that holds the accounts of a business's suppliers. A single control account (which combines the balance of all accounts in the purchase ledger) is held in the nominal ledger. See also *nominal ledger*.

Accounts Receivable: An account in the nominal ledger that contains the overall balance of the sales ledger. See also *nominal ledger, sales ledger*.

Accounts Receivable ledger: A subsidiary ledger that holds the accounts of a business's customers. A single control account (with the total balance of all accounts in the sales ledger) is held in the nominal ledger. See also *nominal ledger, sales ledger*.

accrual method of accounting: Most businesses use the accrual method of accounting (because it's usually required by law). When you issue an invoice on credit (regardless of whether it's paid), it's treated as a taxable supply on the date it was issued for income tax purposes (or corporation tax for limited companies). The same applies to bills received from suppliers. (This does not mean you pay income tax immediately, just that it must be included in that year's Profit and Loss account).

accruals: If, during the course of a business, certain charges are incurred but no invoice is received, then these charges are referred to as *accruals* (they *accrue,* or increase in value). A typical example is interest payable on a loan where you haven't yet received a bank statement. These items (or an estimate of their value) should still be included in the Profit and Loss account. When the real invoice is received, an adjustment can be made to correct the estimate. (Accruals can also apply to the income side.)

accumulated depreciation account: An account held in the nominal ledger that holds the depreciation of a fixed asset until the end of the asset's useful life (because it has either been scrapped or sold). It is credited each year with that year's depreciation, hence the balance increases (or *accumulates*) over a period of time. Each fixed asset will have its own accumulated depreciation account. See also *nominal ledger.*

amortization: The depreciation (or repayment) of a (usually) intangible asset (such as a loan or mortgage) over a fixed period of time. For example, if a loan of £12,000 is amortized over one year with no interest, the monthly payments would be £1,000 a month.

annualize: To convert anything into a yearly figure. For example, if profits are reported as running at £10,000 a quarter, then they would be £40,000 if annualized. If a credit card interest rate was quoted as 1 percent a month, it would be annualized as 12 percent.

appropriation account: An account in the nominal ledger that shows how the net profits of a business (usually a partnership, limited company, or corporation) have been used. See also *nominal ledger.*

arrears: Bills that should have been paid. For example, if you forget to pay your last three months' rent, then you're said to be three months in arrears on your rent.

assets: What a business owns or is due. Equipment, vehicles, buildings, creditors, money in the bank, and cash are all examples of the assets of a business. Typical breakdown includes fixed assets, current assets, and non-current assets. *Fixed* refers to non-cash items such as equipment, buildings, plants, vehicles, and so on. *Current* refers to cash, money in the bank, debtors, and so on. *Non-current* refers to any assets that don't easily fit into the other categories (such as deferred expenditure). See also *deferred expenditure.*

at cost: Usually, the price originally paid for something, as opposed to the retail price, for example.

audit: The process of checking every entry in a set of books to make sure they agree with the original paperwork (for example, checking entries against the original purchase and sales invoices).

audit trail: A list of transactions, arranged in the order they occurred.

bad debts account: An account in the nominal ledger to record the value of unrecoverable debts from customers. Real bad debts, or those that are likely to happen, can be deducted as expenses against tax liability (provided they refer specifically to a customer). See also *nominal ledger.*

bad debts reserve account: An account used to record an estimate of bad debts for the year (usually as a percentage of sales). This estimate can't be deducted as an expense against tax liability.

balance sheet: A summary of all the accounts of a business, usually prepared at the end of each financial year. The term *balance sheet* implies that the combined balances of assets exactly equal the liabilities and equity (meaning net worth). See also *equity.*

balancing charge: Any loss or gain on a fixed asset that you've sold or disposed of that's reclaimed against (or added to) any profits for income tax purposes.

bankrupt: If an individual or unincorporated company has greater liabilities than it has assets, the person or business can petition for, or be declared by its creditors, bankrupt. (To be *bankrupt* means to not be able to afford to pay your bills.) In the case of a limited company or corporation in the same position, the term used is insolvent. See also *insolvent.*

below the line: This term is applied to items within a business that you wouldn't normally associate with the everyday running of a business. If you purchased something but the payment wasn't due until after the accounting period, it's a below the line expense because it doesn't fall into the current accounting period. See also *above the line.*

bill: A term typically used to describe a purchase invoice (for example, an invoice from a supplier).

bought ledger: Another term for purchase ledger. See *purchase ledger.*

burn rate: The rate at which a company spends its money. For example, if a company has cash reserves of £120 million and is currently spending £10 million a month, then you'd say that, at the current burn rate, the company will run out of cash in one year.

CAGR (compound annual growth rate): The year-on-year growth rate required to show the change in value (of an investment) from its initial value to its final value. If a £1 investment was worth £1.52 over three years, the CAGR would be 15% (1 x 1.15 x 1.15 x 1.15) — multiplying by 1.15 increases the figure by 15% over each period, and when you compound it over three years, the total meets the specified financial value.

called-up share capital: The value of unpaid (but issued) shares for which a company has requested payment. See also *paid-up share capital.*

capital: An amount of money put into the business (often by way of a loan), as opposed to money earned by the business.

capital account: Used to describe owners' equity in the business.

capital allowances: In the U.K., relates to the proportion (usually a percentage) of the value of fixed assets that the HM Revenue & Customs allows a business to claim before working out the tax bill.

capital assets: A term also described as fixed assets. See *fixed assets.*

capital employed (CE): There are two elements to this definition — gross capital employed and net capital employed. Gross CE = Total assets; Net CE = Fixed assets plus (current assets – current liabilities).

capital gains tax (CGT): When a fixed asset is sold, the profit may be liable to capital gains tax. Calculating the tax can be a complicated affair: capital gains allowances, adjustments for inflation, and different computations based on the age of the asset all need to be taken into consideration.

cash accounting: An accounting method whereby only invoices and bills that have been paid are accounted for. However, for most types of business in the U.K., as far as the HM Revenue & Customs is concerned, as soon as you issue an invoice (paid or not), you must treat it as revenue and account for it. See also *value added tax (VAT).*

cash book: A journal in which a business's cash sales and purchases are entered. A cash book can also be used to record the transactions of a bank account. The side of the cash book that refers to the cash or bank account can be used as a part of the nominal ledger (rather than posting the entries to cash or bank accounts held directly in the nominal ledger). See also *nominal ledger, three-column cash book.*

cash flow: The flow of money into and out of a business over a period of time.

cash flow forecast: An estimate of the cash flow in the future (usually required by a bank before it will lend you money or take on your account).

cash in hand: See *undeposited funds account.*

charge back: When a credit card order has been processed and is then cancelled by the cardholder directly through the credit card company (rather than through the seller), it results in the credit card company charging the seller for the amount originally credited. (The seller often incurs a small penalty or administration fee.)

chart of accounts: A list of all the accounts held in the nominal ledger. See also *nominal ledger.*

CIF (Cost, insurance, freight): An international contract for the sale of goods in which the seller agrees to supply the goods, pay the insurance, and pay the freight charges until the goods reach the destination (usually a port, rather than the actual buyer's address). After that point, the responsibility for the goods passes to the buyer.

circulating assets: Those assets that turn from cash to goods and back again (hence the term *circulating*). Typically, you buy some raw materials, start to manufacture a product (the asset is called *work in progress* at this point), produce a product (it is now *stock*), and then sell it (which turns it back to cash). The opposite of fixed assets. See also *fixed assets, stock, work in progress.*

closing the books: The journal entries necessary to close the sales and expense accounts of a business at year end by posting their balances to the Profit and Loss account, and ultimately also to close the Profit and Loss account by posting its balance to a capital or other account.

Companies House: The U.K. government department that collects and stores information supplied by limited companies. A limited company must supply Companies House with a statement of its final accounts every year (meaning its trading account, Profit and Loss account, and balance sheet).

compensating error: A double-entry term applied to a mistake that cancels out another mistake.

compound interest: Applying interest to the combination of the capital plus all interest accrued to date. For example, a loan of £1,000 over two years with an annually applied rate of 10 percent would yield a gross total of £1,210 at the end of the period (Year One interest = $1,000 \times .1$, or 100; Year Two interest = $1,100 \times .1$, or 110). The same loan with simple interest applied to it would yield £1,200; interest on both years is £100 per year because it earns interest only on the capital. See also *simple interest.*

contra account: An account created to offset another account. An example of a sales contra account is Sales Discounts. If Sales = £10,000 and Sales Discounts = £1,000, Net Sales = £9,000. This example, affecting the revenue side of a business, is also referred to as *contra revenue.* The telltale sign of a contra account is that it has the opposite balance to that expected for an account in that section; so, in the above example, the Sales Discounts balance would appear in brackets, indicating that it's a debit balance, whereas Sales would show a credit balance.

control account: An account held in a ledger that summarizes the balance of all the accounts in the same or another ledger. Typically, each subsidiary ledger has a control account that's mirrored by another control account in the nominal ledger. See also *nominal ledger, self-balancing ledgers.*

cook the books: Falsify a set of accounts. See also *creative accounting*.

corporation tax (CT): The tax paid in the U.K. by a limited company on its profits. At present, this is calculated at year end and due within nine months of that date. Small and medium-sized companies are exempted from the installment plan for corporation tax and pay any due amount promptly.

cost accounting: An area of management accounting that deals with the costs of a business in terms of enabling the management to manage the business more effectively. See also *management accounting*.

cost-based pricing: Where a company bases its pricing policy solely on the costs of manufacturing, rather than current market conditions.

cost-benefit: Calculating not only the financial costs and benefits of a project, but also the social costs and benefits. This difficult process requires valuations of intangible items, such as the cost of job losses or the effects on the environment. Genetically modified crops are a good example of a project for which a business would conduct a cost-benefit analysis — but it couldn't give an answer with any degree of certainty!

cost center: A cost center allows you to split up your expenses by department. For example, instead of having one account to handle all power costs for a company, you'd open a separate power account for each department. You can then analyze which department is using the most power and hopefully find of way of reducing those costs.

cost of finished goods: The value (at cost) of newly manufactured goods shown in a business's manufacturing account. The valuation is based on the opening raw materials balance, minus the direct costs involved in manufacturing, the closing raw materials balance, and any other overheads. This balance is subsequently transferred to the trading account.

cost of goods sold (COGS): A formula for working out the direct costs of stock sold over a particular period. The result represents the gross profit. COGS = opening stock + purchases – closing stock.

cost of sales: A formula for working out the direct costs of sales (including stock) over a particular period. The result represents the gross profit. Cost of sales = opening stock + purchases + direct expenses – closing stock. See also *Cost of goods sold (COGS)*.

creative accounting: A questionable means of making a company's figures appear more (or less) appealing to people such as shareholders. An example is *branding*, where the value of a brand name is added to intangible assets, which increases shareholders' funds (and therefore decreases the gearing). Capitalizing expenses is another creative-accounting method in which you move the expenses to the assets section of the balance sheet, rather than declaring them in the Profit and Loss account. See also *gearing*.

credit: A column in a journal or ledger that records the From side of a transaction. For example, if you use a check to buy some fuel, the money is paid from the bank to the Fuel account, so you credit the bank for the fuel cost when you make the journal entry.

credit note: A sales invoice in reverse. A typical example is where you issue an invoice for £100, and the customer then returns £25 worth of the goods, so you issue the customer a credit note to say that you owe the customer £25.

creditors: A list of suppliers to whom the business owes money.

creditors (control account): A control account in the nominal ledger that contains the overall balance of the purchase ledger. See also *nominal ledger*.

current assets: Active accounts that relate to money that's yours, such as money in the bank, petty cash, money received but not yet banked (meaning cash in hand), money owed to the business by its customers, raw materials for manufacturing, and stock bought for resale. Money flows into and out of these accounts each financial year, and you need frequent reports of their balances if the business is to survive. (For example, you might ask, "Do we need more stock, and do we have enough money in the bank to buy it?"). See also *undeposited funds account*.

current cost accounting: The valuing of assets, stock, raw materials, and so on at current market value, as opposed to its historical cost. See also *historical cost*.

current liabilities: Active accounts that relate to money you owe that's due to be repaid over a short period of time, including bank overdrafts, short-term loans (loans for less than a year), and what the business owes its suppliers.

days sales outstanding (DSO): How long, on average, it takes a company to collect the money owed to it.

debenture: A type of share issued by a limited company. It's the safest type of share in that it is really a loan to the company and usually tied to some of the company's assets, so if the company fails, the debenture holder has first call on any assets left after the company has been liquidated.

debit: A column in a journal or ledger to record the To side of a transaction. For example, if you're paying money into your bank account, you debit the bank when you make the journal entry.

debtors: A list of customers who owe money to the business.

debtors (control account): An account in the nominal ledger that contains the overall balance of the sales ledger. See also *nominal ledger.*

deferred expenditure: Expenses incurred that don't apply to the current accounting period. Instead, they're debited to a Deferred Expenditure account in the non-current assets area of your chart of accounts. When the expenses become current, they can then be transferred to the Profit and Loss account. See also *chart of accounts, non-current assets.*

depreciation: The amount or percentage that the value of assets decreases as time goes by. Depreciation is normally calculated at the end of every accounting period (usually a year) at a typical rate of 25% of its last value. It's shown in both the Profit and Loss account and the balance sheet of a business. See also *straight-line depreciation.*

dilutive: If a company acquires another company and says the deal is *dilutive to earnings,* it means that the resulting price/earnings (P/E) ratio of the acquired company is greater than the acquiring company.

dividends: Payments to the shareholders of a limited company.

double-entry bookkeeping: A system that accounts for every aspect of a transaction — where it came from and where it went. This From and To aspect of a transaction (called *crediting* and *debiting*) is what the term double-entry means.

drawings: The money taken out of a business by its owner(s) for personal use. Drawings are entirely different from wages paid to a business's employees, or the wages or remuneration of a limited company's directors. See also *wages.*

EBIT (earnings before interest and tax): Profit before any interest or taxes have been deducted.

EBITA (earnings before interest, tax, and amortization): Profit before any interest, taxes, or amortization have been deducted. See also *amortization.*

EBITDA (earnings before interest, tax, depreciation, and amortization): Profit before any interest, taxes, depreciation, or amortization have been deducted. See also *amortization, depreciation.*

encumbrance: A liability (for example, a mortgage is an encumbrance on a property). Also, any money set aside (meaning reserved) for any purpose.

entry: Part of a transaction recorded in a journal or posted to a ledger.

equity: The value of the business to the owner of the business (the *value* is the difference between the business's assets and liabilities).

error of commission: Where one or both sides of a double-entry has been posted to the wrong account (but is within the same class of account). For example, an error of commission occurs if you post a fuel expense to the Vehicle Maintenance account.

error of omission: Where a transaction has been omitted from the double-entry books entirely.

error of original entry: A double-entry transaction has been entered with the wrong amount.

error of principle: One or both sides of a double-entry have been posted to the wrong account (which is also a different class of account). For example, you post a fuel expense to the Fixtures and Fittings account.

expenses: Goods or services purchased directly to run the business. Expenses don't include goods bought for resale or any items of a capital nature. See also *fixed assets, stock.*

FIFO (First In, First Out): A method of valuing stock that means you sell stock in the order you receive it, so it's commonly used by restaurants to ensure stock rotation.

fiscal year: A business's accounting year. The period is usually 12 months, which can begin during any month of the calendar year (for example, a fiscal year might run from 1st April 2013 to 31st March 2014).

fixed assets: Anything that a business owns or buys for use within the business and that still retains a value at year end. Fixed assets usually consist of major items such as land, buildings, equipment, and vehicles, but can also include small items such as tools. See also *depreciation.*

Fixtures and Fittings: A class of fixed asset that includes office furniture, filing cabinets, display cases, warehouse shelving, and the like.

flash earnings: A news release issued by a company that shows its latest quarterly results.

flow of funds: A report that shows how a balance sheet has changed from one period to the next.

FOB (Free on Board): Part of an export contract in which the seller pays all the costs and insurance of sending the goods to the port of shipment. After that, the buyer then takes full responsibility. If the goods are to travel by train, it's called FOR (Free on Rail).

freight collect: A purchase for which the buyer pays the shipping costs.

gearing: The comparison of a company's long-term fixed interest loans compared to its assets. In general, two different methods are used. 1. Balance sheet gearing is calculated by dividing long-term loans by the equity (or proprietor's net worth). 2. Profit and Loss gearing divides fixed interest payments for the period by the profit for the period.

general ledger: Another name for the nominal ledger. See *nominal ledger.*

goodwill: An extra value placed on a business if the owner decides that business is worth more than the value of its assets. Goodwill is usually included if the business is to be sold as a going concern.

gross loss: The balance of the trading account, assuming it has a debit balance.

gross margin: The difference between the selling price of a product or service, and the cost of that product or service; often shown as a percentage. For example, if a product sold for £100 and cost £60 to buy or manufacture, the gross margin would be 40 percent (100 – 60). Gross margin can also be expressed in terms of the total revenue and costs of producing that revenue, as well as on an item-by-item basis.

gross profit: The balance of the trading account, assuming it has a credit balance.

growth and acquisition (G&A): Describes how a company can grow by expanding through its normal operations (growth) and buying other companies (acquisition).

impersonal accounts: Accounts not held in the name of persons (meaning they don't relate directly to a business's customers or suppliers). There are two types of impersonal account — nominal and real. See also *nominal accounts, real accounts.*

imprest system: A method of topping up petty cash. A fixed sum of money is placed in the petty cash box. When the petty cash balance is nearing zero, it's topped up to its original level again (known as *restoring the imprest*).

income: Money received by a business from its commercial activities. See also *revenue.*

HM Revenue & Customs (HMRC): The U.K. government department usually responsible for collecting your tax.

insolvent: When a company has insufficient funds (all of its assets) to pay its debts (all of its liabilities).

intangible assets: Assets of a non-physical or financial nature, such as a loan or an endowment policy. See also *tangible assets.*

integration account: Another name for a control account. See *control account.*

inventory ledger: A subsidiary ledger that is usually used to record the details of individual items of stock. Inventories can also be used to hold the details of other assets of a business. See also *periodic inventory, perpetual inventory.*

invoice: An original document either issued by a business for the sale of goods on credit (a sales invoice) or received by the business for goods bought (a purchase invoice).

landed costs: The total costs involved when importing goods, including buying, shipping, and insuring the goods, as well as associated taxes.

ledger: A book in which entries posted from the journals are reorganized into accounts.

leverage: Leverage is another way to describe gearing. See *gearing.*

liabilities: Money the business owes, including bank overdrafts, loans taken out for the business, and money owed by the business to its suppliers. Liabilities are included on the right side of the balance sheet and normally consist of accounts that have a credit balance.

LIFO (Last In First Out): A method of valuing stock, expressed as the last item you purchased as the first item you sell. This method applies especially to high-value goods. See also *stock.*

LILO (Last In Last Out): A method of valuing stock in which the last item you purchased is the last item you sell. See also *stock.*

long-term liabilities: Money owed by the business for an extended period. For example, a loan that lasts for more than one year, such as a mortgage.

management accounting: A system of accounting in which accounts and reports are tailor-made for the use of the managers and directors of a business (in any form they see fit — there are no rules), as opposed to financial accounts that are prepared for the HM Revenue & Customs and any other parties not directly connected with the business. See also *cost accounting.*

Manufacturing account: An account used to show what it cost to produce the finished goods made by a manufacturing business.

mark up: See *profit margin*.

matching principle: A method of analyzing the sales and the expenses that make up those sales in a particular period. For example, if a builder sells a house, then the builder ties in the cost of all the raw materials and expenses incurred in building and selling the house to one period — usually in order to see how much profit was made.

maturity value: The (usually projected) value of an intangible asset on the date it becomes due. See also *intangible assets*.

MD&A (Management Discussion and Analysis): Information disclosed, usually in a financial report for the benefit of shareholders, that has been derived from analysis and discussions held by the management.

memo billing: Goods ordered and invoiced on approval. There's no obligation to buy.

memo invoicing: See *memo billing*.

memorandum accounts: A name for the accounts held in a subsidiary ledger, such as the accounts in a sales ledger. See also *sales ledger*.

minority interest: When an individual holds a small shareholding in a company, whereas the rest of the shares are owned by larger corporate bodies or the company itself. If that company is bought, this smaller shareholder may still retain his or her shareholding with the implication that the company isn't a wholly owned subsidiary of its new owner. The minority shareholdings are shown in the holding company accounts as long-term liabilities. See also *long-term liabilities*.

moving average: A way of smoothing out (meaning removing the highs and lows) of a series of figures (usually shown as a graph). For example, if you have 12 months of sales figures and decide on a moving average period of 3 months, you add 3 months of figures together and divide that number by three to end up with an average for each month of the 3-month period. You then plot that single figure in place of the original monthly points on your graph. A moving average is useful for displaying trends. See also *normalize*.

multiple-step income statement: An income statement (meaning a Profit and Loss account) that has had its revenue section split into subsections in order to give a more detailed view of its sales operations. For example, if a company sells services and goods, the statement could show revenue from services and associated costs of those revenues at the start of the Revenue section, then show goods sold and cost of goods sold in a separate section below the Revenue section. The two sections' totals can then be amalgamated at the end to show overall sales (or gross profit). See also *Profit and Loss account, single-step income statement.*

narrative: A comment appended to an entry in a journal. It can be used to describe the nature of the transaction and, often, in particular, where the other side of the entry went to (or came from). This follows the basic principle of double-entry bookkeeping — keeping track of where your money goes, and from where it's come.

net loss: The value of expenses less sales, assuming that the expenses' value is greater than the sales' value (meaning if the Profit and Loss account shows a debit balance).

net of tax: The price less any tax. For example, if you sold some goods for £12, which included £2 sales tax, then the net of tax price would be £10.

net profit: The value of sales less expenses, assuming that the value of sales is greater than the value of expenses (in other words, if the Profit and Loss account shows a credit balance).

nominal accounts: A set of accounts, which usually don't relate to an individual person, held in the nominal ledger. The accounts that make up a Profit and Loss account are nominal accounts (as is the Profit and Loss account itself), whereas an account opened for a specific customer is usually held in a subsidiary ledger (the sales ledger) and referred to as a personal account. See also *personal accounts, sales ledger.*

nominal ledger: A ledger that holds all the nominal accounts of a business. The nominal ledger usually includes a control account to show the total balance of a subsidiary ledger, such as a sales ledger.

normalize: To average or smooth out a set of figures so that they're more consistent with the general trend of the business. You usually normalize figures by using a moving average. See also *moving average.*

opening the books: Every time a business closes the books for a year, it opens a new set of books. It does this at the end of each tax year, then by opening the books, you can start recording the transactions for the new year. The new, empty books must have the balances from the last balance sheet copied into them (via journal entries) so that the business is ready to start the new year. See also *journal(s).*

ordinary share: A type of share issued by a limited company. It carries the highest risk but usually attracts the highest rewards.

original book of entry: A book that contains the details of the day-to-day transactions of a business. See also *journal(s)*.

overheads: The costs involved in running a business, as recorded in expense accounts (for example, rent, insurance, fuel, staff wages, and so on).

P/E (price/earnings) ratio: An equation that gives you a very rough estimate about how much confidence there is in a company's shares (the higher the P/E ratio, the greater the confidence). P/E ratio = (current share price × earnings) ÷ number of shares. (*Earnings* in this equation means the last published net profit of the company.)

paid-up share capital: The value of issued shares that have been paid for. See also *called-up share capital*.

pay on delivery: The buyer pays the cost of the goods (to the carrier) on receipt of those goods.

PAYE (Pay As You Earn): The U.K. income tax system in which an employee's tax and national insurance contributions are deducted before the wages are paid.

periodic inventory: An inventory in which the balance is updated on a periodic basis — for example, every week, month, or year. See also *inventory ledger*.

perpetual inventory: An inventory in which the balance is updated after every transaction. See also *inventory ledger*.

personal accounts: The accounts of a business's customers and suppliers. These are usually held in the sales and purchase ledgers.

petty cash: A small amount of money held in reserve, normally used to purchase items of small value for which a check or other form of payment isn't suitable.

petty cash slip: A document used to record petty cash payments for which an original receipt wasn't obtained (sometimes called a petty cash voucher).

phoenix firm: A firm that has been about to become insolvent but has then been repackaged, restructured, and sold back to the management — so called because it rises from its ashes.

point of sale (POS): The place where a sale of goods takes place — for example, a shop counter.

posting: Copying entries from the journals to the ledgers.

preference share: A type of share issued by a limited company. To own a share in a company means to own a part of that company; for example, if you were to own 10 shares in a company that has issued 100, you would be said to own a 10-percent shareholding. A preference share carries a medium risk but has the advantage over ordinary shares in that preference shareholders get the first slice of the amount, per share, that each shareholder receives when a dividend is declared (but usually at a fixed rate). If the example company issued a dividend of 40p per share, with your holding of ten shares, you'd receive a dividend of £4.00.

prepayments: One or more accounts set up to account for money paid in advance (for example, insurance, where part of the premium applies to the current financial year and the remainder to the following year).

price change accounting: Determining the value of assets, stock, raw materials, and so on by their current market value, rather than the more traditional historic cost. See also *historic cost.*

prime book of entry: See *original book of entry.*

profit: What you earn from your work, after the cost of your work. As a simple example, if a pie costs £1 to make and you sell it for £2, your profit is £1 per pie. See *gross profit, net profit, Profit and Loss account.*

Profit and Loss account: An account, made up of revenue and expense accounts, that shows the current profit or loss of a business (meaning whether a business has earned more than it has spent, or vice versa, in the current year). Often referred to as a P&L.

profit margin: The percentage difference between the costs of a product and the price at which it is sold. For example, if a product costs £10 to buy or produce and it is sold for £20, the profit margin is 100 percent. This is also known as the *mark up.*

pro-forma accounts: A set of accounts prepared before the annual accounts have been officially audited. Often done for internal purposes or to brief shareholders or the press. Also called pro-forma financial statements. ***Note:*** Not all types of business have to be audited.

pro-forma invoice: An invoice that requires payment before any goods or services have been dispatched.

provisions: One or more accounts set up to handle expected future payments (for example, a business creates a provisions account when it is expecting a bill but hasn't yet received it). A provisions account would be used to allow for that payment, on a set date, each month.

purchase invoice: See *invoice.*

purchase ledger: A subsidiary ledger that holds the accounts of a business's suppliers. A single control account held in the nominal ledger shows the total balance of all the accounts in the purchase ledger. See also *nominal ledger.*

raw materials: The materials bought by a manufacturing business in order to manufacture its products.

real accounts: Accounts that deal with money, such as bank and cash accounts, as well as accounts that deal with property and investments. In the case of bank and cash accounts, they can be held in the nominal ledger or balanced in a journal (for example, the cash book), where they can then be regarded as a part of the nominal ledger when compiling a balance sheet. Property and investments can be held in subsidiary ledgers (with associated control accounts, if necessary) or directly in the nominal ledger itself. See also *nominal ledger.*

realization principle: The value of an asset can be determined only when it is sold or otherwise disposed of, thus identifying its real (or realized) value.

rebate: A refund of some of the money paid for a service after the service has been cancelled. (For example, if you've paid for a one-year insurance policy but cancel after three months, you may get a rebate for the remaining nine months.)

receipt: Confirmation of a payment. For example, if you buy some fuel, you normally ask for a receipt to prove that the money was spent legitimately.

reconciling: Comparing entries made in a business's books with those on a statement sent by a third person (for example, checking a bank statement against your own records).

refund: The money repaid to you if you return goods you bought (for whatever reason).

reserve accounts: Accounts usually set up to make a balance sheet clearer by reserving some of a business's capital against future purchases or liabilities (such as the replacement of capital equipment or estimates of bad debts). For example, a company carries forward to the following year the residue of any profit after all the dividends have been paid to use in payment towards any further dividends.

retail: A term usually applied to a shop that resells other people's goods. This type of business requires a trading account, as well as a Profit and Loss account.

retained earnings: The amount of money held in a business after its owner(s) have taken their share of the profits.

retainer: A sum of money paid in order to ensure that a person or company is available when required.

retention ratio: The proportion of the profits that remain in the business after all the expenses (usually including tax and interest) are taken into account. Retention ratio = total profits ÷ profits available for ordinary shareholders (or available for the proprietor/partners in the case of unincorporated companies).

revenue: A business's sales, together with any other taxable income (for example, interest earned from money on deposit).

run rate: A forecast for the year based on the current year-to-date figures. If a company's first quarter profits were £25 million, for example, they may announce that the run rate for the year is £100 million.

sales: Income received from selling goods or services. See also *revenue*.

sales invoice: See *invoice*.

sales ledger: A subsidiary ledger that holds the accounts of a business's customers. A control account is held in the nominal ledger (usually called a debtors' control account), which shows the total balance of all the accounts in the sales ledger. See also *nominal ledger*.

self assessment: In the U.K., a means by which individuals can calculate their own income tax if they're self-employed or receive an income that's untaxed at source.

self-balancing ledgers: A system that makes use of control accounts so that each ledger balances on its own. To have a ledger balance means to have both sides — the money out and the money in — add up to the same figure. A control account in a subsidiary ledger is mirrored by a control account in the nominal ledger. See also *nominal ledger*.

self-employed: Someone who's the owner of (or partner in) a business and is legally liable for all the debts of the business. This relates to all types of business, from the one-man band carrying out freelance work through to a corner shop.

selling, general and administrative (SG&A): The expenses involved in running a business.

service: A term usually applied to a business that sells an activity, rather than manufactures or sells goods (for example, an architect or a window cleaner are service businesses).

shareholders: The owners of shares in a limited company or corporation.

share premium: The amount paid above the face value of a share. For example, if a company issues its shares at £10 each and you later buy one share on the open market at £12, you're paying a share premium of £2.

share: A document supplied to an individual or company that has bought a partial ownership in another company. The value of shares varies depending mostly on market factors: if the company has had a good year, the share value rises; a bad year, and the share value falls. This document states how many shares in the company each shareholder has bought and what percentage of the company the shareholder owns. See also *stock*.

shares issued: The number of shares a company has made available for sale to shareholders.

simple interest: Interest applied only to the original sum invested (as opposed to compound interest). For example, £1,000 invested over two years at 10 percent per year will yield a gross total of £1,200 in simple interest at the end of the period (10 percent of £1000 = £100 per year). See also *compound interest*.

single-step income statement: A statement in which all the revenues are shown as a single total, instead of being split up into different types of revenue. (The single-step income statement is the most common format for very small businesses because it allows for the simplification of the preparation of business accounts.) See also *multiple-step income statement, Profit and Loss account*.

sinking fund: An account set up to reduce another account to zero over time (by using the principles of amortization or straight-line depreciation). After the sinking fund reaches the same value as the other account, both can be removed from the balance sheet. An example could be the way an NHS trust repays money loaned to it.

SMEs (small and medium-sized enterprises): A classification for businesses. The distinction between what's small and what's medium varies depending on where you are and who you talk to.

sole proprietor: The self-employed owner of a business. See also *self-employed*.

sole trader: An individual who carries out business. See *sole proprietor*.

source document: An original invoice, bill, or receipt to which journal entries refer.

stock: The shares of a limited company; also, the goods manufactured or bought for resale by a business. See also *shares*.

stock control account: An account held in the nominal ledger that holds the value of all the physical stock held in the inventory subsidiary ledger. See also *nominal ledger*.

stockholders: See *shareholders*.

stock taking: Checking a business's physical stock for total quantities and value.

stock valuation: Calculating the worth value for goods bought for manufacturing or resale.

straight-line depreciation: Depreciating something by the same (meaning a fixed) amount every year, rather than as a percentage of its previous value. For example, if a vehicle initially costs $10,000 and you depreciate it at a rate of $2,000 a year, it will depreciate to zero in exactly five years. See also *depreciation*.

subordinated debt: The amount of money owed to the unsecured creditors if a company is liquidated (meaning it becomes insolvent). See also *insolvent*.

subsidiary ledgers: Ledgers opened in addition to a business's nominal ledger. Subsidiary ledgers are used to keep sections of a business separate from each other (for example, a sales ledger for customers and a purchase ledger for suppliers). See also *control account, nominal ledger, purchase ledger, sales ledger*.

suspense account: A temporary account used to force a trial balance to balance if there is only a small discrepancy (or if an account's balance is simply wrong and you don't know why). For example, if you have a small error in petty cash, you can make a transfer to a suspense account to balance the cash account. After you determine what happened to the money, you make a transfer entry in the journal to credit or debit the suspense account back to zero and debit or credit the correct account.

T an account: A particular method of displaying an account in which the debits and associated information are shown on the left, and credits and associated information on the right.

tangible assets: Assets of a physical nature. Examples include buildings, motor vehicles, plants and equipment, and fixtures and fittings. See also *intangible assets.*

three-column cash book: A journal that deals with the day-to-day cash and bank transactions of a business. The side of a transaction that relates directly to the cash or bank account is usually balanced within the cash book and used as a part of the nominal ledger when compiling a balance sheet (so only the side that details the sale or purchase needs to be posted to the nominal ledger). See also *nominal ledger.*

Total Cost of Ownership (TCO): The real amount an asset will cost. For example, an accounting application retails at £1,000. Support — which is mandatory — costs a further £200 per annum. Assuming the software will be in use for five years, TCO will be £2,000 (£1,000 + [5 years × £200]).

trading account: An account that shows the gross profit or loss of a manufacturing or retail business (for example, sales less the cost of sales).

transaction: Two or more entries made in a journal that, when looked at together, reflect an original document, such as a sales invoice or purchase receipt. See also *journal.*

trial balance: A statement showing all the accounts used in a business and their balances.

turnover: The income of a business over a period of time (usually a year). This figure is usually stated before allowing for running costs — for example, staffing, travel, and so on.

undeposited funds account: An account used to show the current total of money received (meaning money not yet banked or spent), including money, checks, credit card payments, bankers drafts, and so on. This type of account is also commonly referred to as a cash-in-hand account.

value added tax (VAT): A sales tax that increases the price of goods. VAT is added to the price of goods so, at the U.K. rate of 20 percent (correct at the time of writing), an item that sells at £10 will be priced £12 when VAT has been added.

wages: Payments made to the employees of a business for their work on behalf of the business. Wages are classed as expense items and must not be confused with drawings taken by sole proprietors and partnerships. See also *drawings.*

work in progress: The value of partly finished (meaning partly manufactured) goods.

write-off: To depreciate an asset to zero in one go. Also applies if you're not paid for work carried out — you may elect to write off the value before spending a fortune on recovery proceedings. See also *depreciation*.

Zero-Based Account (ZBA): An account (usually a personal account, such as a current account) in which the balance is kept as close to zero as possible by transferring money between that account and another, such as a deposit account.

Zero-Based Budget (ZBB): Starting a budget at zero and justifying every cost that increases the budget.

Index

creating a new view, 148–149, 170–171
deleting a view, 149
Filter tab, 148
showing deleted transaction templates, 131–132
showing or hiding, 146
View tab, 148
View tab (View Editor panel), 148
views. *See also* charts
  Accounts view, 144–145
  Chart Filter view, 178
  Charts view, 152, 173–174, 177–179
  column widths for, 149–150, 242
  conditions available for, 172, 217, 218
  Constrain Col Widths check box, 149–150
  creating, 137–139, 148–149, 170–171, 215–218
  customizing, 149–151
  defined, 137
  deleting, 149
  drop-down list of, 146
  Filter view, 131–133
  filtering, 242
  forecasting, 215–218
  foreign-currency, 137–139
  predefined, 147, 169–170
  printing, 195
  for recent transactions, 235–236
  searching within, 146
  showing or hiding columns in, 138–139, 151, 171–173
  sorting by column, 150–151, 240
  for transactions, 145–146
  uses for, 143

• W •

wages, 258, 270
Warning icon, 4
warning messages
  data validation, 78, 79
  enabling or disabling, 81
  status information warning-level values, 75, 80
Windows computers. *See* PCs
work files
  opening, 230
  restoring from BAK folder, 229
work in progress, 271
write-off, 271

• Y •

YouTube videos, 12

• Z •

zero (0) as number formatting code, 83
Zero-Based Account (ZBA), 271
Zero-Based Budget (ZBB), 271